Organizational
Architecture

DAVID A. NADLER
MARC S. GERSTEIN
ROBERT B. SHAW
AND ASSOCIATES

Organizational Architecture

DESIGNS FOR CHANGING ORGANIZATIONS

Jossey-Bass Publishers · San Francisco

For sales outside the United States contact Maxwell Macmillan International Publishing Group, 866 Third Avenue, New York, New York 10022

Printed on acid-free paper and manufactured in the United States of America

 The paper used in this book meets the State of California require-ments for recycled paper (50 percent recycled waste, including 10 percent postconsumer waste), which are the strictest guidelines for recycled paper currently in use in the United States.

Library of Congress Cataloging-in-Publication Data

Nadler, David.
    Organizational architecture : designs for changing organizations / David A. Nadler, Marc S. Gerstein, Robert B. Shaw. — 1st ed.
      p.   cm.—(The Jossey-Bass management series)
    Includes bibliographical references and index.
    ISBN 1-55542-443-0
    1. Organizational change. I. Gerstein, Marc S. II. Shaw, Robert B., date. III. Title. IV. Series.
HD58.8.N33   1992
658.4'063—dc20   92-4071
                                                        CIP

FIRST EDITION
HB Printing   10 9 8 7 6 5 4   *Code 9244*

The Jossey-Bass
Management Series

CONTENTS

PREFACE

Organizational Architecture emerged as a direct consequence of our work at Delta Consulting Group, an organization that provides counsel to managers and companies in periods of significant transition. Rather than a comprehensive survey or a highly integrated theoretical discussion, the book is a practice-driven collection of chapters that reflect the issues in organizational architecture that we have been encouraged to examine through our work with our clients. In contrast to the traditional academic model of moving from theory to practice, in our work and in this book we move from practice to theory: we reflect on our experiences and from them derive insights and observations that may be relevant in a variety of organizational settings. The thread running through this collection is the nature of the challenges that senior managers of leading-edge organizations face today.

Our approach to consulting is to form highly collaborative relationships with our clients. Part of that collaboration involves transferring our technology (concepts, methodologies, and tools) to help clients enhance their capacity to design, build, and manage effective organizations. Thus, part of our core mission involves continually refining our practical knowledge about organizations and inventing tools that enhance organizational effectiveness. Invention in our domain, however, does not occur in a laboratory, an academic office, or a library; it occurs as the direct result of working with our clients to manage large-scale organizational change. In this way, our clients have not been just customers; they have been collaborators in the development of knowledge. Each chapter in this collection is the result of clients' interest in or concern about a particular issue and their encouragement for us to learn and discover with them.

Overview of the Contents

Organizational Architecture is our attempt to draw broadly applicable conclusions from what we have learned through our problem-solving work on issues of organizational architecture. In the Introduction, David A. Nadler describes the major forces exerting pressure on organizations in the 1990s and outlines the basic organization of the book. The chapters that follow are structured around five major topics: understanding the architectures of change, designing formal organizational arrangements, transforming the informal organization, designing senior management, and traveling the road from decline to competitiveness.

The first part of the book introduces the concept of organizational architecture. In Chapter One, Marc S. Gerstein draws on themes in the architecture of physical space to define and illustrate the concept of the architecture of organizational space. He focuses on how information technology can enable the development of new types of architectures. The second chapter presents a framework, based on open-systems theory, for thinking about the design of organizations. David A. Nadler and Michael L. Tushman present the framework as consisting of four components—work, people, the formal organization, and the informal organization—and describe the ways in which these components do and do not work together.

The second part of *Organizational Architecture* addresses topics such as acquisitions, joint ventures, and high-performance work systems that relate to designing formal organizational arrangements. In Chapter Three, David A. Nadler and Terry M. Limpert present a model for effective acquisition management that focuses on sources of strategic leverage, critical success factors for acquisition, and degree and pace of integration. The fourth chapter examines the dynamics of joint ventures and other strategic alliances that involve the creation of new jointly owned entities. Charles S. Raben presents different models of joint venture design and management and offers guidelines for joint venture organizational development. Chapter Five integrates and advances much of the work done on high-involvement management of sociotechnical systems and provides a perspective on the development of different organizational forms. David A. Nadler and Marc S. Gerstein outline a set of design principles for high-performance work systems and lay out the key steps in the design process.

Part Three discusses the process of transforming the informal organization and related issues such as total quality management (TQM), capacity to act, and organizational learning. Chapter Six discusses what the authors have learned from designing and implementing TQM strategies. Jeffrey D. Heilpern and David A. Nadler present their views of TQM as primarily a cultural change and discuss approaches for change management and quality improvement. Chapter Seven reports on results from applied research on some of the dysfunctions found in large organizations and focuses in particular on problems related to lack of initiative and risk taking. Robert B. Shaw identifies and discusses the concept of "insufficient capacity to act," presents a paradigm of the factors that cause the problem, and makes recommendations for actions to reverse it. In Chapter Eight, Robert B. Shaw and Dennis N. T. Perkins present models of organizational learning and discuss actions that have the potential to either block or facilitate it.

Part Four of *Organizational Architecture* discusses the design of senior management, with a focus on such topics as executive selection, executive teamwork, and collaborative strategy development. Chapter Nine describes an applied approach for making staffing decisions at the level of the executive team. David A. Nadler and Marc S. Gerstein report on the results of several years of effort to put theories of strategically driven selection into action. In Chapter Ten, David A. Nadler and Deborah Ancona discuss the emergence of executive teams in major corporations as a new type of design for senior management. The authors spell out the significant differences between executive teams and other types of teams, list common team dysfunctions, and present a model of executive team effectiveness. Chapter Eleven focuses on strategy development as one of the key tasks of the executive team. David R. Bliss presents both a way of thinking about collaborative strategy and a process for developing one.

In Part Five, we draw conclusions and present directions for the future. This part begins with Chapter Twelve, which summarizes the themes developed in the book by presenting an analysis of the key issues for U.S.-based companies trying to regain competi-

tiveness. David A. Nadler presents ten common misconceptions that
ensure decline and then urges executives to work four leverage
points—strategy, organizational design, quality, and learning—to
improve competitiveness. In Chapter Thirteen, Marc S. Gerstein
and Robert B. Shaw build on the ideas presented in the previous
chapters to identify major trends in organizational architecture and
the types of organizations that will be most effective in the twenty-
first century.

Acknowledgments

This book is the reflection of the collaborative work that goes on
at Delta. Many of our colleagues at Delta who are not listed as
authors have been collaborators in the effort. In particular, Michael
Chayes, Jean Freeman, Kathleen Gunderson, Larry Kacher, and
Kathy Morris were active participants in much of the work reflected
here. The model presented in Chapter Eight was developed as part
of an organizational learning research project in which six in-depth
case studies were prepared. The researchers on the project—Jamie
Holmes, Hermi Ibarra, Dennis Schoor, Robert Silvers, and Joan
Slepian—contributed significantly to our ideas. Special thanks also
go to Jim Barrow, John Seely Brown, Roger Levin, and Hal Tra-
gash for commenting on an earlier draft of Chapter Eight.

We would also like to express our appreciation to a number
of our client organizations who have been particularly supportive
of our efforts to break new ground. These include Alcoa, American
Express, AT&T, Citicorp, Corning, GTE, and Xerox. Their contribution is reflected in many of the chapters included here. GTE, in
particular, was quite generous in its financial support for the R&D
used to develop Chapter Four. Paul Allaire, chairman and chief
executive officer of Xerox, has urged us to work with Xerox and to
use it as a laboratory. Jamie Houghton, chairman and chief executive officer of Corning, and the Corning Management Committee
have provided us with a unique opportunity to learn by allowing
us to work with them to design and build a twenty-first century
organization. We are deeply indebted to both of these companies
and their leaders.

Finally, the operations staff at Delta has had a major role in producing this book. Kathy Mahon collaborated in the development process, and Annie Matta had the responsibility for publications and graphics. Kate Linnihan did a tremendous job of managing the production of the final manuscript.

Although we recognize and thank the individuals and organizations who have helped us in this project, we, of course, take responsibility for the content and the opinions expressed here.

New York, New York David A. Nadler
March 1992 Marc S. Gerstein
Robert B. Shaw

THE AUTHORS

Deborah Ancona currently serves on the faculty of the Sloan School of Management at the Massachusetts Institute of Technology, where she specializes in group dynamics, team performance, organizational diagnosis, and organizational design. She received her B.S. (1976) and M.S. (1977) degrees from the University of Pennsylvania in psychology, and her Ph.D. degree (1982) from Columbia University in organizational behavior.

David R. Bliss is practice leader for strategy at Delta Consulting Group, where he works in the areas of strategy formulation and implementation, executive leadership, organizational design, and total quality management. He formerly held various executive and strategic planning positions at Xerox Corporation. He received his B.S. degree (1965) from Babson College in marketing and finance.

Marc S. Gerstein is managing director and practice leader for technology and organization at Delta Consulting Group, where he works in the areas of strategy development, information technology, organizational design, high-performance work systems, and management of change. He received his B.S. degree (1967) from Rensselaer Polytechnic Institute in electrical engineering and his M.S. (1969) and Ph.D. (1974) degrees from the Sloan School of Management at the Massachusetts Institute of Technology in organizational behavior and information systems.

Jeffrey D. Heilpern is practice leader for total quality management at Delta Consulting Group, where he works in the areas of organizational diagnosis and change, organizational culture, and executive leadership. He formerly served as vice president of human resources and organizational development at Yankelovich, Skelly &

White. Heilpern received his B.A. degree (1973) from Tufts University in political science and his M.B.A. degree (1977) from Harvard University.

Terry M. Limpert works in the areas of organizational diagnosis, change management, merger and acquisition management, quality improvement, team development, and leadership at Delta Consulting Group. He formerly served as senior corporate consultant at Union Carbide Corporation. Limpert received his B.S. degree (1965) from Marietta College in chemistry.

David A. Nadler works with senior management at Delta Consulting Group on organizational change, organizational design, senior team development, management succession, and leadership. He formerly served on the faculty of the Graduate School of Business at Columbia University and the staff of the Survey Research Center at the University of Michigan Institute for Social Research. He received his B.A. degree (1970) from George Washington University in political science and international affairs, his M.B.A. degree (1972) from Harvard University, his M.A. degree (1973) from the University of Michigan in psychology, and his Ph.D. degree (1975) from the University of Michigan in psychology.

Dennis N. T. Perkins specializes in survey feedback, survey methodology, career development, organizational culture, and evaluation research at Delta Consulting Group. He is a former faculty member of the Yale University School of Organization and Management and a former staff member of the Survey Research Center at the University of Michigan Institute for Social Research. He received his B.A. degree (1964) from the U.S. Naval Academy in engineering, his M.B.A. degree (1971) from Harvard University, and his Ph.D. degree (1977) from the University of Michigan in organizational and community psychology.

Charles S. Raben is practice leader for survey-based consultation at Delta Consulting Group, where he works in the areas of organizational design, organizational change, business restructuring, and executive leadership. He formerly served as director of organizational planning and development at the ARCO Oil and Gas Company and served on the faculties of the University of California, Berkeley, and the University of Maryland. He received his B.S. degree (1969) from Farleigh Dickinson University in psychology and his M.A. (1970) and Ph.D. (1973) degrees from Ohio State University in industrial and organizational psychology.

Robert B. Shaw specializes in strategic design, high-performance work systems, and large-scale organizational change at Delta Consulting Group. He received his B.A. degree (1982) from the University of California, Santa Cruz, in psychology, and his M.S. (1985) and Ph.D. (1989) degrees from the Yale University School of Organization and Management in organizational behavior.

Michael L. Tushman is Hettleman Professor of Management and director of the Research Center in Entrepreneurship and Innovation at the Columbia University Graduate School of Business, where he specializes in organizational design and management of innovation and strategic change in organizations. He received his B.S. degree (1970) from Northeastern University in electrical engineering, his M.S. degree (1972) from Cornell University in industrial and labor relations, and his Ph.D. degree (1976) from the Sloan School of Management at the Massachusetts Institute of Technology in organizational studies.

INTRODUCTION

Organizational Architecture: A Metaphor for Change

DAVID A. NADLER

Corporations based in the United States face increasing pressures in the 1990s. In industry after industry, senior managers are dealing with conditions that make success more elusive. The days of easy and effortless global dominance by U.S. firms clearly have passed, replaced by conditions that require executives to use every possible tool at their disposal to create and maintain organizational effectiveness. These new conditions create the need to develop new architectures of organization.

Sources of Increased Pressure

What are the sources of this newly intense environment? Several forces that arose during the 1980s appear to have contributed to the current situation (see the table on p. 3). First, technological change has continued to accelerate. This has led to major shifts in the competencies that are critical to maintaining a competitive advantage and has placed a premium on time-based competition, or the ability to develop and commercialize products quickly. Second, competition has increased and intensified. As each year passes, fewer industries are characterized as monopolistic, either by law or through the dominance of a few unchallenged players. This competition is more intensive and less courteous than in the past. Third, there is oversupply on a global basis. Except perhaps for the commodities industries, there are more suppliers with more capacity than there are consumers ready and able to purchase. Fourth, "globalism" has become a reality. Companies now compete in global

1

markets against global competitors. This means it is impossible to think about purely domestic markets with a set of known and comparable domestic competitors. Fifth, as a consequence of the preceding four forces, customer expectations are rising. The driving element in these rising expectations is the fact that customers have a larger range of choices and alternatives than ever before. Confronted with choice and newly discovered buyer power, their expectations for quality, value, and service are exploding.

Sixth, economic competition has become the primary world dynamic, forcing governments to become inexorably involved in the success of their own home industries. Government, particularly outside of the United States, has become an active participant in the marketplace, supporting companies through explicit or implied national industrial policies. Seventh, as concentrated institutional ownership of corporations increases (as opposed to highly distributed individual ownership), owners are becoming more militant and aggressive about their stakeholder interests. They continue to push for more involvement in key decisions within the organization.

Finally, more women and racial minorities are entering the work force than ever before, with white males ultimately in the minority. At the same time, because of problems in the education system, work force entrants have fewer skills to handle the increasingly demanding jobs. Demographics indicate that there will continue to be a shortage of skilled workers as the "baby boomers" reach retirement age.

Each one of these forces by itself poses considerable challenges to the creation and management of effective organizations. More distressing, however, is that many companies are experiencing the effects of most or all of these forces at the same time. The net result is that increasing rate of change has become a fact of life.

Responses to the Pressures

The companies that survive will be those that are able to respond to these challenges. The companies that succeed will be those that anticipate change and develop strategies in advance. This puts a premium on certain qualities of organization, in particular adaptability, flexibility, responsiveness, decisiveness, and speed. Or-

Forces Contributing to Increased Pressures on Organizations.

Force	Change Component
Technology	The increasing rate of change threatens existing positions and investments.
Competition	An increasing number of effective competitors are emerging in major industries.
Oversupply	The capacity to supply most products and services exceeds the demand.
Globalism	Competition now occurs on a global scale.
Customer expectations	Given more choices, customers expect greater value, quality, and service.
Government participation	Governments have become more active supporters of industry in their countries.
Ownership	Changes in patterns of corporate ownership are leading to greater expression of the requirements of owners.
Work force dynamics	Changes in work force make-up, including sex, race, education level, and age distribution, are creating a work force radically different from that of the past

ganizations have no choice but to be anticipators and managers of change.

Organizations can increase their flexibility and ability to anticipate in a number of different ways. Obviously, the development of effective core resources—financial, technological competencies, people, and so on—strengthens the capacity of an organization to face new challenges. One source of adaptive strength which has implications for all of the others, however, is the way in which the efforts of the enterprise are organized. How the firm organizes its efforts can be a source of tremendous competitive advantage, particularly in times where premiums are placed on flexibility, adaptation, and the management of change. When we say "organization" we mean all of the various systems, structures, management processes, technologies, strategies, etc., that make up the "modus operandi" of the firm. The term we have used to encompass all of these elements is *organizational architecture.*

Organizational Architecture

When executives talk about organization, they frequently focus on the elements of organizational design, or the formal structures and systems that they create to execute strategies. During the past few years, many of us who have been working with complex organizations on problems of structure and design have begun to think less about the specifics of organizational structure—what is in the boxes and which lines connect them—and more about a broader concept called *organizational architecture*. By architecture we mean a much more inclusive view of the elements of design of the social and work systems that make up a large complex corporation. (This term is discussed in more detail in Chapter One). Architecture therefore includes the formal structure, the design of work practices, the nature of the informal organization or operating style, and the processes for selection, socialization, and development of people.

What has become clear is that organizational architecture can be a source of competitive advantage to the degree that it motivates, facilitates, or enables individuals and groups to interact more effectively with customers, the work, and each other. As companies gain equal access to capital, and as many technologies mature and become generic, organizations will gain a sustainable competitive advantage from their ability to deploy and leverage the efforts of the people who are members of the organization. What has also become clear is that many of our cherished assumptions about organizational architecture may no longer hold true. In many different settings, industries, and markets, companies are searching for new architectures that will serve them more effectively in a new and changing environment.

The forces that are causing the rethinking of organizational architecture have become fairly evident: increasing competition, massive social and technological change, increasing government participation in economic affairs, and the evolution of global markets and thus global competition. Perhaps most importantly, the rate of change is increasing. Organizations therefore need to increase their capacity to deal with uncertainty.

This change presents some very specific challenges, particularly to large, complex organizations. Competition has forced companies to search for ways to decrease the cost in both time and money of internal coordination. Customer demand for quality has led companies to recognize the need to motivate employees by providing them with an increased sense of the meaning of their work. The need for competitive innovation has required many firms to search for ways to increase both the sense of accountability and the degree of empowerment for teams at all levels. The global economy has pushed corporations to search for their true competitive advantage and to broaden their reach and scale without creating the "mass" that traditionally has been required.

Perhaps the largest single influence on organizational architecture and design has been the evolution of information technology. Most modern theories of organizational design view the core task of organizational structure as information processing—moving information among individuals and groups in the organization to coordinate their work activities. The basic information processing device is hierarchy, built through the grouping of jobs and roles into work units that are linked through common reporting relationships and successive levels of management control.

Information technology has begun to revolutionize organizational design by providing alternatives to hierarchy as the primary means of coordination. Information systems, common architectures, shared data bases, decision support tools, and expert systems facilitate the coordination of behavior without control through hierarchy, thus enabling the creation of autonomous units linked together through information. It also allows more loose coupling (versus tight coupling) without the risks of lost coordination and control. The combination of the great potential of information technology with the great demands of the competitive environment has led to innovations in organizational design.

What organizational forms will we see? Although it is difficult, and potentially foolhardy, to predict what organizations will look like, it is possible to identify some evolving architectural forms and features that we will see in the future:

> *Autonomous work teams.* Self-managed teams that are responsible for an entire piece of work or a complete segment of a work process will become more prevalent. Such

teams provide their own supervision, cross train and change roles, and in many ways are empowered to take responsibility for their own process and results. Autonomous work teams have been used extensively in factory settings, but they will start to become more prevalent—first in the production elements of the office and then in knowledge-intensive work.

High-performance work systems. High-performance work systems is a term describing an approach to organizational design that emphasizes the deliberate integration of the social and technical systems of work, using both advanced technology-based tools (for example, expert systems, knowledge-based power tools) and state-of-the-art human system design (for example, autonomous work teams, enriched job design, flat hierarchies). Typically, this type of design moves beyond the specific work group or team and encompasses other elements, including the broad flow of work, the nature of the hierarchy (usually much fewer levels), reward systems (frequently gain sharing), and symbols (egalitarian). Again, although the pioneering work in high-performance work systems has been in manufacturing environments and some "paper factories," the use of this approach will broaden into other settings.

Alliances and joint ventures. An increasing number of companies will find they cannot go it alone. They will recognize the need to focus their talents, particular strengths, and resources on those areas in which they have a competitive advantage and let others perform functions that can be done better elsewhere. This will lead to the establishment of alliances and joint ventures that can capitalize on and leverage the particular strengths of the individual partners. Alliances and joint ventures will become a normal, accepted feature of organizational design. Successful joint venturers will have the capacity to create organizational learning from these arrangements, rather than simply profit in the short term. To date, Japanese and European companies have outperformed U.S. companies in their ability to gain insight, acquire technology, and build capacity as a consequence of their participation in collaborative ventures.

"Spinouts." As corporations search for the means to promote and leverage innovation, many will find that when they unleash human creativity, they end up with many more opportunities than there is time, attention, and capital to support. Rather than lose the innovators, they will "stake" entrepreneurs in the creation of new organizational entities in which the parent retains some equity. These "spinouts" may evolve into joint ventures, become fully independent companies, or continue to be associated with the parent, but they usually will not end up as fully integrated operations. Companies of the future will be surrounded by many of these satellite spinouts, with various degrees of coupling to the core.

Networks. Those companies that become particularly adept at shaping themselves to face uncertainty will evolve into a combination of wholly owned operations, alliances, joint ventures, spinouts, and acquired subsidiaries. They will not be holding companies, but will be linked together in what will be called organizational networks through shared values, people, technology, financial resources, and operating styles. Examples of such organizational networks are Benetton in Europe and Corning, Inc., in the United States.

Self-designed organizations. Accompanying the increasing rate of change is the need for organizations to develop the capacity to redesign themselves to meet different conditions. Thus, mechanisms will evolve that enable organizations to learn from their successes and failures and to reshape themselves in response to changes. Organizations will be able to create design teams quickly with the aid of technology-supported organizational design tools.

Fuzzy boundaries. The boundaries that define organizations will become less clear. The architectural elements of joint ventures, spinouts, and networks will contribute to this fuzziness. The main factor, however, will be technology. When a customer can hook into networks and interact

with organizational tools, and when the customer becomes a codesigner of products by participating in the
design and development process, who is in and who is out
become less clear. Mechanisms developed to manage the
fuzzy boundaries will enhance the ability of organizations
to interact positively with their environments.

Teamwork at the top. Lastly, as all of these new forms evolve,
a change will occur at the top of the organization. The
diversity, uncertainty, and multiple relationships to be
managed will place greater demands on the executive level
of management. Although institutions will still require
the single chief executive officer (CEO), fewer companies
will find themselves with a single chief operating officer
(COO). Instead, team structures will emerge at the top of
organizations, and collective intellect and collaborative
action will become more evident.

These eight architectural elements do not constitute an all-
inclusive list. By definition, the responses of organizations to increased uncertainty are difficult to predict; however, we should expect to see these features. Those companies that are creative in
designing new organizational architectures will be those that gain
significant competitive advantage in this new era of change.

PART ONE

Architectures of Change

As the principal means for the accomplishment of productive work and the creation of economic value, organizations are among society's most important institutions. Organizations are also an important means through which people satisfy their needs for individual achievement and social affiliation and through which cultural values are perpetuated from generation to generation.

The degree to which organizations fulfill their various purposes is intimately tied to the efficacy of their design. Although not the sole determinant of success, the design of organizations is fundamental to their performance and is the most accessible, perhaps the most important, of managerial tools.

The two chapters in Part One provide an important conceptual foundation for organizational design and an overview of the material to follow. First, we elaborate the concept of organizational architecture through the metaphor of physical architecture. Second, we present an organizational model that has been useful for both the design of organizations and the diagnosis of organizational problems.

In Chapter One, Marc S. Gerstein, drawing on physical architecture as a foundation, describes organizational architecture in depth. Organizational designers can learn a great deal from architects and master builders, and this chapter outlines principles that can be used to guide the process of organizational design. In addition, Gerstein positions information technology as a "structural material" capable of supporting organizations quite different from those of the past. Finally, this chapter provides a picture of the future of organizational design, concentrating on the features of the network organization and team-based designs introduced in the Introduction.

In Chapter Two, David A. Nadler and Michael L. Tushman portray organizations as "open systems" with four major components—work, people, the formal organization, and the informal organization. This "congruence model" provides the organizational architect with an important tool to use in understanding current organizational problems or plotting the evolution of the organization as conditions change.

ONE

From Machine Bureaucracies to Networked Organizations: An Architectural Journey

MARC S. GERSTEIN

In the 1880s, Britain was the heart of the Industrial Revolution and the center of a global merchant shipping empire. By sail and steam, it was possible to ship goods inexpensively virtually anywhere in the world—to Europe, the Americas, and the Far East. This allowed British companies to virtually control world trade in a number of vital commodities.

William Lever, founder of Unilever, was a hands-on, detail-oriented manager who single-handedly directed his soap business's worldwide operations. Lever handpicked British expatriates to run his overseas subsidiaries and personally made frequent visits abroad to check on the company's operations. Lever's ability to run a far-flung global enterprise despite the communications and transportation limitations of the day was possible because of weak local competition and the highly favorable economics created by centralized production and the British merchant fleet.

After Lever's death in 1925, however, the new overseas committee chairman, H. R. Greenhalgh, faced a different situation (Table 1.1). The inherently low technology of early twentieth-century soap manufacture had given rise to a number of indigenous local competitors, while significant differences in consumer preferences around the world encouraged product differentiation, which changed the basis of competition. In addition, rising trade barriers in the 1920s and 1930s blunted Unilever's cost advantages, permitting local competitors to flourish despite their relatively small size. Unilever needed to change its strategy if it was to avoid losing its competitive position.

Table 1.1. Summary of Differences Between Unilever Before and After 1925.

Unilever Pre-1925: Integrated Global Business	Unilever Post-1925: Federation of Independent Businesses
Compelling economics and limited competition	Increased competition, differentiated markets, and national protectionism
Handpicked British expatriate country heads	Local nationals as managers
Centralized leadership and decision making by the founder	Decentralized management norms and practices
Frequent visits by headquarters to gather information and exercise control	Headquarters' role of planning/ review, capital allocation, executive development

Therefore, starting in the 1930s in India, Unilever began to fill management and technical positions with local nationals and increase their freedom to make decisions. This trend was dramatically accelerated by World War II, which made communications and travel between overseas subsidiaries and headquarters in London quite difficult. By the time the war ended, Unilever's management philosophy had almost completely changed from that established by its founder. Each subsidiary was expected to run its local business as an independent entity. Country managers had maximum freedom to develop and implement strategies that reflected local market needs and competitive conditions; headquarters now acted in a supportive rather than a controlling role (Bartlett and Ghoshal, 1989).

Unilever's early history underscores a well-accepted management principle articulated by Chandler (1962), Woodward (1965), and Lawrence and Lorsch (1967): there is no one "best" way to organize. Organizational form is the complex product of the organization's history, strategy, and environmental circumstances. However, this "contingency theory," as it is known, does not fully reflect the richness of organizational design. As suggested by the Unilever example, management processes (such as information, reporting, and control systems); staff capabilities, attitudes, and values (such as the characteristics of the country general managers); and the overall culture of the organization are equally important characteristics of the organization, particularly with respect to how it is to work in practice rather than how it looks on paper.

Recognizing the limits of the term *organizational structure*, we have adopted the phrase *organizational architecture* to refer to a wider set of organizational characteristics. The notion of architecture encourages us to focus not only on the fit between the organization and its environment but also on the harmony among constituent design elements. In other words, the notion of architecture encourages a holistic approach to design. Architecture also encourages us to think about the process of *building* organizations, not just designing them. Whether an organization is a "new construction" or a "renovation," it must be brought into being through a complex process of human interaction that involves hundreds and often thousands of people. The notion of architecture is an effective reminder that design is only one part of the process.

The purposes of this chapter are to use examples of physical architecture to illustrate the value of both a holistic approach to design and the principles of good architecture, to discuss the evolution of organizational design from the machine bureaucracy of the late nineteenth century to the "network organization" that we expect to be the dominant form of organization in the next century, and to discuss the unique opportunities available to organizational designers arising from the capabilities of information technology. We view information technology as a structural material (analogous to concrete or structural steel) that makes possible architectures previously unrealizable.

As the treatment of the material in this chapter is somewhat unusual, it might be useful to establish the reader's expectations. We spend more time exploring the content of the architecture metaphor than is typical for a business text. Physical architecture has much to teach us about organizational design, but to learn its lessons, we must have more than a cursory understanding of its principles. Therefore, approximately half of the material in this chapter is about physical architecture. Also, instead of a sequential treatment of physical architecture followed by organizational issues, the chapter alternates between discussions of key aspects of physical architecture and examinations of their implications for organizational design.

In reviewing the material presented, I encourage the reader to think as much as possible like the "master builders" of earlier ages.

These highly skilled individuals combined the abilities of architect, general contractor, and construction manager. Master builders were responsible for both the design and its execution, and without their unique abilities there would have been little architectural progress over the centuries. As executives are responsible for both the architecture and the construction of organizations, the role of master builder seems an apt metaphor.

The Nature of Architecture

We begin our exploration with a set of basic definitions and core ideas. According to art historian F. W. Janson (1991, p. 84), the ancient Greeks coined the term *architecture:* " 'Architecture' meant something higher than ordinary 'tecture' (that is, 'construction' or 'building'). [It is] a structure distinguished from the merely practical, everyday kind by its scale, order, permanence, or solemnity of purpose." Janson defines architecture as "the art of shaping space to human needs and aspirations." It is considered to be a very special art: "It confines space so that we can dwell in it, creat[ing] the framework around our lives" (Rasmussen, 1991, p. 10).

In the context of this definition, we might ask what general lessons we can learn from physical architecture that will help us to design more effective organizations. Several are listed below that seem particularly applicable:

1. Architecture is a "practical art." "Ordinary people" are its consumers. Because people have to work and live in that which is created, the ultimate test of any architecture is its utility measured in human terms.
2. Architecture provides a framework for the conduct of life, not a specification for what that life should be. Architecture should facilitate, guide, and provide a context; it should not provide a rigid blueprint for conduct.
3. When conceived, new designs have to be "ahead of their time" so that they will endure. The architect's "building should pref-

erably be ahead of its time when planned so that it will be in keeping with the times as long as it stands" (Rasmussen, 1991).

4. Unlike a painting, which is produced by a single artist, architecture is produced by large numbers of people working together to achieve the vision of the architect. Architecture is, by definition, a social rather than a solitary activity (Rasmussen, 1991).

Borrowing from Janson, we might define organizational architecture as the art of shaping organizational space to meet human needs and aspirations. But what is the "space" that organizational architects shape? Conventional architects work in the three-dimensional space in which people move. In a similar way, organizational architects work in the "behavioral space" in which people act. Creating opportunities for action, which we often call *empowerment,* and creating constraints to action are central to the organizational architect's job.

Physical architects also design with light. Light shapes space, models forms, and reveals texture. Analogously, the organizational architect can be seen to design the organization's "information space." Information illuminates the organization by revealing the current state of its activities and the historical pattern of transactions, events, and decisions. The information space can also be seen to contain the knowledge and expertise of the organization—that is, the learning arising from its cumulative problem-solving experience.

In many cases, the design of the information space will parallel and reinforce the formal structure. For example, financial consolidations are likely to flow along structural lines. Other times, however, information will be made to flow from unit to unit or between the organization and its customers and suppliers. This is the organizational equivalent of creating a "room with a view."

Organizational units with views onto other units, or customers who are directly tied to the organization's information system, will possess a greater sense of contact and control than can be provided by conventional structures. In our complex, rapidly changing world, the design of the information space is among the most important aspects of organizational architecture. We deal with this key aspect of organizational design in greater detail later in this chapter.

Finally, organizational architects must design the "informal organization" as defined in the congruence model introduced in Chapter Two. This might be referred to as the design of the organization's "value space." A company's customer orientation; its attitudes toward excellence, innovation, and quality; and its preference for employee autonomy versus control are not accidental developments, nor can they be changed like a coat of paint. The organization's value space is a fundamental part of its architecture and thus an essential aspect of organizational design. In view of its importance, Chapters Six, Seven, and Eight discuss the informal organization.

Having defined what organizational architecture is, let us now turn to the conditions that lead to excellence in design. From physical architecture, we have learned that four factors are essential to the creation of effective designs:

1. Primacy of purpose—the principle of "form follows function"
2. Architectural fit—having an "architectural style" capable of fulfilling the vision of the architect, the requirements of the situation, and the needs of the people living in it
3. Use of structural materials capable of implementing the architecture
4. Availability of the necessary collateral technologies

Next, we describe and illustrate these principles using examples from both physical and organizational architecture. Subsequently, we describe the potential of information technology as a structural material and outline the organizational design possibilities it opens up. Finally, we outline the future of organizational design at both the enterprise level and the unit level. Included is a description of the network organization and specific design principles for business units, plants, and offices.

Primacy of Purpose

To understand the relationship between purpose and architectural form, we look at the plans of one Greek and two Roman temples (Figure 1.1). (A plan is a bird's-eye view of a building through a

Figure 1.1. Architectural Plans for One Greek Temple and Two Roman Temples.

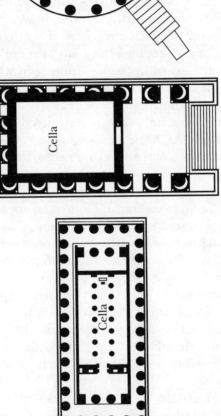

Temple of Poseidon
Paestum
c. 460 B.C.

Temple of Fortuna Virilus
Rome
Late 2nd century B.C.

Temple of the Sibyl
Tivoli
Early 1st century B.C.

horizontal "slice" or section.) In classical Greek temples, such as the Temple of Poseidon, the cella (or sanctuary, where the image of the deity was kept) tended to be small and divided into three parts. Access to the cella was restricted and ceremonies tended to take place outdoors, with the facade of the temple in the background (Janson, 1991). Although the Romans adopted many elements of Greek temple design, they needed a more spacious temple interior to display the trophies of their conquests. In the Temple of Fortuna Virilus, we see a cella consisting of a single room; however, the essential design, built around the basic functions of the temple, persisted even when the Romans adopted the round temple design for the Temple of the Sibyl, based upon the building in which the flame of the city of Rome was kept (Temple of Vesta) (Janson, 1991).

These three examples illustrate that when an architectural design fulfills the needs for which it was intended, it will endure for many generations. As the next example shows, however, marked changes in functional requirements may necessitate an alteration in the basic design.

When Constantine the Great made Christianity the Roman Empire's state religion in the fourth century, an appropriate setting was needed for the new official faith. The new church had to combine the traditional role of the temple as a sanctuary with that of an assembly hall in which the Christian congregation could worship together. In other words, the participative character of Christian worship demanded a type of sacred building very different from the Roman temple that had preceded it. The basilica, with its large interior space based on the design of the Roman baths, served as the basis for a new design. Old St. Peter's, the church built from that design, became the model for Christian churches that persisted well into the Renaissance.

The design of Old St. Peter's is a perfect example of the principle that form follows function, and it contains an important lesson for organizational architects (Figure 1.2). Managers who attempt to make their organizations perform functions for which they were not designed invite frustration and failure. For example, trying to make a functional organization adopt a customer focus may be extremely difficult, if not impossible. The architecture of the functional form is essentially inward-facing, not outward-facing. Only a fundamental redesign is likely to make a real difference.

Figure 1.2. Design of Old St. Peter's.

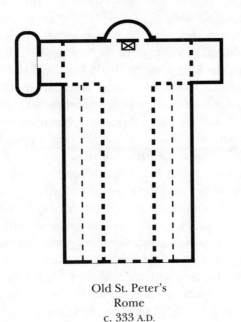

Old St. Peter's
Rome
c. 333 A.D.

    As executives contemplate the appropriate form for their organizations, it is critical that they objectively reassess their organizations' strategic intent (Hamel and Prahalad, 1989) and core mission (Beckhard and Pritchard, 1992). Changes in these fundamentals may suggest that historical organizational forms, appropriate for so many years, may need to change.

Architectural Fit

The early Christian church was only the beginning of a long process of architectural evolution. As shown in the next example, the Gothic style developed in the Middle Ages to satisfy needs that could not be fulfilled by earlier designs. The focus of our architectural example is the rebuilding of the Abbey Church of St.-Denis, just outside Paris, in early twelfth-century France. As architecture is always created in context, we begin our story with some important history (von Simson, 1956).

In the twelfth century, the power and wealth of the king of France were eclipsed by those of his nobles. In fact, the only region ruled directly by the king was the Île-de-France, a small geographic region with Paris at its center. Abbot Suger, chief advisor to King Louis VI, forged a landmark political alliance between the monarchy and the Church. A council was convened on French soil at Reims in October 1119. Then, in the presence of the French king, Pope Calixtus II excommunicated German Emperor Henry V as an enemy of the Church. This brought to a head a longstanding struggle between the papacy and the German empire.

Although forced to concede diplomatically to the Church's demands in 1123, the emperor was less gracious with the French, with whom he had been feuding for some time and without whose support at the Reims council the excommunication would have been impossible. Consequently, in August 1124, Henry V invaded France with the support of his father-in-law, Henry I of England.

In this crisis, Louis VI retreated to Suger's church, the Abbey of St.-Denis, to ask for the intercession of his "special patron" St. Denis, who, "after God, [was the] singular protector of the realm." After acknowledging his vassalage to St. Denis, the king appealed to contingents throughout France to join him in his defense of the realm. The response to the royal summons was unprecedented.

With the relationship between the Church and the king cemented by these events, Suger sought to make St.-Denis the religious center of France, ending a century-long struggle for independence from the bishops of Paris. In addition, Suger sought to make St.-Denis a pilgrimage church to outshine all the others, most of all Santiago de Compostela, the most celebrated pilgrimage center of Western Europe. Together, these two acts constituted a significant shift in power within the Church, and the rebuilt St.-Denis was to be the concrete symbol of the reshaped political landscape.

St.-Denis was perfect for Suger's ends, because it was the shrine of the apostle of France and the chief memorial of the Carolingian dynasty, from which the kings of France derive their claim to rule. (Charlemagne and his father, Pepin the Short, had been consecrated kings at St.-Denis, and the remains of Pepin and other important figures were interred there.) Although there is reliable historical evidence that Suger did not have a clear plan in mind when he took his first steps toward rebuilding St.-Denis immediately after the events of 1124 (von Simson, 1956), two longstanding principles underlie his vision:

> *A symbolic interpretation of light.* The metaphysics of light (light flooding through "most sacred" choir windows to become the Light Divine, a mystic revelation of the spirit of God) was central to Christian doctrine in the Middle Ages (Janson, 1991). "Light and luminous objects conveyed an insight into the perfection of the cosmos, and a divination of the Creator" (von Simson, 1956).
>
> *Perfect mathematical relationships among design elements.* Suger believed that a harmonious relationship between the parts of the design would result from perfect mathematical ratios. This idea goes back to ancient times, had a long tradition in Christian thought, and would remain central in Renaissance architecture (Brunelleschi, Alberti, and Palladio) and the modern work of Le Corbusier.

By driving the architecture of St.-Denis along these two powerful principles, Suger designed the church quite differently from any that preceded it. The vaulted ceilings were higher, and a greater proportion of the walls were windowed, leading to a lightness and gracefulness that communicated a sense of spirituality quite different from the heavy solidity of the Romanesque churches built in the late eleventh and early twelfth centuries. In addition, the plan of the church is far more rational, symmetrical, and carefully proportioned than any that had preceded it. Instead of a series of closed rooms, the choir of St.-Denis is one large open space.

On reflection, the significance of Gothic architecture lies neither in its inspirational design principles nor in its technical achievements. As mentioned, the symbolic interpretation of light and the idea of mathematically based harmony had existed for centuries. Furthermore, each of the design elements in St.-Denis had been used in one form or another in previous designs. But no church had united all the design elements as they were united in St.-Denis. Most importantly, however, the Gothic style as conceived by Suger was the right architecture for the times and for the purpose for which it was conceived. As prototyped in St.-Denis and refined in Sens, Chartres, Notre Dame, and other churches throughout Europe, the Gothic cathedral is the fusion of a clear purpose, a compelling vision, and technical mastery in design and execution. As such, it is the very quintessence of architecture.

   If we return to the example of global and multinational business organization that started this chapter, we see some striking parallels. Just as the architecture of Unilever after William Lever's death was clearly shaped by protectionist sentiments and the isolation forced on subsidiaries by World War II, the rebuilding of St.-Denis was shaped by the political forces and theological vision of the Middle Ages. Equally important, each architecture had to "work" in both philosophical and practical terms for the people inhabiting it—that is, the managers and employees of Unilever in the first half of the twentieth century and the clergy, nobility, and laypeople of France in the first half of the twelfth century.

   To complete our discussion of the appropriateness of the "fit" between architectural form and the requirements of the situation, in Table 1.2 we summarize and elaborate the organizational frameworks introduced in the Unilever case (global and multinational organization) and add a new one (international organization) (Bartlett and Ghoshal, 1989). The international form emerged shortly after the end of World War II as American companies expanded abroad. The major thrust of the international form is knowledge transfer. It provides subsidiaries with greater freedom than the global organization but not as much as the classical multinational organization. In the international form, freedom occurs within the context of a sophisticated set of management practices and reporting systems. For instance, in such firms, it is not unusual to require upwardly mobile foreign nationals to spend time in the home country to learn "how things are done."

   The purpose of describing these three types of organizations is to clarify their similarities and differences as architectural forms.

Table 1.2. Characteristics of Global, Multinational, and International Organizations.

Global Organization	Multinational Organization	International Organization
Theme: World is one integrated global market.	*Theme: Decentralize federation—a portfolio of national businesses—and become multinational.*	*Theme: Transfer knowledge/expertise to "less advanced" overseas environments.*
Earliest of the international corporate forms (Henry Ford, J. D. Rockefeller, William Lever)	Adopted in the pre–World War II period, for example, Lever post-1925	Emerged early post–World War II
Centralized assets, resources, responsibilities		
Role of subsidiaries to reach foreign markets/ build scale		Role of subsidiary to leverage capabilities/resources of the parent company
Little freedom to modify products and strategies for local subsidiaries	Responses by subsidiaries to differences in local markets	Because of professional management and sophisticated controls, more freedom than global organizations but less than multinational organizations
Fits managerial norms of Japanese companies	Well suited to "informal" management practices of European companies	Good fit with U.S. management culture

From Table 1.2, it is clear that they are very different types of organizations despite superficial similarities in their formal structure.

There are critical differences between the components of these organizational architectures with respect to culture, values, skills required, and the management processes within subsidiaries and headquarters. The resulting characteristic behavioral patterns that define the functioning of each organizational form are also quite different. For example, decisions on how capital is spent, how people are assigned to jobs, which products will be manufactured and how they will be distributed and priced, and other subjects vary so greatly that they constitute *architectural differences*, not simply minor variations of a common design.

The table also reminds us that political, economic, and competitive forces, the home country national culture, and the personal-

ities of founding managers play a key role in determining the type
of organizational architecture created. Later in this chapter, we will
identify the forces that are shaping the organizational architecture of
the twenty-first century.

Structural Materials

We now turn to a deeper level of design, specifically to the materials
out of which architecture is created. As building materials are generally insufficiently appreciated, two examples will clearly illustrate
their importance.

Concrete had been developed in the Near East prior to 1000
B.C.; however, this material was used only for fortifications. The
Romans legitimized the use of concrete and developed its application until it became their primary building material. For example,
in the Temple of the Sibyl discussed earlier, the walls of the cella
are made of concrete sheathed with an aesthetic covering to harmo-
nize with the pillars, doors, and window frames, which were made
of cut stone. The famous Roman Colosseum, completed about A.D.
80 as an amphitheater for gladiatorial combat is, in terms of mass,
one of the largest single structures ever created. The Colosseum
clearly illustrates the inseparability of architecture and structural
materials, because such an undertaking would have been impossible
without the capabilities of concrete.

The relationship between structural materials and architecture is even more vividly highlighted by the history of the skyscraper, perhaps the most distinctive icon of the modern era. The earliest
roots of the skyscraper go back to the middle of the nineteenth
century, a time during which the world was enjoying a love affair
with the machine. Technological breakthroughs such as photogra-
phy, the telephone, and electric lighting captivated the public and
transformed Victorian society into "modern times."

Borrowing both the iron beam and the interior spaciousness
of railroad stations and roundhouses, Sir Joseph Paxton built an
international exhibition hall called the Crystal Palace in London
in 1850. Paxton's design proved too far ahead of its time; it would
take another seventy years before its machine aesthetic would have
its full effect on mainstream architecture. Nevertheless, by the turn
of the century, a new architecture based on the structural capabil-

ities of the steel beam had emerged. Rather than load-bearing walls, the steel beam permitted structures whose weight could be shouldered entirely by the interior skeletal frame. And although early examples, such as the Wainright building in St. Louis, Missouri, built in 1891 by American architect Louis Sullivan, were clearly transitional because of their solid exterior walls, they were clearly indicative of what was to come.

In the 1920s, a distinctly "modern" architecture emerged that severed completely the characteristic look of load-bearing wall construction. Walter Gropius, founder of the avant-garde Bauhaus school in Germany, pioneered the radical glass "curtain wall" in his Bauhaus buildings. Gropius's "glass box" quickly evolved into the International Style that would come to dominate architectural design for the next fifty years.

The principal lesson from these examples is that new materials make possible new architectures, and that new architectures may make certain elements of the old architecture obsolete. Equally clearly, the mere existence of a revolutionary material does not ensure that a new architecture will emerge to take advantage of it. Depositing a large pile of structural steel on the building site of St.-Denis would not have given the church a new architecture. Not only was Suger's vision quite different, but the aesthetics of the times were different, and it is not likely that St.-Denis's master builder (who is unnamed in Suger's extensive writings) would have had the engineering know-how or the building methods to use it.

In organizational terms, the role of the hierarchy as the principal means to coordinate, control, and facilitate communication is dramatically impacted by the capabilities of information technology, which we position here as a structural material. The existence of these capabilities, however, does not determine the organizational architecture of the future; it merely makes a new architecture possible. Furthermore, as people have to work in any new organizational form, there are profound social consequences arising from new organizational architectures that are at least as complex as their technical challenges. In the next section, we explore the capabilities of information technology and its implications for organizational design in greater detail.

Information Technology as a Structural Material

To use any structural material, one must understand its capabilities. Toward the end of developing architectures "ahead of their time," we consider the capabilities of information technology that push the limits of current practice without, it is hoped, crossing into science fiction.

Communications

Communications is the foundation of the organization's infrastructure and one of the basic purposes fulfilled by its formal structure. It should soon be possible to deliver sound, data, and image to any person, any time, anywhere on the globe, either fixed or mobile (Table 1.3). The principal message of the benefits outlined in Table 1.3 is the creation of organizations that are free from the communications constraints imposed by geography and time zones. In the past, individuals working remotely were second-class citizens, irrespective of how important they might be to the organization's mis-

Table 1.3. Some Technical Capabilities Offered by Emerging Information Technology Communications Capabilities and Some Resulting Organizational Design Benefits.

Communications Capabilities of Information Technology	Organizational Design Benefits of Enhanced Communications
"Go anywhere" electronic mail, facsimile, and data interchange	Organizational functioning independent of time and distance
Desktop video teleconferencing	Greater dissemination of information and expertise, particularly to people located remotely
Voice and video annotated documents and electronic mail	
Joint authoring and other "groupware" applications	Creation of ad hoc groups and organizations tied together electronically
	Enhancement of collaboration, in physical proximity and at a distance

sion. In addition, temporary organizations, such as task forces, often had to make do with a less-than-adequate communications infrastructure, even if their projects were vital. All of these constraints will be a thing of the past in coming years as technology improves.

Linkage

Since the early 1980s, the benefits of using information technology to achieve closer integration or "linkage" between parts of the organization and between the organization and its customers and suppliers have been documented by management researchers, consultants, and the business press (Table 1.4). Many treatments of this subject have discussed these systems-based improvements independently of organizational factors, although a few writers saw them as steps leading to a "rearchitecting" of the organization (Nolan and Pollack, 1986; Gerstein, 1987).

Using information technology to achieve closer linkage does not constitute a new organizational architecture any more than using steel structural beams would automatically turn a building into a skyscraper; however, the creation of technology-supported work processes that cross traditional organizational boundaries and the design of team-based work processes aided by systems-based tools

Table 1.4. Linkage Capabilities of Information Technology and Resulting Organizational Design Benefits.

Linkage Capabilities of Information Technology	Organizational Design Benefits of Enhanced Linkage
Across organizational boundaries with customers and suppliers	Business processes that reach directly into customers' or suppliers' value chain; integration possible at the industry as well as at the company level
Across functions, such as between sales and manufacturing	Business processes that integrate company's value chain more effectively
Within individual functions, teams, and so on	Enabling of parallel processes and facilitation of reciprocal interdependencies

are clearly directional moves. Although it is not a manager's purpose to create a new architecture, merely to get the work done, it may be beneficial to managers if they recognize that they may be working toward a new organizational design paradigm in their attempt to stretch the application of the sophisticated technology at hand.

In addition to reshaping the organizational architecture, increasing linkage will tend to blur external boundaries and facilitate multicompany alliances. When linkage becomes extensive, an electronic "marketplace" emerges to replace previous rigid structures of buyers and sellers. Increased liquidity in the marketplace usually means better prices for buyers, slimmer margins for producers, and a threat to the existence of many intermediaries. We have seen this phenomenon many times in recent years, particularly in the world's securities and currency markets.

Knowledge Enhancement

One of the most exciting areas of information technology application is artificial intelligence (AI). Unfortunately, in the early 1980s, AI was a media darling, and people's expectations tended to rise faster than results could be achieved. Although many difficult problems remain to be solved, steady progress has been made in the application of robotics, artificial vision, speech recognition, and knowledge-based systems. Of the areas likely to have the greatest impact on organizational architecture, knowledge-based systems that seek to incorporate human know-how into computer software and equipment are among the most important. (As it turns out, significant value can be generated even without employing the specialized programming methodologies generally associated with AI. We therefore make no presumption in this section about the underlying technology employed.) Table 1.5 outlines a few of the technological benefits we can expect to impact organizational design in the coming years. This table is not exhaustive, however. Its purpose is to provide a sense of direction to the reshaping of work in the coming decades that will occur as complex systems grow smarter and thus simpler for people to use.

Table 1.5. Knowledge Enhancement Capabilities of Information Technology and Resulting Organizational Design Benefits.

Knowledge Enhancement Capabilities of Information Technology	Organizational Design Benefits of Knowledge Enhancement
Codification of technical knowledge and subject matter expertise	"Smart" transaction processing systems with higher levels of automation
Representation of knowledge of "how things work" to facilitate use	Less reliance on human expertise to solve problems and operate complex systems
Creation of "smart tools," software "agents," and "knowbots" that accomplish communication, computing, and administrative tasks previously requiring human intervention	Increased "democratization" of computer-based tools Reduction of training costs when systems are redesigned and enhanced More efficient extraction of information from complex networked data bases

Collateral Technologies

Imagine designing a skyscraper. Think first of those capabilities required to achieve its characteristic height. Next, think about providing the means to fulfill its principal use, for example, as an office building. There are many capabilities required of a skyscraper that are critical to its usability but not central to either its basic architecture or mission. We call these required capabilities *collateral technologies*. For the skyscraper, collateral technologies include indoor plumbing, high-speed elevators, heating and ventilation systems, and fire prevention/control systems. An understanding of the collateral technologies for any new architecture is critical because the efficacy of the architecture is often as dependent on them as on the technologies associated with accomplishing the core functions for which the structure was created. Listed here are a number of collateral technologies consistent with the requirements of emerging organizational architectures.

- People selection methods geared to the needs of new work designs

- Education and training systems consistent with redefined work
- Consistent feedback, evaluation, and reward systems, particularly those that are geared to group-based work structures and use high levels of automation
- Privacy/security methods and technology for more automated work systems
- Design tools for creating, viewing, and modifying automated work processes

The last item may require a little explanation. In most organizations today, much of the work process is visible, consisting of a series of "islands of automation" connected by a manual process. As more technology is introduced into the work process, however, a greater percentage of the total work will become invisible. In many cases, a work product will be visible at one step in the production process only to disappear and reappear somewhere else in a more advanced state. In such an environment, it is critical to have an automated tool capable of showing the entire work process, both manual and automated. Ideally, such a tool would have computer-aided design/computer-aided manufacturing (CAD/CAM) capabilities with which changes in the work process could be made electronically. One would still have to change what people do, of course, but the necessary systems modifications would be created automatically.

Although we are far from possessing such capabilities today, systems designers are working in this area, and there is no reason to believe that such capabilities are not achievable.

Twenty-First–Century Organizational Architecture: Where Are We Going?

The "Design Problem"

Following our principles of good architecture, we should root our new architecture in the functions such an architecture must serve. This might be expressed as a "design problem" comprising several elements:

- Being cost competitive with the most efficient producers while supplying products that reliably exceed customer requirements
- Addressing differentiated and changing needs in local markets ("micromarkets" for small companies, regionally or demographically distinct submarkets for a national company, or country-sized markets for the transnational organization)
- Learning from both successes and failures
- Exploiting innovation companywide whether ideas arise inside or outside the company
- Achieving compatibility with relevant community values and cultures

In developing architectural solutions to this design problem, the organizational architect typically approaches design at two levels: enterprise-level design and unit-level design.

Enterprise-Level Design

When Thomas Edison founded the Edison Electric Light Company in 1878 to exploit the possibilities of electric lighting, he took a step that has often powered the innovation process in America: he started his own company. Just fourteen years later, however, in 1892, Edison Electric merged with other companies to form the General Electric Company, one of the largest industrial companies in the United States.

Organizations such as General Electric, like the railroads and steel companies before them, were large, geographically distributed, and functionally diverse in order to muster the knowledge required in many different disciplines and markets. To govern themselves, these organizations adopted an architecture characterized by its unity of command and steep hierarchy (Chandler, 1988). This machine bureaucracy, which arose during the same period as the skyscraper in response to the requirements of the industrial age, was a major step forward in the structuring of human enterprise. It was in no small part responsible for the monumental achievements of that era. Today, however, we must recognize that the utility of this basic architectural style has come to an end. (See Jaques, 1990, for a discussion of the strengths and weaknesses of hierarchy.) The external environment and the knowledge requirements necessary to manage in it have become increasingly more complex over the decades. In addition, the pace at which new knowledge is created has accelerated, and the increased interconnections needed between knowledge areas have forced specialized groups into greater contact with one another, thereby adding internal complexity. Together, these forces make the traditional solutions to organization obsolete. As indicated graphically in Figure 1.3, traditional organizations increasingly find that their core businesses are changing more rapidly than their organizations can adapt; however, coping with this change by starting a new company—the traditional route of entrepreneurship—is increasingly less effective. The financial, manufacturing, and distribution resources required to cope with greater environmental complexity often exceed the capabilities of startup companies. Both types of organization are therefore being pushed in the direction of what is called the *network organization* (Nolan, Pollack, and Ware, 1988).

As a different architecture, the network organization goes beyond its formal structure. Pools of assets, knowledge, and competence are "distributed"; that is, they reside in multiple locations. Resources are neither solely concentrated in the center nor disbursed to business units. Not all businesses or units play the same role in the organization ("designed asymmetry"). In developing new products or marketing strategy, some units lead while others play a supportive role. The interdependence among entities is facilitated as necessary through shared goals, management processes, and common incentives (Bartlett and Ghoshal, 1989).

In the network organization, patterns of interaction (flow of information, product, and people) are dynamic and established by need rather than by a rigid plan. Some interaction patterns change very slowly and thus are nearly permanent, similarly to more traditional organizations. Other patterns of interaction are established rapidly, endure for the duration of a new product design cycle or special project, and are then dissolved, returning the resources to their home bases.

Whenever required, direct contact is initiated between individuals and groups who need to work together. The hierarchy is not

Figure 1.3. Factors in the Trend Toward Network Organization.

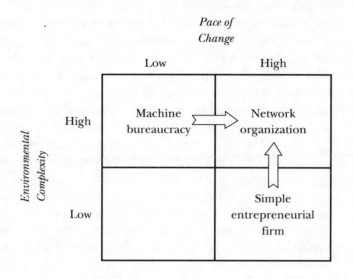

Source: Adapted from Nolan, Pollack, and Ware, 1988, p. 2.

used as the primary means of communication, coordination, or initiation of action.

The organization's value system is characterized by sharing and collaboration versus ownership and turfism, trust versus suspicion, authority of knowledge versus position, and value on learning versus "not invented here."

The network organization is clearly more than the simple sum of these elements. As a result of the attitudes of its people, the management and work processes employed, and the structures that establish the framework for behavior, the network has scale without mass. The network's wide reach and deep technical knowledge can be deployed rapidly to deal with problems and opportunities, and the results of these efforts, whether successes or failures, enhance organizational learning.

The network would be a panacea if it were not painfully difficult to build and maintain one. Its very nature makes it impossible to plan centrally and roll out to the field. The network must be grown. This takes time, typically many years, and its success is highly dependent on its people and a complex set of interpersonal relationships nurtured over time.

A new concept in organizational design has recently emerged that bears watching. The *platform organization* (Ciborra, 1991) takes its name from the architecture of computer workstations, specifically those built using the UNIX operating system. A number of UNIX workstations have been created as "computing platforms," capable of being configured for many different uses, in contrast to other computers designed as single-purpose machines. Therefore, rather than a new "stable" architecture (such as the network), the platform organization is envisioned to rapidly reconfigure its resources in fundamental ways based on the changes required in mission and basic strategy. For example, suppose a computer company must emphasize specialized hardware manufacture one year, low-cost generic hardware manufacture two years later, and applications software development a few years after that. None of the conventional organizational forms, including the network, are capable of transforming themselves rapidly enough. The platform organization's strength, therefore, is *fundamental change* (Beckhard and Pritchard, 1992).

Viewed in this way, a snapshot of the platform organization would not reveal its essential character. Only its history over time, with particular attention paid to the interval required to achieve a fundamental change in mission and strategy, would reveal the platform organization's unique strengths. In fact, day-to-day, the platform organization may function at a lower performance level than a more specialized organization, which has optimized its resource mix and processes to implement a specific strategy.

Though the platform organization is an elegant idea, we are a long way from understanding either the practice or the theory of such "meta-level architectures."

Unit-Level Design

Despite the value of an appropriate design at the enterprise level, most of the people in an organization spend the bulk of their working lives as employees of one of the organization's many units, for example, a plant or an office. Equally important, most of the work of the organization—making and selling the product, fulfilling orders, providing product support—takes place at this level. Obviously, effective design at the unit level of the organization is crucial to success. It is equal in importance to the macro level design at the enterprise level.

Listed below are guidelines to help shape organizational architecture at the unit level. In contrast to design at the enterprise level, which focuses on the distribution of businesses and resource groups and their relationship to one another, design at the unit level deals with engineering work flows, the configuration of work groups, and the nature of individual jobs. The ideas presented here constitute an architecture for work at the unit level. Structure, process, information flow, and values are included, and it is intended that these design elements be configured to work in concert toward the creation of a coherent design.

1. Use micro-enterprise units as the basic building blocks within the network. Each unit should consist of a set of capabilities that permit the fulfillment of an entire segment of the work process—that is, the provision of a product or service to a designated set of customers. If possible, each unit should have external suppliers and customers, although internal customers operating "at arms length" are a workable alternative.
2. Instead of designing from the top downward, design from the center outward, starting with the micro-enterprise units. The administrative superstructure should be kept to a minimum.
3. Design work processes prior to designing organizational structure. Instead of building an organization around the division of labor and the creation of a hierarchy, analyze the steps in the work process and redesign as necessary to create subgroups based on natural breaks and meaningful jobs for individuals and teams.
4. In designing work processes, automate as much as is practically possible. Pushing for maximum practical automation encourages a work design in which people do those tasks that uniquely use human skills and capabilities. Since the automation frontier will always be changing, maximum practical automa-

tion is more an orientation to design rather than a fixed technological frontier.

5.   Engineer work processes for zero defects and no after-the-fact inspections or reconciliations. Data should be entered only once, and inspection should be built into each step in the work process to ensure that mistakes are not exported down the line. Reconciliations arising from multiple copies of the same data element or timing differences should be designed out of the work process.

6.   Use teams, not individuals, as the basic organizational building block. In most cases, the wider scope of teams will ensure that the output is measurable and meaningful to the people producing it. Teams also permit the flexibility to respond to day-to-day fluctuations in available staff. For teams to operate most effectively, groups should be self-managed, not traditionally supervised; people should be multifunctional; and tasks should be defined with minimum boundaries and maximum freedom.

7.   Share the wealth. It is likely that people will wish to share in the prosperity created by their work, though the benefits they seek may not solely be financial. In addition to recognition and fair pay, therefore, the means to understand the work force's values and satisfy them financially and nonfinancially should be created.

Summary

Organizational historians will look back at our time as one of transition and innovation. They will point to examples of organizations that foreshadowed the still immature organizational architecture of the twenty-first century.

For these innovative organizations to be successful, there must be harmony between people's attitudes and values and the new structures, processes, and technology. Because values change very slowly, organizational architecture will evolve incrementally, even during periods of rapid environmental flux. Unlike technology, which can make breakthrough leaps that leave earlier generations behind, organizational architecture is essentially a social art form that must remain grounded in the needs of its consumers, the people who work in the organization day-to-day.

As long as we keep the needs of these ultimate customers in mind, those of us who design organizations and manage change will find the coming years an era of unprecedented opportunity, challenge, and reward. Now is the time to build the organizational architecture of the future, one that will last for generations.

References

Bartlett, C. A., and Ghoshal, S. *Managing Across Borders*. Boston: Harvard Business School Press, 1989.

Beckhard, R., and Pritchard, W. *Changing the Essence: The Art of Creating and Leading Fundamental Change in Organizations*. San Francisco: Jossey-Bass, 1992.

Chandler, A. *Strategy and Structure: Chapters in the History of the Industrial Enterprise*. Cambridge, Mass.: MIT Press, 1962.

Chandler, A. "The Railroads: Pioneers in Modern Corporate Management." In T. K. McCraw (ed.), *The Essential Alfred Chandler: Essays Toward a Historical Theory of Big Business*. Boston: Harvard Business School Press, 1988.

Ciborra, C. U. "A Platform for Surprises: The Organization of Global Technology Strategy at Olivetti," Unpublished dissertation, Universita di Trento, 1991.

Gerstein, M. *The Technology Connection: Strategy and Change in the Information Age*. Reading, Mass.: Addison-Wesley, 1987.

Hamel, G., and Prahalad, C. K. "Strategic Intent." *Harvard Business Review*, May/June 1989, 63-76.

Janson, F. W. *History of Art*. New York: Abrams, 1991.

Jaques, E. "In Praise of Hierarchy." *Harvard Business Review*, Jan./Feb. 1990.

Lawrence, P., and Lorsch, J. *Organization and Environment*. Cambridge, Mass.: Harvard Business School Research Division, 1967.

Nolan, R., and Pollack, A. "Organization and Architecture, or Architecture and Organization." *Stage by Stage*, 1986, *6*(5).

Nolan, R., Pollack, A., and Ware, J. "Creating the 21st Century Organization." *Stage by Stage*, 1988, *8*(4).

Rasmussen, S. E. *Experiencing Architecture.* Cambridge, Mass.:
  MIT Press, 1991.
von Simson, O. *The Gothic Cathedral: Origins of Gothic Architecture and the Medieval Concept of Order.* New York: Pantheon,
  1956.
Woodward, J. *Industrial Organization.* New York: Oxford University Press, 1965.

TWO

Designing Organizations That Have Good Fit: A Framework for Understanding New Architectures

DAVID A. NADLER, MICHAEL L. TUSHMAN

The primary job of senior management is to design, build, and operate organizations that function effectively. Achieving organizational effectiveness is difficult, however. Understanding one individual's behavior is challenging in and of itself; understanding the behavior of a group made up of different individuals and comprehending the many relationships among those individuals are even more complex. Imagine, then, the mind-boggling complexity of a large organization made up of tens of thousands of individuals and thousands of groups with myriad relationships among them. Organizational behavior must be shaped and managed despite this overwhelming complexity. Ultimately the organization's work is achieved by people, individually or collectively. Influencing organizational behavior is therefore at the center of the leadership role.

Leaders have a rather limited set of tools with which to influence the patterns of organizational behavior. They can make discrete resource allocation decisions, they can choose which individuals will sit in key positions, and they can attempt to influence others through their own actions, but their influence is limited to the decisions, jobs, and people with whom they come in contact regularly. Ultimately, the tool with the largest potential leverage is the design of the organization, including the systems, the structures, and the processes by which work gets done.

We have chosen to label the broad set of decisions managers make about organizations *organizational architecture.* We use this term because organizational design is typically viewed as a narrowly defined set of decisions concerning the basic structure of the organization (Nadler and Tushman, 1988), and we believe the task that senior management faces is much broader. Over time, executives must make decisions concerning the configuration, dynamics, and aesthetics of how the various elements of organization combine to create a productive enterprise. These sets of decisions constitute what we refer to as organizational architecture.

The purpose of this chapter is to provide a way of thinking about organizational architecture. We focus on thinking about organizations as behaviorial systems, and we will begin by discussing some broad perspectives on architecture. Then, drawing from open systems theory, we describe our basic view of how organizations function. We build on that view to describe in detail a particular framework, which we call a *congruence model of organizations.* We conclude with some of the broad implications of this model for organizational architecture.

The Architecture of Organizations: A Question of Balance

What are the issues, or conflicting demands, that the organizational architect must keep in mind? Architects should consider two sets of questions (see Table 2.1). On one hand, they must consider how the architecture will enable the organization to execute its various strategies and accomplish the required work (strategy/task performance perspective). On the other hand, they must consider how the architecture will fit with or have an impact on the individuals who work for the organization (social/cultural perspective).

Both perspectives are valid, but each by itself is incomplete and will lead architects into trouble. Those who consider only strategies are likely to design organizations that look effective but that somehow do not work, are not implemented, or create as many new problems as they solve. On the other hand, those who consider only the social/cultural perspective may create organizations in which many people feel satisfied but which fail to implement strategies and accomplish the work.

Table 2.1. Two Architectural Perspectives.

Strategy/Task Performance	Social/Cultural
Design supports the implementation of strategy.	How will existing people fit into the design?
Design facilitates the flow of work.	How will the design affect power relationships among different groups?
Design permits effective managerial control.	How will the design fit with people's values and beliefs?
Design creates doable, measurable jobs.	How will the design affect the tone and operating style of the organization?

To some extent, these diverse perspectives reflect very different underlying views on the fundamental nature of organizations. From the strategy/task performance perspective, organizations are purely devices created to get work done—to execute strategies, create value, and thus benefit customers, shareholders, and the society at large. An organization is fundamentally an economic mechanism created to achieve ends that could not be achieved by individuals working alone. On the other hand, from the social/cultural perspective, organizations are devices created to satisfy the needs, desires, and aspirations of various stakeholders, both inside and outside of the organization. An organization thus exists to meet individual needs, aid in the exercise of power, and express individual or collective values.

Our view is that both perspectives are valid, and both are usually considered during the process of design. Therefore, the frameworks used for understanding organizations must be able to encompass both points of view.

A Basic View of Organizations

There are many different ways of thinking about organizations. At first, most managers think about organizations in terms of the formal structure as represented by the classical organization chart. This model views the stable, formal relationships among the jobs and work units as the most critical factor in an organization. This very limited view excludes leadership behavior, impact of the environment, informal relationships, and power distribution. Such a model can capture only a fraction of what actually goes on in organizations. Its perspective is narrow and static.

The past three decades have seen a growing consensus that a viable alternative to the classical static models of organizations exists: the organization as a social system. This approach stems from the observation that social phenomena display many of the same characteristics as natural or mechanical systems. In particular, a number of theorists have argued that organizations can be better understood if they are considered dynamic open social systems (Katz and Kahn, 1966; von Bertalanffy, 1968; Buckley, 1967; March and Simon, 1959).

What is a system? Most simply stated, a system is a set of interrelated elements; a change in one element affects other elements. An *open system* interacts with its environment. It is more than a set of interrelated elements; rather, the elements constitute a mechanism that takes input from the environment, transforms the input, and produces output. At the most general level, it should be easy to visualize organizations as systems. For example, a manufacturing plant is made up of different but related components (departments, jobs, and technologies). The plant receives input from the environment—labor, raw material, production orders—and transforms these inputs into products. Organizations display basic system characteristics. Some of the most critical characteristics are described next.

Internal Interdependence

Changes in one component of an organization frequently have repercussions for other components because the parts are interconnected. For example, in the manufacturing plant cited, changes made in the skill levels of employees will affect the productiveness of equipment, the speed or quality of production, and the nature of the supervision needed.

Capacity for Feedback

Information about the output can be used to control the system. Organizations can correct errors and even change because of this feedback. In the manufacturing plant, if management receives information that product quality is declining, it can use this information to identify factors in the system that contribute to the problem; however, unlike mechanized systems, feedback does not always lead to correction. Organizations have the potential to use feedback for self-correction but they do not always realize this potential.

Equilibrium

When an event puts the system out of balance, the system reacts by moving back into balance. If one work group in the manufacturing plant were suddenly to increase its performance dramatically, it would throw the system out of balance. This group would be making increasing demands on the groups that supply it with the information or materials it needs; the groups that work with the output would be pressured by the increasing inventory. If an incentive is in effect, other groups might perceive inequity as this one group begins to earn more. We can predict that some actions would be taken to bring the system back into balance. Either the rest of the plant would be changed to increase production, and thus be put back in balance with the single group, or (more likely) there would be pressure on the group to modify its behavior in line with the performance levels of the rest of the system (by removing workers or limiting supplies, for example). Somehow the system would develop the energy to move back toward a state of equilibrium.

Equifinality

Different system configurations can lead to the same end or to the same type of input/output conversion. There is no universal, or "one best," way to organize. This point is particularly critical to keep in mind when designing organizations. Although there is no one best way to structure an organization, clearly some ways are better than others. The challenge is to identify those architectures that are relatively comparable based on technical concerns and then make the ultimate choice based on other factors (individual, political, or cultural).

Adaptation

For a system to survive, it must maintain a favorable balance of input and output transactions with the environment, or it will run down. If the manufacturing plant produces a product for which there are fewer applications over time, the company that owns the plant must adapt to new demands and develop new products; otherwise, the plant will ultimately have to close its doors. Any system, therefore, must adapt as environmental conditions change. Prosperous organizations can fail if they do not respond to environmental changes.

Open systems theory provides a way of thinking about the organization in more complex and dynamic terms. Although the theory provides a valuable basic perspective, it is limited as a problem-solving tool because it is too abstract for use in day-to-day analysis of organizational behavior problems. We need to develop a more specific and pragmatic model based on the concepts of the open systems paradigm.

Congruence Model of Organizational Behavior

Over the years, we have developed, worked with, and refined a model that reflects the basic open systems concepts and characteristics but is more specific and thus more viable as an analytical tool. It specifies the critical input, the major output, and the transformation processes that characterize organizational functioning.

This model emphasizes the transformation process and specifically illustrates the critical characteristic of system interdependence. It views organizations as constructed of components that interact. These components exist in states of relative balance and consistency—they "fit" with each other. The parts of an organization can fit together well and function effectively, or they can fit poorly and lead to dysfunctions. This *congruence model of organi-*

zational behavior is based on the degree to which components fit together—the congruence among the components. The effectiveness of an organization reflects the congruence of the key components (Homans, 1950; Leavitt, 1965; Seiler, 1967; Lorsch and Sheldon, 1972; Galbraith, 1977).

It is important to remember that we are concerned about creating a model for the behavioral system of an organization—the system of elements that ultimately produces behavior patterns and, in turn, organizational performance. Put simply, we must understand the input with which the system has to work, the output it must produce, the major components of the transformation process, and the ways in which these components interact.

Input

In the congruence model, the input includes the elements that at any one time make up the context the organization faces, including the material with which the organization has to work. There are several types of contextual factors, each of which presents a set of givens to the organization (see Table 2.2 for an overview of organizational input).

The first contextual factor is the *environment,* or factors outside of the organization. Every organization exists within a larger environment, which includes individuals, groups, other organizations, and larger technological and social forces, all of which have a potentially powerful impact on how the organization performs. Specifically, the environment includes markets (clients or customers), suppliers, governmental and regulatory bodies, technological conditions, labor unions, competitors, financial institutions, and special-interest groups. Three critical features of the environment affect organizational functioning. First, the environment makes demands on the organization. For example, it may require certain products or services at certain levels of quality or quantity. Market pressures are particularly important here. Second, the environment may place constraints on organizational action. It may limit the activities in which an organization may engage. These constraints range from the limitations imposed by scarce capital or technology to prohibitions set by government regulations. Third, the environ-

Table 2.2. Organizational Input.

Input	Environment	Resources	History
Definition	All factors, including institutions, groups, individuals, and events, that are outside the organization being analyzed but that have a potential impact on that organization	Various assets to which the organization has access, including human resources, technology, capital, and information, as well as less tangible resources (recognition in the market and so forth)	Patterns of past behavior, activity, and effectiveness of the organization that may affect current organizational functioning
Critical features for analysis	What demands does the environment make on the organization?	What is the relative quality of the different resources to which the organization has access?	What have been the major stages or phases of the organization's development?
	How does the environment put constraints on organizational action?	To what extent are resources fixed rather than flexible in their configurations?	What is the current impact of such historical factors as strategic decisions, acts of key leaders, crises, and core values and norms?

ment provides opportunities for the organization to explore. When we analyze an organization, we must consider these factors in its environment and determine how they, singly or collectively, create demands, constraints, or opportunities.

The second contextual factor is the organization's *resources.* Any organization has access to a range of assets. These include employees, technology, capital, and information. Resources may also include less tangible assets, such as the perception of the organization in the marketplace or a positive organizational climate. Organizations can shape or deploy resources in various ways. For the purpose of analysis, two features are of primary interest: the relative quality of those resources, or their value in the context of the current or future environment, and the extent to which resources can be reshaped, or their flexibility.

The third contextual factor is the organization's *history.*

There is growing evidence that the way an organization functions today is greatly influenced by past events. It is particularly important to understand the major stages of an organization's development over time, as well as the current impact of past events—for example, prior strategic decisions, the behavior of key leaders, the nature of past crises and the organization's responses to them, and the evolution of core values and norms.

Environmental conditions, organizational resources, and history are contextual factors that cannot be changed in the short run; they are givens that provide the setting within which managers make strategic decisions. A fourth, different type of input (for purposes of organizational architecture) is *strategy*. Strategy comprises the decisions that allocate scarce resources against the constraints and opportunities of a given environment. More explicitly, strategy can be defined as specific choices of markets, offerings, technology, and distinctive competence. Given explicit attention to environmental opportunities and threats, organizational strengths and weaknesses, and organizational history, managers need to make decisions on the types of products to offer, the markets in which to sell the products, and the manner in which to distinguish the firm (for example, first mover, low-cost producer, or niche player). These long-term strategic objectives must then be factored into a set of internally consistent shorter-term objectives and supporting strategies, or tactics.

Decisions on markets, offerings, technology, and distinctive competence are the most important decisions for managers. Those organizations that make inappropriate strategic decisions will underperform or fail. No amount of organizational architecture can help an ill-conceived strategy; however, given a viable strategy and internally consistent objectives, management's challenge is to build an organization to accomplish those strategic objectives. Strategy, then, determines both the nature of the work and critical organizational output.

Output

Output is what the organization produces, how it performs, and how effective it is. There has been much discussion about the definition of an effective organization. For our purposes, it is possible to identify several critical aspects of organizational output. First, we need to think about system output at different levels. In addition to the system's basic output (that is, the products and services or economic return), we need to think about other types of output that contribute to organizational performance, such as the functioning of groups or units and individuals within the organization.

At the organizational level, three factors must be kept in mind when evaluating organizational performance: (1) goal attainment, or how well the organization meets its objectives (usually as specified by strategy); (2) resource utilization, or how well the organization makes use of available resources (not simply whether it meets its goals, but whether it realizes all of its potential and achieves its goals by building resources or by "burning them up"); and (3) adaptability, or whether the organization continues to position itself in a favorable position with respect to its environment, that is, whether it is capable of adapting to environmental changes.

Obviously, the functioning of organizational units contributes to organizational output. Organizational output is also influenced by individual behavior, and certain individual output (affective reactions such as satisfaction, stress, or good-quality working life) may be desired output in and of itself.

The Organization as a Transformation Process

So far, we have defined the nature of the input and output of the organizational system. This leads us to the transformation process. Given an environment, a set of resources, and history, the question is how to implement a strategy to produce effective performance at the individual, group, and organizational levels. In this model, the organization and its major components are the fundamental means for transforming energy and information from input into output. To understand this process, we need to identify the key components of the organization.

Organizational Components

There are many different ways of thinking about what makes up an organization. The challenge is to find useful approaches to describing organizations, simplifying complex phenomena, and identifying patterns in what may at first seem to be random activity. This model views four major components of organizations: the work, the people, the formal organization, and the informal organization (Table 2.3).

The first component is the *work*—the basic activity in which the organization is engaged, particularly in light of its strategy. The emphasis is on the specific work activities that need to be done and their inherent characteristics (as opposed to the work characteristics resulting from how the work is structured in this particular organization at this particular time). Task analysis would include a description of the basic work and work flows. This analysis must characterize the different tasks required and the specific work flows—for example, the knowledge or skills required, the rewards provided, the degree of uncertainty, and the inherent constraints (such as critical time demands and cost constraints). As it is assumed that a primary (although clearly not the only) reason for the organization's existence is to perform the task consistent with strategy, the task is the starting point for analysis. As we will see, the assessment of the adequacy of other components depends to a large degree on an understanding of the nature of the tasks to be performed. This is particularly critical in analyzing the organization for architectural purposes. Because we organize to get work done, it is critical to understand the nature of that work.

The second component of organizations is the *people* who perform tasks. The issue here is identifying the characteristics of the employees or members. The most critical aspects to consider include the nature of individual knowledge and skills, the different needs or preferences of individuals and the perceptions or expectancies that they develop, and such demographic factors as age and sex that potentially influence individual behavior.

The third component is the *formal organizational arrangements,* the structures and procedures that are explicitly and formally developed to get individuals to perform tasks consistent with organizational strategy.

The final component is the *informal organization.* Despite the set of formal organizational arrangements that exists in any organization, another set of arrangements tends to emerge over

Table 2.3. The Four Organizational Components.

Component	Work	People	Formal Organization	Informal Organization
Definition	Basic tasks to be done by the organization and its parts	Characteristics of individuals in the organization	Various structures, processes, and methods that are formally created to get individuals to perform tasks	Emerging arrangements including structures, processes, and relationships
Critical Features of Each Component	Degree of uncertainty associated with the work, including such factors as interdependence and routineness Skill and knowledge demands of the work Rewards the work inherently can provide Performance demands inherent in the work (given a strategy)	Knowledge and skills individuals have Individual needs and preferences Perceptions and expectations Background factors Demography	Grouping of functions, structure of units Coordination and control mechanisms Job design Work environment Human resources management systems Reward systems Physical location	Leader behavior Norms, values Intragroup relations Intergroup relations Informal working arrangements Communication and influence patterns Key roles Climate Power, politics

time. These arrangements are usually implicit and unwritten, but they can exert considerable influence on behavior. Such arrangements are frequently referred to as the informal organization and also have been described by the term organizational culture. They include the structures and procedures that emerge while the organization is operating. These sometimes complement formal organizational arrangements by providing structures to aid work accomplishment; in other situations, they may emerge in reaction to the formal structure—to protect individuals from it. Thus, they may either aid or hinder organizational performance. A number of aspects of the informal organization have a critical effect on behavior, including the leadership, values and beliefs, and relationships within and between groups.

An organization can therefore be thought of as a set of components—the task, the individuals, the formal organization, and the informal organization. In any system, however, the critical question is not what are the components, but what is the nature of their interaction and how do the relationships among the components affect how they combine to produce output.

The Concept of Congruence

A relative degree of congruence exists between each pair of organizational components. The congruence between two components is defined as the degree to which the needs, demands, goals, and structures of one component are consistent with the needs, demands, goals, and structures of another component. Congruence is therefore a measure of how well pairs of components fit together. Consider, for example, two components: the task and the individual. At the simplest level, the task presents skill and knowledge demands on the individuals who would perform it. At the same time, the individuals available to do the tasks have certain characteristics (their skill and knowledge). Obviously, if an individual's characteristics match the demands of the task, his or her performance will be more effective. Obviously, too, the individual-task congruence relationship encompasses more factors than knowledge and skill. Similarly, each congruence relationship in the model has its own specific characteristics. Research and theory can guide the assessment of fit in each relationship. For an overview of the critical elements of each congruence relationship, see Table 2.4.

The Congruence Hypothesis

The aggregate model, or whole organization, displays a relatively high or low degree of system congruence in that pairs of components have high or low congruence. The basic hypothesis of the model is as follows: other things being equal, the greater the total degree of congruence among the various components, the more effective will be the organization, effectiveness being defined as the degree to which actual organizational output is similar to expected or planned output as specified by strategy.

The basic dynamic of congruence sees the organization as most effective when its pieces fit together. If we also consider strategy, this view expands to include the fit between the organization and its larger environment; an organization is most effective when its strategy is consistent with its environment (in light of organizational resources and history) and when the organizational components are congruent with the task necessary to implement that strategy.

The Model

We can think of organizations in the terms laid out in Figure 2.1. The organization is a system that takes input from its context. The three major elements of context are the environment, the available resources, and history. A major organizational input is strategy, the basic decisions made about what businesses the enterprise will engage in. Within each business, decisions are made about markets, offerings, and the basis of competition.

The organization is the mechanism that takes strategy, in the context of environment, resources, and history, and transforms it into output. The organization is viewed as being composed of four key elements, and the critical dynamic is how those elements fit with one another, or their degree of congruence. The more congruent an organization is the more effective it will be.

Table 2.4. Definitions of Fit Among Components.

Fit	Issues
Individual/ organization	How are individual needs met by the organizational arrangements? Do individuals hold clear perceptions of organizational structures? Is there a convergence of individual and organizational goals?
People/work	How are individual needs met by the tasks? Do individuals have skills and abilities to meet task demands?
People/informal organization	How are individual needs met by the informal organization? How does the informal organization make use of individual resources consistent with informal goals?
Work/organization	Are organizational arrangements adequate to meet the demands of the task? Do organizational arrangements motivate behavior that is consistent with task demands?
Work/informal organization	Does the informal organization structure facilitate task performance? Does it help meet the demands of the task?
Organization/informal organization	Are the goals, rewards, and structures of the informal organization consistent with those of the formal organization?

Summary

The view of organizations expounded in this chapter leads to a number of implications about architecture. First, this is a contingency view (rather than a universal view) of organizational effectiveness and architecture. Effectiveness is driven by the relationship among components (congruence) rather than by the inherent characteristics of individual components; thus there are very few universally good approaches to organizational architecture. Different ways of organizing will be more or less effective for different contexts, for different technologies, and for different people.

Second, the model is driven by strategy and work. Although organizations exist for different purposes, corporations as economic

Figure 2.1. Organizational Model.

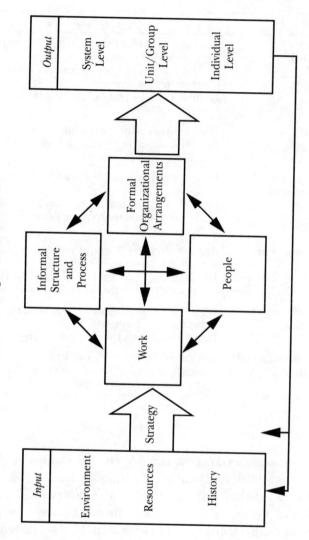

enterprises are fundamentally organized around a core business proposition that involves the provision of offerings to customers who pay for them, leading to return for owners, employees, and other stakeholders. The primary variable is thus strategy, or the achievement of purpose. In line with that assumption, the architecture of organizations is driven by a set of core strategic decisions (who are our customers? with what will we provide them? why should they choose us?) that in turn shape the dimensions of the work to be done. The task of the architect is to find different combinations of people, formal organization, and informal organization that meet the needs of the strategy (and thus the work).

Third, the model implies a dynamic view of organization. Although it is difficult to convey in the two-dimensional, static space of a book page, the model does view organizations as dynamic—the different components are always in a state of change. New external forces constantly impose new demands on the organization. These forces push the components out of fit; at the same time, the forces of the system seek to restore fit. An analysis of an organization using the congruence model at one point in time is, at best, a snapshot. One can fully understand an organization only by observing it over time. Thus, architectures need to be created that can function in that dynamic space.

On a day-to-day basis, managers face three different challenges. The first challenge is *strategic fit,* making appropriate and effective strategic decisions that enable the organization to respond to and capitalize on the demands, constraints, and opportunities presented by the environment. The second challenge is *strategy-organization fit*—to develop a basic approach, or organizational architecture, that meets the demands of the business strategy. The third challenge is *internal organization fit*—to make sure that the four components of the organization remain congruent.

Another point should be made concerning fit. Over the long term, fit is usually desirable, and the task of the architect is to tune the architecture to maintain congruence. However, there frequently are times when major changes occur in the environment that require significant change in all elements of an organization: work, people, formal organization, and informal organization. At these times, the goal may be to destroy the fit that previously existed. In fact, fit may become the enemy of change. The forces that strive to maintain equilibrium may be the very forces that resist change. The architect's task here is to develop new architectural paradigms that fit the new conditions.

The congruence model does not guide us toward specific architectural decisions, but it does provide us with a way of thinking about the environment in which these decisions are made. It also gives us a way of understanding and analyzing the potential impact of architectural decision, as well as provides us with a common language for discussing the elements of organization and the activities of architecture.

References

Buckley, W. *Sociology and Modern Systems Theory.* Englewood Cliffs, N.J.: Prentice Hall, 1967.

Galbraith, J. R. *Organization Design.* Reading, Mass.: Addison-Wesley, 1977.

Homans, D. C. *The Human Group.* Orlando, Fla.: Harcourt Brace Jovanovich, 1950.

Katz, D., and Kahn, R. L. *The Social Psychology of Organizations.* New York: Wiley, 1966.

Leavitt, H. J. "Applied Organization Change in Industry." In J. G. March (ed.), *Handbook of Organizations.* Skokie, Ill.: Rand-McNally, 1965.

Lorsch, J. W., and Sheldon, A. "The Individual in the Organization: A Systems View." In J. W. Lorsch and P. R. Lawrence (eds.), *Managing Group and Intergroup Relations.* Homewood, Ill.: Business One Irwin, 1972.

March, J., and Simon, H. *Organizations.* New York: Wiley, 1959.

Nadler, D. A., and Tushman, M. L. *Strategic Organization Design.* Glenview, Ill.: Scott, Foresman, 1988.

Seiler, J. A. *Systems Analysis in Organizational Behavior.* Homewood, Ill.: Business One Irwin, 1967.

von Bertalanffy, L. *General Systems Theory: Foundations, Development, and Applications* (rev. ed.). New York: Braziller, 1968.

PART TWO

Designing Formal Organizational Arrangements

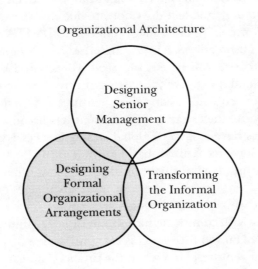

Organizational Architecture

Designing Senior Management

Designing Formal Organizational Arrangements

Transforming the Informal Organization

Although organizational architecture encompasses far more than the structure of an organization, a discussion of structure is nevertheless a very good place to begin. As in physical architecture, structure establishes the characteristic shape of the entity by delineating its boundaries with the environment. In the case of organizational design, in particular, structure establishes a key framework within which other aspects of the architecture are developed, as well as a context for all subsequent organizational activity.

As mentioned in Chapter One, it is useful to think of organizational design at two levels. The first, enterprise-level design, deals primarily with the overall form of the organization—for example, a set of distinct business units, a group of specialized functions, a "matrix" of product groups and geographies, or a complex network of resource centers and areas of focus. The second, unit-level design, deals with the design of individual business units, divisions, and plants as well as the work groups and individual jobs that they comprise. As the two levels of design are interdependent, the prudent organizational architect must pay attention to both.

In this section, we address important issues that have arisen in recent years as organizations have pushed the limits of design at both the enterprise and unit levels. These discussions assume some grounding in the fundamentals of organizational design, but because of space limitations the text does not provide that background. For additional information, the reader is directed to David A. Nadler and Michael L. Tushman's *Strategic Organization Design: Concepts, Tools, and Processes* (Glenview, Ill.: Scott, Foresman, 1988).

At the enterprise level, the issues covered in this section deal with the use of acquisitions and joint ventures as vehicles to implement strategy. As the external environment has become more complex and firms have embraced global strategies as essential to their success, they have recognized that "going it alone" may not be the most effective approach for reasons of resource availability, timing, and market access; however, the enormous advantages of obtaining vitally needed capabilities through acquisition or a new venture with a partner with complementary strengths carry significant risks. Firms have had far too little success integrating new acquisitions or building joint ventures, even when the financial and strategic characteristics of the deals are highly attractive.

In Chapter Three, David A. Nadler and Terry M. Limpert develop a framework for viewing the potential benefits of a strategic acquisition, as well as the requirements for success. Specifically, their framework addresses opportunities for leverage, degree of integration required to achieve this leverage, changes required to achieve the needed integration, and the "critical success factors" necessary for the acquisition to achieve its potential.

In Chapter Four, Charles S. Raben explores the circumstances in which a joint venture is the correct architectural choice, the logic of partner selection, and the governance options for the new entity, and offers some thoughts about relationship management with a strategic partner and management of the joint venture.

Despite its critical importance, enterprise-level design does not completely determine organizational behavior. In fact, most people spend the bulk of their work lives in local business units, plants, and offices. In these settings, the impact of the larger structure is felt, but its effects are indirect. Equally important are the design of the local work process, the design of individual jobs, and the nature of supervision. Therefore, Chapter Five deals with a key opportunity at the unit level: the creation of local work organizations that are dramatically more productive than those of the past. These organizations are the result of more than forty years of research and practice on the creation of work systems based on "sociotechnical" principles rather than the classical bureaucratic management ideas developed in the early 1900s.

In Chapter Five, David A. Nadler and Marc S. Gerstein trace the evolution of high-performance work systems from their roots in F. W. Taylor's scientific management and Max Weber's bureaucracy through the human relations school to the breakthrough 1940s British coal mining studies that challenged the classical work paradigm. The principles of high-performance work systems (HPWS) are discussed and contrasted with traditional work design principles, and the relative benefits are described. On the practical level, the steps for applying HPWS thinking to current organizations are outlined, and the relationship of HPWS to other work improvement strategies, such as employee involvement and total quality management, is discussed.

In total, the application of new structural ideas at the enterprise and unit levels is likely to lead to organizations that are architecturally quite different from those of the past. In the place of monolithic organizations grown entirely from within, we will increasingly see organizations built from "modular pieces," potentially with shared ownership. In the place of narrow jobs, steep hierarchies, and close supervision, we will see self-managed, client-centered teams responsible for an entire work process. Such organizations appear to possess the characteristics required to succeed in the years ahead.

THREE

Managing the Dynamics of Acquisitions: Successfully Moving from Decision to Integration

DAVID A. NADLER, TERRY M. LIMPERT

The last quarter of the twentieth century is witnessing the restructuring of much of U.S. business. In response to changes in the economy, technology, competition, regulation, and ownership patterns, major changes have been initiated in the form, structure, governance, and functioning of many companies. This restructuring has taken many forms, including mergers, acquisitions, leveraged buy-outs, joint ventures, divestitures, and liquidations. In addition, new organizational forms, such as joint ventures, alliances, and networks, have begun to move into greater use.

Restructuring poses significant strategic and organizational challenges for many managers and leaders. These challenges are particularly interesting in the case of acquisitions. What do we mean by acquisition? For our discussion, it is one organization (the parent) gaining controlling ownership of another company (the acquiree), where there is intent on the part of the parent to hold and operate the acquiree. This definition therefore excludes those situations in which a company is acquired as a passive investment or as part of a short-term deal to be used as a stake for subsequent transactions. It includes some combinations that may be called mergers, as many so-called mergers are in truth acquisitions.

During the 1980s, acquisition became commonplace in the United States. The theory of the acquisition is one of scale and synergy, that the combination of two companies can provide significant strategic advantage because of complementary strengths, competencies, market positions, assets, products, and technology. The results of acquisition have, however, been somewhat disappointing (Porter, 1987). There are various estimates of the success of acquisitions, but the consensus is that somewhere between 65 and 85 percent of acquisitions do not meet the expectations the parent had when making the decision to acquire.

Why is the track record of acquisitions so poor? Part of the answer lies in strategic factors. The strategic factors responsible for acquisition failure include unclear or poor strategic match, industry differences leading to lack of transferable knowledge, bad timing, resource shortages, and overvaluation of assets. Many companies thus make acquisitions that, in hindsight, simply were the wrong choices.

In other cases, however, the acquisition appears to be strategically appropriate—the right company has been acquired at the right time for the right price—but the acquisition does not work out as expected because of problems that arise in the process of taking hold of and operating the acquiree. Case studies report problems of cultural incompatibility, employee stress in reaction to acquisition, failure to gain potential operating advantages, and problems in combining different functions, units, and activities. These human and organizational issues appear to play a significant role in the ultimate success or failure of an acquisition.

This chapter articulates a framework for thinking about the organizational dynamics of acquisitions and, thus, is intended to guide managers in planning and implementing the integration of acquired organizations. This approach is based on our work with companies that have made acquisitions in a variety of different industries, including financial services, chemicals, telecommunications, office equipment, medical services, and building materials. It also builds on the growing body of research on the organizational issues arising from acquisition (Marks, 1982; Mirvis and Marks, forthcoming). We begin by discussing different ways of thinking about acquisitions and argue for the concept of acquisition as a class of organizational change. We then present a model for acquisition integration and discuss the core elements of that model. In the final section, we identify some specific implications for management of acquisitions.

Perspectives on Acquisition

In recent years, two perspectives on acquisition have emerged. The first is what can be called the *strategic perspective,* and the focus is on the decision to acquire and the choice of what to acquire. This perspective has focused primarily on financial concerns, although recent attention has been given to the strategic issues, questioning the efficacy of many acquisitions as valid strategic moves (Porter, 1987). Clearly, an effective acquisition, one that meets the expectations of the parent, is composed of the right strategic purpose, the right choice of acquisition, and the right financial terms (Management Analysis Center, 1986).

A second viewpoint might be called a *human resources perspective.* The focus of this work is on the problems of postacquisition integration (Levinson, 1981; Sales and Mirvis, 1984; Mirvis, 1985; Perry, 1986). Much of the attention is on the impact of acquisitions on individuals and how they cope with and respond to the potentially traumatic act of acquisition, or what has been called "merger syndrome" (Marks and Mirvis, 1985; Mirvis and Marks, 1986). A number of researchers have moved beyond the individual to look at the whole issue of organizational culture and how potentially incompatible cultures are merged in the wake of an acquisition.

Although both perspectives are important, they are frequently unlinked, both in theory and in practice. Those who write about strategic issues pay little attention to the integration problems. Those who focus on human resources issues frequently do so in a strategic vacuum. A third perspective is therefore necessary to bridge this gap. An *organizational dynamics perspective* concerns the link between strategic concerns and human resources impact. It focuses on the planning and analysis that occur after the deal but before the integration to determine what type of integration is necessary and appropriate, given the strategic context of the acquisition. Most importantly, it conceives of acquisition as a special class of organizational change and, therefore, implies that an understanding of change management concepts can be helpful in managing the acquisition process.

Organizational change can be thought of as a movement from a current state of affairs to a desired future state (see Figure

3.1). The critical insight of change management is the recognition of a third state, the transition state, which occurs when the organization is no longer what it was but not yet what it will be (Beckhard and Harris, 1977; Nadler, 1981). Change management requires an understanding of the current state, a vision of the future state, a grasp of the gaps between the current and future states, and attention to the predictable problems and challenges that occur during transitions.

Acquisition can be seen as a special case of change (see Figure 3.2). Prior to the acquisition, there are two separate organizations: the parent and the acquiree. The future state is some combination of the parent and the acquiree into a new organization that encompasses both. The transition state is that period during which acquisition integration occurs. Change management theory says that the transition state is critical; the management of transition may be disproportionately influential in determining how effective a change will be. In acquisition terms, a good acquisition decision followed by poorly planned and managed integration may fail despite the fact the correct purchase was made.

In terms of the change model, we focus on integration as the entire series of events that begin with the decision to make an acquisition and extend to the point where the future state (parent and acquiree as part of a functioning and relatively stable new organization) is achieved. Effective integration occurs when the future state is achieved, when that future state meets the performance expectations that motivated the acquisition, and when the costs as-

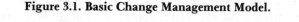

Figure 3.1. Basic Change Management Model.

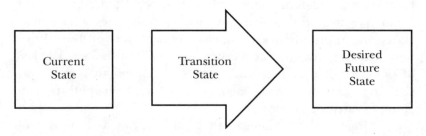

Figure 3.2. Acquisition as Change Management.

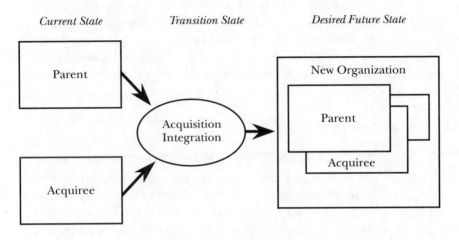

sociated with the acquisition (to employees, customers, or the organization) are managed and minimized.

Acquisition Integration and Management Model

Research on successful and unsuccessful acquisitions indicates that there are some systematic differences in how they evolve over time. A recent review of mergers and acquisitions in the financial services industry (Management Analysis Center, 1986) described some of these differences. Acquisition is seen as having three phases: preacquisition, negotiation, and postacquisition. Typically, emphasis is placed on finances during preacquisition, politics during negotiation, and damage control during postacquisition. In the more successful cases, the preacquisition emphasis is strategic; during negotiation, the focus is on integration planning; and postacquisition, the emphasis is on integration management.

The question, then, is how to develop an effective integration strategy, an approach for shaping and managing the transition state. Our experience has led us to develop a model for thinking about the various factors that interact to potentially influence the integration of acquisitions. It is a normative model, describing what one should consider and do to develop and implement an integration strategy. A simple depiction of that model is shown in Figure 3.3. The strategic context and history of the specific acquisition decision influence the nature of the integration strategy. That strategy, in turn, determines the specific integration process employed. Each of the three elements of the model comprises a number of different factors. In the following sections, we discuss each element in more detail.

Strategic Context and History

An acquisition decision evolves over time and is the result of many different forces. The elements of the decision, the parties involved, and their relationships during the period leading up to and including the agreement to acquire (and be acquired) all set the context for integration. Who the players are and how they have interacted have major implications for the problems and opportunities that will be encountered during integration. These historical and contextual factors are usually shaped prior to the planning of integration. The integration strategy needs to be built on a knowledge of what these factors are and what the implications will be, both positive and negative.

Parent Characteristics. Integration is influenced by who the parent is; what motivated the parent to make the acquisition; how the acquisition fits into the parent's business strategy, vision, or objectives; and why the parent chose to acquire the particular company that it did. Also important is the acquisition history of the parent and, therefore, the fantasies about acquisition held by the parent.

Figure 3.3. Acquisition Integration and Management Model.

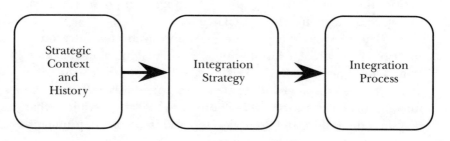

Finally, the general condition of the parent, including financial health, cash position, depth-of-management resources, and management style, need to be considered.

Acquiree Characteristics. Integration is also greatly influenced by the factors that motivated the acquiree to enter into the deal (to the extent that there was a choice). The general health of the acquiree is also an important consideration, as are its previous history with acquisitions and, thus, its fantasies and expectations. Of particular importance is the recent history of the acquiree, including the specific events that led to the acquisition event.

Degree of Difference. A third element of context and history is the degree of compatibility between the parent and the acquiree. How different or similar are the two organizations in terms of management style, business definition, organizational culture, operating systems, skills, and orientations? Some of these differences can be complementary; some will lead to potential conflict. A key question to ask is whether these differences are related to the core values or basic assumptions of the two companies, and thus how much difficulty they might present during integration.

Third-Party Stakeholders. In addition to the two principal parties to an acquisition, there are frequently numerous third parties who have some stake in the outcome of the acquisition. These parties include shareholders, other potential acquirers, regulators, competitors, customers, employees, suppliers, and labor unions. Integration planning needs to consider who these stakeholders are, what their perceived stake is, and how much power they have to influence events during the period of integration. In some cases, these stakeholders may present problems; in other cases, stakeholders may be enlisted to assist in integration.

Context of the Deal. The way in which the acquisition deal develops and is concluded is an important contextual factor. Different deals evolve through different scenarios. The acquisition could be perceived as a rescue, a collaboration, a contest, a hostile raid, or a merger. Each scenario brings with it different perceptions, fantasies, and psychological baggage, which are carried over into the integration period.

Integration Strategy

At the core of the model is integration strategy, the approach developed to integrate the acquiree and the parent. Integration strategies can be thought of as having three components: strategic leverage, critical success factors, and degree and pace of integration (see Figure 3.4).

Strategic Leverage. Acquisitions are made because of the expectation that the combination of two entities will create a new entity that has greater value in its combined form rather than in separate forms. Acquisition is motivated by value creation, the idea that either the parent or the acquiree will benefit significantly from the combination. It is this belief that justifies the price paid for an acquisition. This is the "theory" of acquisition, that the combination will lead to leverage of the resources of one or both of the parties.

Strategic leverage can take different forms. Leverage can come from resources or competencies that the parent brings to the acquisition that enhance the value of the acquisition. Conversely, the acquiree might have resources or competencies that increase the value of certain assets of the parent. Leverage in either direction has many forms:

> *Market access.* One party provides entry into new market segments, relationships with customers, or geographic coverage.
> *Products or services.* The acquisition produces complementary combinations of the offerings of the two entities.
> *Capital access.* One party brings capital, or access to sources of capital, to leverage the activities of the other.
> *Technology.* The technologies of one party have value for the other party.

Figure 3.4. Integration Strategy.

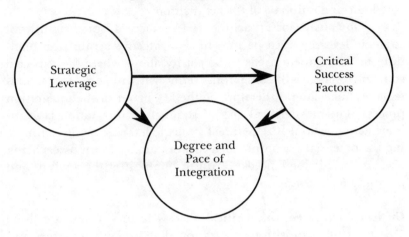

Distribution networks. The two companies have complementary relationships with distributors, channels, and agents.

Management resources. One company has specific skills, experiences, and competencies in management that bring unique value when combined with those of the other.

People. People in one company have capacities, technical capabilities, knowledge, and competence that can be used or enhanced by the other.

Name and reputation. The image, brands, or marketplace perception of one company can enhance that of the other.

Economies of scale. Similar or redundant operations in the two companies can be combined into shared resource units with true scale advantages.

Diversification. The combination expands the scope of the parent into different industries and completely different markets, thus changing the risk profile and competitive set of the combined organization.

These are some, but not all, of the potential dimensions of strategic leverage that motivate, justify, and ultimately reward the investment made in an acquisition. Strategic leverage therefore defines the core logic and rationale of the acquisition.

Obviously, for an acquisition to succeed, some significant strategic leverage must be present. For effective acquisition planning to occur, there needs to be clarity about where the expected strategic leverage will come from and how it will be achieved. Strategic leverage should therefore be the key driver of the integration process. The most critical task of acquisition integration is to initiate activities to realize planned strategic leverage while minimizing the potential for unintended cost or damage to the assets being leveraged. This logic needs to run through all of the analysis and planning for integration.

Critical Success Factors. Critical success factors (CSFs) are those aspects of the acquisition integration that are both *necessary* and *sufficient* for success. These factors must be attended to if the acquisition is to meet expectations and achieve the intended strategic leverage.

What determines the acquisition CSFs? Obviously, the contextual factors (parent and acquiree conditions and differences, third parties, and nature of the deal) all suggest potential areas where problems could arise during integration. For example, if a commercial bank buys a savings and loan that has been close to default because of problems in its loan portfolio, one of the CSFs would be to quickly assess the portfolio, set credit standards and controls, and develop a workout process to limit the damage and "stem the bleeding." The key elements of strategic leverage also should point the way to the CSFs. For example, if that bank buys that particular savings and loan because of the location of its branches and its customer base, then a CSF during integration would be to maintain the confidence of the customer base and avoid loss of customers. Similarly, if a company is acquired because of the unique talents and disciplines represented in its management, the CSF would be to retain senior managers in the business.

As with strategic leverage, the key issue related to CSFs in integration planning is clarifying what they are and developing some sense of their relative priority, in terms of both time and importance. Given differences in history and strategic leverage, different acquisitions will end up having radically different CSFs. Once integration has begun, new information may also come to light that may change the nature of the CSFs, and as problems are dealt with, the CSFs may evolve.

Degree and Pace of Integration. The final element of integration strategy comprises the degree of integration needed between the parent and the acquiree and the pace at which that integration needs to proceed. It appears that acquirers, in general, have given little thought to this area and, thus, have had to learn difficult lessons from trial and error.

Consider the case of a large technology company that over more than fifteen years purchased a number of smaller entrepreneurial companies to gain leverage through the addition of technology, management talent, and products. In case after case, the parent moved in quickly and imposed its own policies and procedures for financial control, measurement, personnel, and investment. In most of these cases, the managements of the acquired companies left shortly thereafter, followed by key technical staff. The acquisitions failed to realize the intended strategic leverage because the integration was too intense and too fast. In contrast, another manufacturing company purchased a large financial services company for diversification purposes. The financial services company sale was initiated by a group of senior managers who were reaching retirement age and saw value in the combination with a large industrial firm. The parent, feeling that there were significant industry differences, kept a largely hands-off attitude toward the acquiree and operated it as a separate holding. Following retirement of the original senior managers of the financial services company, however, the new managers (chosen by the departing team) immediately steered the company into significant trouble through bad investments and loss of control. These problems were remedied only when the parent company management stepped in and brought order and discipline through its financial staff. From that point forward, the acquisition became much more effective. In this second case, the mistake was too little integration.

The point is that each acquisition presents the parent with a choice about how intensively to integrate the acquiree. Integration is not an either/or choice but a range (Figure 3.5) of alternatives. At one extreme, there is no integration; the acquiree is placed in the portfolio of the parent as a separate holding. Aside from limited financial controls and reviews of results at the board level, it remains autonomous. Examples of this approach are seen in diversified financial services acquisitions, such as Dillon-Read by Travelers Insurance. At the other extreme, integration can be complete; the acquiree is absorbed and consolidated into the parent so that the acquiree ceases to exist as a separate entity. An example of this second case would be the airline acquisitions, where the acquired airline (for example, National by Pan Am, Mohawk by U.S. Air, Northeast by Delta, and People Express by Continental) is no longer recognizable from the parent.

Between these two extremes are a range of integration alternatives. In the middle is what can be called coupled integration: some of the activities and functions of the acquired company are integrated with the parent and some are left separate and independent. Loosely coupled acquisitions are those in which a minimum of activities are integrated to achieve strategic leverage, but the acquiree still largely functions as an independent entity. Operationally integrated acquisitions are not fully consolidated; they can still be identified as entities, but all key operations and procedures are tightly linked with the parent, as in the case of a normal division or operating unit of the parent company.

Figure 3.5. Degree of Integration.

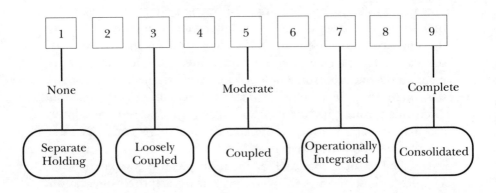

What is the appropriate degree of integration during the initial stages of the acquisition? As strategies evolve and more is learned, the degree of required integration may change. In addition, in those cases other than the extremes (separate holding and consolidation), there is the important choice of which operations to integrate and which ones to leave separate. Potential points of integration might include staffing, technology, channels of distribution, control systems, resource allocation, personnel practices, product development, and manufacturing suppliers. Mirvis and Marks (forthcoming) have proposed an approach to this question (Figure 3.6). For each activity, one needs to consider the degree of strategic importance (does it relate to strategic leverage and does it appear as part of a CSF) and the ease of integration (easy or difficult). In general, those activities that are strategically critical and easy to integrate should be consolidated; those that are hard to integrate and less important should be left separate. The remaining activities should be coupled with varying degrees of intensity, as required.

Degree and pace of integration should be determined by an analysis of strategic leverage and CSFs. In the light of this analysis,

Figure 3.6. Integration Intensity Model.

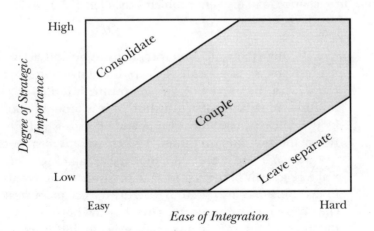

Source: Adapted from Mirvis and Marks, forthcoming.

the question of risk needs to be considered. The risk of moving fast and integrating completely is the potential cost of doing the wrong things and destroying some of the value of the assets acquired. On the other hand, the risk of moving too slowly is that of inaction—events may occur during the first days and weeks of acquisition because of the inattention of the parent. Both types of risk need to be assessed and weighed.

Integration Process

The third element in the acquisition integration and management model is the integration process. With an integration strategy in hand, the question is: How can we implement the integration strategy so that it protects the value of the acquired assets and leads to achievement of the intent of the acquisition? The answer lies in our earlier observation that acquisition integration is the transition state in a change.

Problems. If we think of acquisition as a complex and significant organizational change, there are some predictable problems that can be anticipated during this transition period. In addition to the strategic and operational issues encountered in the course of the acquisition, three change management problems (Nadler, 1981) typically occur:

> *Power.* In any change, counterproductive political activity tends to emerge as a result of the political dynamics associated with the impact of changes on the informal organization. In the case of acquisition, this is brought about by the potential clash of cultures and operating styles between the two organizations. To achieve any degree of integration, there must be a major reshaping of the political topography of the acquiree, with distinct winners and losers. This may also result in decreased trust and a weakened capacity for teamwork. Different interest groups in the parent and the acquiree compete to influence the course and outcomes of the integration, and that competition may become destructive.

Anxiety. Any significant change causes people to experience anxiety and stress as they question what will become of them. If they do not receive a satisfactory answer to this question, they may act in seemingly irrational, unproductive, and even self-destructive ways. At the very least, there is resistance. Acquisition is psychologically charged because, for the acquiree, it represents potential death. Acquisition raises profound fears about success, failure, and survival. Self-preservation becomes the dominant motivation. Many of the rules that govern behavior may be suspended because there is frequently a feeling that "all bets are off" until it becomes clear what the new parent will do. People spend a good deal of time and energy figuring out who is staying and who is leaving, finding out what the new rules are, and attempting to determine how to survive. During this time, limited information may be available to individuals and they may feel cut off from their normal support networks. As a result, they may develop fantasies about what will happen to them. Many individuals (including those in the parent who are assigned to the acquiree) may be experiencing simultaneous personal transitions—job changes, moves, and family dislocations—that add to the general level of stress.

Control. The third predictable transition problem is the maintenance of managerial control. Control may be difficult as the current state is disassembled. This is particularly salient in acquisitions, as the current state falls apart psychologically the moment the acquisition is announced or, possibly, when rumors of an aquisition spread. During this period, there is the de facto suspension of the control and reward system in the acquiree. People are not sure what the parent will do and frequently succumb to "acquisition paralysis." This can result in loss of momentum, which competitors may see and exploit.

Components. Given these change management issues and the imperatives for action emerging from the integration strategy, an integration process needs to include four major components. The first is *strategic action,* or the initial steps necessary to realize the strategic leverage expected. For example, if an acquisition is made to gain economies from the combination of sales and distribution channels, the integration process must include specific steps to identify redundant channels, design the new integrated distribution network, and sell off or redeploy redundant assets. Closely related is a second component, *business repair and maintenance.* These are the actions needed to fix any immediate and threatening problems (such as the credit problems in the savings-and-loan example above) as well as actions necessary to ensure that the acquiree continues as a going concern (such as reassuring customers and suppliers). The third component of the integration process is *transition management,* the use of change management tools and concepts to shape the political dynamics in the acquiree, to motivate constructive behavior, and to manage the transition state to maintain control. It implies the use of various transition mechanisms and techniques (Delta Consulting Group, 1983) such as transition teams, participation, intensive communications, data collection and feedback, symbols and language, and carefully crafted leader behavior. Finally, the integration process needs to create methods for *personal support* for individuals who may be impacted psychologically by the acquisition. Although implied in transition management techniques, it is such a significant issue in acquisition that it needs to be considered separately. Acquisition can be a very traumatic event; personal counseling, support groups, psychiatric referral, and other mechanisms for support need to be built into the integration process.

      Each of these four components needs to be designed and implemented differently in varying situations. In a vacuum, many actions are possible, but the development of an integration strategy (strategic leverage, CSFs, and degree of integration) based on an analysis of the strategic context and history of the acquisition can provide very significant direction as to where to put the emphasis and resources during the integration process.

Summary

This chapter has proposed a way of thinking about the organizational dynamics of acquisition. Recognizing the value of the stra-

Figure 3.7. Acquisition Integration and Management Model.

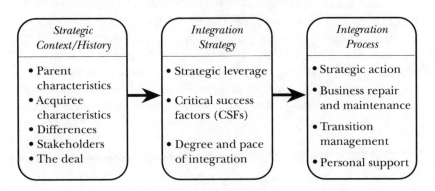

tegic and human resources perspectives on acquisitions, we have proposed a third perspective that links these two. This perspective has been represented as a model for acquisition integration and management (Figure 3.7).

Planning needs to start with an analysis and understanding of the strategic context and history of the acquisition, including parent and acquiree characteristics and differences, stakeholders, and the deal itself. On the basis of this analysis, an integration strategy can be developed that clearly identifies the points of strategic leverage, the critical success factors, and the appropriate degree and pace of integration. Finally, the integration process, including necessary strategic action, required business repair and maintenance, vital transition management actions, and the provision of personal support, can be designed.

With this model in mind, what are the implications for those planning and implementing significant organizational acquisitions?

1. Link integration planning and deal management. Integration issues are profoundly influenced by the nature of the deal; thus, the roots of effective integration strategies and processes frequently lie in the evolution of the acquisition decision and the deal itself. The implication is that those who will be responsible for developing integration strategies and processes should

be involved as part of the deal team. They can thus help to shape some of the events that will influence integration, they can collect data during the deal development process that can help in developing appropriate integration strategies, and they may also bring a perspective to the deal and the valuation of assets that may lead to more effective acquisition decisions.

2. Where possible, conduct a preacquisition organizational diagnosis. One of the problems in integration planning is the sense of time urgency. Acquisitions frequently have a "stop-start" quality, and once agreement is reached and announced, there is tremendous pressure to get on with the integration. At that point, it may be difficult to take the time to collect data, integrate information, and develop an integration strategy. Therefore, it is important to use any and all opportunities to collect data about the acquired organization as early as possible; this allows the work to begin on integration strategies while the deal is in progress.

3. Push for clear identification of points of strategic leverage and critical success factors. Those engaged in the acquisition decision and deal development and those who are responsible for integration and management of the acquisition need to invest the time and energy to clarify the strategic leverage being sought from the acquisition. In light of the desired strategic leverage, what are the true critical success factors associated with the integration of the acquisition?

4. Make a deliberate decision about degree and pace of integration. Integration is too important to be done casually. Prior to entry of any parent management into the acquisition, a careful and thoughtful decision should be made about the appropriate degree and pace of integration of the new acquisition. This is true at the firm level (how integrated will the acquisition be as a whole), as well as at the functional level. All of the members of the parent company who are entering the acquisition should have a clear understanding of the integration strategy being implemented.

5. Where possible, have the initial stages of the integration process already planned, supported, and ready to go prior to announcement of the deal. Integration begins with the

announcement, despite anything that is said or done to the contrary. Thus it is critical to have plans before the announcement is made so that the integration process can begin as soon as possible.

6. Use transition management concepts and devices. Acquisition integration is a transition, and thus methods for managing transition states should be employed. To ignore the transition management issues is to invite failure.

7. Create systems to learn and modify as you go. Even the best analysis cannot account for all the uncertainties that will be encountered during transition integration. At a minimum, integration strategy development and integration process planning will have been done with limited information. It is inevitable that surprises will be encountered once the transition management team (or the new senior managers of the transition) "hit the ground." Thus, during the early phases of integration, it is critical that those responsible for managing integration be involved in very intensive, continuous data collection to assess the situation, test the impact of early actions, and revise the integration strategy and plan as appropriate. The integration managers need to be quick and efficient learners during this period.

References

Beckhard, R., and Harris, R. *Organizational Transitions*. Reading, Mass.: Addison-Wesley, 1977.

Delta Consulting Group. *Concepts for the Management of Organizational Change*. New York: Delta Consulting Group, 1983.

Levinson, H. "A Psychologist Diagnoses Merger Failures." *Harvard Business Review*, 1981, *48*, 138-147.

Management Analysis Center. *Making Mergers Work in the Financial Services Industry*. Cambridge, Mass.: Management Analysis Center, 1986.

Marks, M. L. "Merging Human Resources: A Review of the Current Research." *Mergers and Acquisitions*, Summer 1982, 38-43.

Marks, M. L., and Mirvis, P. H. "Merger Syndrome: Stress and Uncertainty." *Mergers and Acquisitions*, Summer 1985, 50-55.

Mirvis, P. H. "Negotiations After the Sale: The Roots and Ramifications of Conflict in an Acquisition." *Journal of Occupational Behavior,* 1985, 65–84.

Mirvis, P. H., and Marks, M. L. "Merger Syndrome: Management by Crisis." *Mergers and Acquisitions,* Jan./Feb. 1986, 70–76.

Mirvis, P. H., and Marks, M. L. *Making Mergers Work.* (Forthcoming)

Nadler, D. A. "Managing Organizational Change: An Integrative Approach." *Journal of Applied Behavioral Science,* 1981, *17,* 191–211.

Perry, L. T. "Merging Successfully: Sending the 'Right' Signals." *Sloan Management Review,* Spring 1986, 47–57.

Porter, M. E. "From Competitive Advantage to Corporate Strategy." *Harvard Business Review,* 1987, *3,* 43–59.

Sales, A. L., and Mirvis, P. H. "When Cultures Collide: Issues in Acquisition." In J. R. Kimberly and R. E. Quinn (eds.), *Managing Organizational Transitions.* Homewood, Ill.: Business One Irwin, 1984.

FOUR

Building Strategic Partnerships: Creating and Managing Effective Joint Ventures

CHARLES S. RABEN

Over the past several years, an increasing number of companies have chosen to pursue joint ventures as a strategic option. The lure is easy to understand. Many companies see joint ventures as a readily accessible means to new technologies and new markets or as a way to gain momentum within their industry by joining forces with a winning team. What company would not be attracted to a business opportunity that offered a potentially high payoff and yet lessened risk, financial investment, and time to market? It is not, however, as simple as it may appear. Plunging ahead without an understanding of the commitment and its requirements can substantially reduce the chances for the venture's success. The purpose of this chapter is to provide some practical information and advice that can guide companies in their efforts to establish and manage successful joint venture enterprises. It is based on recent studies of joint ventures as well as actual experience in their implementation (Harrigan, 1985; Killing, 1983).

Reasons for Formation of a Joint Venture

A joint venture is merely one of a growing number of strategic business alliances that companies have begun to form in response to rapid changes in the structure of American business. Changes in technology, macroeconomics, and a vast array of legal and regulatory issues have forged a much more complex and competitive world in which to conduct business. Many companies are having

81

to consider some form of strategic alliance if they want to grow or, in some instances, even maintain their traditional market positions. This struggle for competitive strength has given rise to many diverse alliances including mergers, acquisitions, leveraged buy-outs, divestitures, and joint ventures.

Corning, Inc., for instance, a company that has become synonymous with successfully managed joint ventures, believes that the world has simply become too complicated for organizations to enter new markets or form new businesses on their own. Jamie Houghton, Corning's chairman, fervently believes that joint ventures provide an effective form of leverage. Indeed, many predict that within the next ten to twenty years, most companies will be members of teams that compete against one another in a struggle to control markets. Individual companies will find it increasingly difficult to go it alone.

Figure 4.1 provides a further understanding of why companies wanting to introduce new products find joint ventures attractive. As the data suggest, the success rate for a new product is at its highest when that product is being introduced into an existing or known market with existing or known technology. The chances of success are considerably lower if the product is being introduced into a new market or with a new technology. From this point of view, joining forces with a partner who offers a knowledge of markets, technology, or both that makes up for what the other partner does not have becomes a very pragmatic course of action.

Despite their growing popularity, joint ventures have become very complex and problematic forms of organization. They fail as often as they succeed. For example, in a recent study of joint ventures formed between 1924 and 1985, Harrigan (1985) found that only 46 percent succeeded. The average life span was only three and one-half years. What can be done to increase the likelihood of success?

The material presented in this chapter is intended to help managers increase the probability of forming and managing successful joint ventures by alerting them to the array of issues that require managerial attention. By identifying critical success factors and potential problems, managers can work to lessen the risk of failure and, at the same time, increase the likelihood of success.

Figure 4.1. Success Rates for New Products.

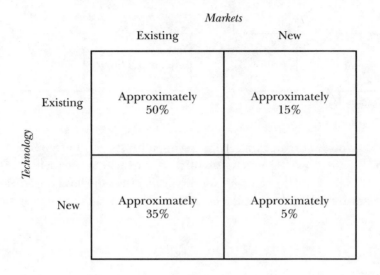

Markets

	Existing	New
Existing	Approximately 50%	Approximately 15%
New	Approximately 35%	Approximately 5%

Technology

Stages of a Joint Venture

The development or evolution of a joint venture consists of a series of stages as shown in Figure 4.2. Each stage is unique in terms of its characteristics and task requirements. The cycle is initiated (stage 1) when an organization begins to examine the possibility of a joint venture and the various factors that must be assessed in making the decision to proceed. Once a partner is found and the decision to proceed has been made, the partner organizations must then design and plan the venture's structure and operation (stage 2). Stage 3 consists of implementing the design and dealing with the numerous issues that arise when introducing the new organization. Stage 4 describes the period during which the venture develops an identity as an organization. Ultimately, the partners must decide what to do with the venture over the long term. This decision, as we will see, should be guided by the original strategic objectives set in forming the venture and how they continue to serve the strategic purposes of the partner organizations.

Figure 4.2. Four Stages of a Joint Venture.

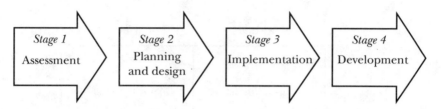

How an organization considering a joint venture responds to stage 1 and how the newly established partners subsequently respond to the remaining stages significantly affect the level of success the venture is likely to experience. Let us look at each stage in some detail.

Stage 1: Assessment

Stage 1 is the period during which a joint venture is being considered and evaluated. As shown in Figure 4.3, an organization should collect and assess three kinds of information during this stage. First, the organization must assess itself—its own strategic plan, its ability to accept the operating requirements of a venture, and its readiness to manage change. Second, it must assess the business opportunity being sought. Third, the organization must assess the potential partners that can provide that opportunity. These activities together constitute the period during which the deal is made. Partly because of the excitement and enthusiasm that accompany this process, many of these assessment activities are not done systematically. Poor assessment therefore produces the first of the problems that can besiege a joint venture.

Assessment of Organization

Strategic Plan. Perhaps foremost of all the issues an organization needs to address early in the assessment of a joint venture is strategic choice. Is a joint venture the most appropriate strategic mechanism to address the problem needing to be resolved or the opportunity

Figure 4.3. Assessment Activities.

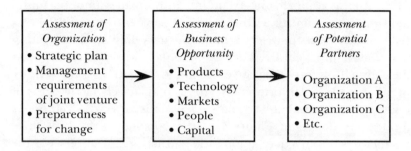

being sought? Are other, less complicated alternatives more appropriate for the situation?

Joint ventures are often undertaken to deal with temporary problems. A company may be trying to gain quick access to a potentially profitable market or offset limited financial resources necessary for new product development. Once the immediate need has been satisfied, many firms regret having formed the venture in the first place. Their interest in it lessens considerably as does the behavior required of them to make it successful. In such circumstances, some other, less complicated alternative should be seriously considered. For instance, hire managers who already possess needed market knowledge, seek out a license agreement as a way of acquiring technology, or review alternative financial structures as a means of offsetting limited financial resources.

A company should be absolutely clear on the strategic purpose being served by the venture and should have concluded that it is the most appropriate path. This will result in a clearer set of expectations for the venture that in turn can be used to guide decisions about it and its operation. Agreement on long-term goals is particularly important. It helps provide direction and stability in overcoming any difficulties the venture may experience in the short term. Unless long-term goals and commitments are discussed and agreed on at the outset, conflicts will emerge later in the form of differences over resource allocations and investments in future development.

A clear strategic understanding also provides an opportunity to assess compatibility with a potential partner. Typically, potential partners share some set of complementary objectives in wanting to initiate a joint venture. These commonly held objectives are often the compelling forces that give rise to the formation of the venture in the first place. Unfortunately, they can also overshadow areas of potential conflict that become evident only after the venture is formed. As shown in Figure 4.4, it is possible to think of three distinct sets of objectives among the partner organizations and the joint venture.

First, the convergent objectives serve as the basis of the relationship among the three organizational entities. These are the commonly shared objectives and activities that typically receive the most attention in the initial consideration and formation of the venture. They represent the primary reasons the venture has been created. Each organization also has another set of objectives that are unique to itself and compatible with the other two. These objectives do not interfere with the performance of either the partner or the venture. The third set of objectives contains the potential for conflict. Whether they be differences in strategy, operating characteristics, or management style, this area represents an array of potential threats to the viability and success of the venture.

Acknowledging and understanding these objectives make it possible to more accurately discern potential problem areas before a venture is formed. In some instances, full knowledge of how much conflict may lie ahead could be enough reason to rethink the decision to form the venture. In other instances, the potential conflict may be easily managed or avoided by reading an agreement early in the negotiation process between the partners. The point, however, is that potential threats to the venture's success cannot be handled without first understanding one's own objectives in forming the venture.

Management Requirements of a Joint Venture. The internal management and operating requirements of a venture are often underestimated or misjudged at the outset of a venture. Partnerships

**Figure 4.4. Relationship of Objectives Among
Partner Firms and Joint Venture.**

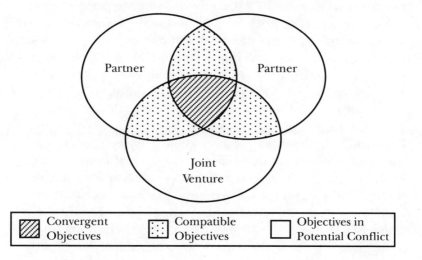

▨ Convergent Objectives	⬚ Compatible Objectives	☐ Objectives in Potential Conflict

require behavior different from that traditionally required of many organizations. Partners must cooperate, be flexible, and often share responsibility for the management of the venture. Giving up control is very difficult for some managers. It runs counter to fundamental beliefs about accountability and obligations to shareholders. Organizations often enter into these partnerships without an understanding of what will be required of them to make it successful.

What needs to be assessed at this stage is the willingness of the organization to accept the conditions implied by these internal requirements. These requirements, as will be evident later, may suggest a style of management and degree of control very different from what the firm is accustomed to or can accept. It is better that these issues be confronted and resolved early so as to avoid mismanagement later and thus threaten the probability of the venture's success.

Preparedness for Change. Other important issues to assess are the readiness of the organization to manage organizational change and the impact the change is likely to have on the company and its people. Problems with resistance, power, and control typically arise when introducing any major change into an organization (Nadler, 1981). In the case of joint ventures, predictable problems are likely to emerge in the venture itself as well as in the partner organizations. For example, problems with job security are likely to arise when employees are recruited to staff the venture. Many may see it as a risky, temporary, and otherwise unstable environment. Such perceptions are likely to result in considerable anxiety and resistance among employees. These and similar problems serve as additional threats to the success and effectiveness of the venture.

The problems associated with the introduction of change are best handled by developing a specific and deliberate plan to manage the implementation of that change. The successful introduction of a joint venture is no exception. It is not enough to assess and decide on the right content for the venture—that is, its structure, design, staff, and so on. The process of creating and implementing that content is also critical and needs to be effectively managed if the anticipated benefits of the venture are to be realized.

More specific information on the dynamics of organizational change is provided later in conjunction with stage 3, the joint venture implementation. The important point to be emphasized at this stage is the need to assess the organization's readiness to manage the change and its ability to develop a deliberate course of action that will minimize disruption in the partner organizations while ensuring the successful implementation of the venture. The more the partner organizations can anticipate and be prepared to handle the organizational issues that will arise within their own respective organizations as well as in the venture, the better able the venture will be to conduct its business.

Assessment of Business Opportunity

Misreading the business opportunity is often cited by venture partners as a primary reason for their eventual dissatisfaction with a venture enterprise. Firms have admitted to misjudging such things as market size, market growth rate, product/service preferences, and buying patterns. Clearly, an understanding of the opportunity being sought and its boundaries is essential in making an informed judgment about engaging in a joint venture. Otherwise, it may be difficult to know whether the original strategic intention is achieved.

This information is also critical in linking the venture to other elements of the strategic plan. The venture may simply be one in a series of initiatives on a critical path to achieving some larger strategic objective. Knowing the specific business dimensions of the venture may be essential to the execution of the larger plan. Taken in their entirety, these findings suggest the importance of conducting a thorough examination of the opportunity by doing sufficient market research prior to the initiation of any formal venture collaboration.

Assessment of Potential Partners

In selecting a partner, successful firms logically seek out an organization that offers the skills, resources, and attributes that satisfy the requirements of the business opportunity they desire. Some of these (like possession of needed technology, market knowledge, or financial and human resources) may be immediately evident or easily assessed. Other characteristics like cooperation, integrity, honesty, trustworthiness, and the style of general management are less clear and not easily determined. These attributes are best assessed through experience in working with an organization.

Successful firms rely first on this experience in selecting a partner. When there is no history of having worked with a potential partner, the firms typically pursue a lengthy courtship period during which they get to know one another and develop an experiential base. With new partners, it is advisable to proceed sequentially. Conduct a small project first and evaluate its success before committing to a large, ambitious joint venture. This gives each partner the time to look closely at the other. A critical attribute to be assessed as part of this exposure is trust. Partners, fundamentally, must be able to trust one another. The absence of trust will create a very difficult relationship that will affect how they subsequently manage the venture. Ultimately, it will interfere significantly in how the venture operates and the level of success it experiences.

The importance of accurately assessing and understanding such things as management style and cooperation cannot be overemphasized. Whereas resource differences between partners can become a strength when those resources are combined to support a joint venture, management style differences can become a serious liability. Incompatible styles and cultures make it very difficult for partners to reconcile differences in how they believe the joint venture should be managed. Their inability to agree on a process of conflict resolution and on respective management responsibilities as defined by the needs of the venture can seriously threaten the venture's success.

Successful venturers consider whether or not the potential partner has had any previous experience with joint ventures. Those with previous experience tend to be more knowledgeable about the strengths and weaknesses of joint ventures and how to manage them effectively. This experience can be invaluable to a firm that is considering a joint venture for the first time.

It is also important in establishing a successful relationship that the partners share common views on at least a few critical issues. For instance, the partners should have a similar need for growth. This similarity is more likely to ensure that they are equally motivated to make the venture work and that they agree on a long-term time frame (including objectives) for the venture. The partners must also share a willingness to commit time to the venture as required. The time needed simply to maintain the relationship is often woefully underestimated by partners.

Generally speaking, it is also desirable for the two partners to be similar in the overall level of importance they attribute to the venture. The size of the partner organization is often a clue in this regard. Whereas a venture may be critically important to a small partner, it can be insignificant to a large partner. These differences are likely to emerge in the form of differences between the two partners in their accessibility to discuss or work venture issues, to allocate resources to the venture, or to respond to venture priorities. The best partners also tend to be those that understand the business activities of the venture and are perceived as making equal contributions to it. Partners that contribute only cash and do not understand the business become a problem as the joint venture proceeds. Conflicts typically arise when managers within the passive partner firm do not understand what they are being told about the business activities of the venture and begin to question the truthfulness of the information they receive.

Combining all of these considerations results in a profile of desirable partner characteristics shown in the following list. Selecting a partner with these characteristics in mind is more likely to yield a successful partnership.

- Offers resources required
- Is financially sound
- Is trustworthy and respected
- Has compatible management style and culture
- Is able to resolve conflicts and differences
- Is cooperative and flexible
- Is experienced with joint ventures
- Shares need for growth
- Agrees on venture's long-term objectives
- Is willing to commit to relationship
- Attributes similar level of importance to venture
- Makes comparable contribution
- Understands venture's business

Before leaving this assessment stage, it is important to discuss one final issue—the formal venture agreement. The agreement documents the understanding, responsibilities, and commitments of the partners to the venture. To maximize the success of a joint venture from the start, partners should be as thorough as possible in identifying the issues on which they need to agree. Working out a clear understanding at the contract writing stage will avoid many of the surprises, misunderstandings, and conflicts that can arise after the venture has been formally initiated. Some key issues should be anticipated and included in the formal contract agreement:

- Mission of the joint venture
- Short- and long-term objectives
- Markets to be served
- Products and services to be offered
- Basic organizational structure of the venture
- Obligations and responsibilities of the partners

- Management responsibilities of the venture
- Definition of roles
- Process by which venture will be dissolved

The final issue listed, terminating the venture, requires elaboration. It is important to include some clear-cut mechanism for ending the venture in the initial agreement because the dynamics of the venture change over time. Partners typically perceive a win/win situation at the outset of the enterprise. They both see themselves as benefiting from their joint efforts to create and achieve wealth; however, as the venture matures and thought is given to its termination, the focus shifts to the division of rewards and the creation of a win/lose situation. This can be most effectively handled when it is clearly defined at the beginning of the venture and documented in the contract agreement.

One mechanism partners often choose as a means of terminating a venture is a buy/sell agreement that allows either party to offer a price at which it will buy the other out. The second firm, however, has the option of either selling at that price or buying the first party's shares at the same price. This kind of agreement ensures that only fair offers are made.

Including as many of these anticipated issues as possible in the contract agreement will increase the ease of implementing and operating the venture. Another way of ensuring consideration of all such issues is to involve managers in the joint venture negotiations. They can anticipate issues that may not be apparent to lawyers. The process of talking through these topics with their partner counterparts will also enable them to learn more about one another, establish the trust necessary for the relationship to work, and generate a high level of commitment to the venture.

Stage 2: Planning and Design

After agreeing to embark on a joint venture, the partners must turn their attention to the planning and design of their newly established enterprise. This work occurs both before and after the legal closing of the deal. A major focus of this second stage is on the appropriate organization and management structure and the staffing of the venture. How involved should each partner organization be in the operations of the venture? How should the venture report organizationally? How much control should the partners have over the decisions and activities of the venture? How should the venture be staffed? How are the partner organizations expected to relate to one another? These are only a few of the many complex questions that partners must address in planning and designing a venture.

Structure and Staffing

As shown in Figure 4.5, research and experience indicate that there is a much higher failure rate for joint ventures when both partner organizations are heavily involved managerially in the venture than when just one partner dominates. Dual reporting relationships, operational complexities created by functional links across all three organizations, and competing decision-making structures are a few of the problems that arise when both partners are heavily involved. Chances for survival increase when one partner dominates and manages the joint venture as if it were a wholly owned subsidiary.

Research also indicates that the success of the venture increases with the autonomy of the venture general manager (see Figure 4.5). Successful joint ventures typically require a high degree of competitive responsiveness. When both or even one of the partner

Figure 4.5. Structural Factors Involved in Success/Failure of Joint Ventures

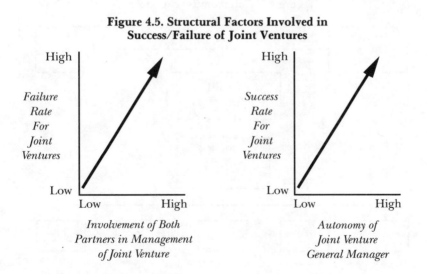

High

Failure Rate For Joint Ventures

Low

Low   High

Involvement of Both Partners in Management of Joint Venture

High

Success Rate For Joint Ventures

Low

Low   High

Autonomy of Joint Venture General Manager

organizations is heavily involved in the decision-making process, it is difficult for the venture manager to act quickly and achieve the responsiveness required to make the venture successful.

These data pose an interesting design challenge. How can both partners share responsibility for managing the venture without restricting the independence of the venture general manager? A collaborative structure (Figure 4.6) is the most straightforward of the design possibilities, yet it is the most difficult to make work. In this design, the venture general manager reports directly to a board of directors composed of managers from each of the partner organizations. The board is responsible for strategic decision making, oversight and guidance, approval of budgets and resource allocations, and so on. The venture manager and the venture staff typically come from one or both of the partner organizations.

The difficulty of this design lies in the need to negotiate any and all differences between the partner organizations on issues that affect the venture and its operation. The structure of the arrangement and the role of the board certainly imply considerable involvement in the venture. When differences are significant and no fast, effective mode of conflict resolution exists, the interference is likely to be substantial and the process of decision making slow. To make this structure work, the partner organizations must be especially

Figure 4.6. Collaborative Structure.

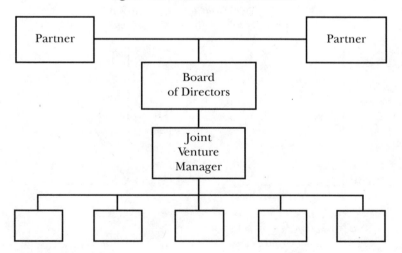

compatible in style and orientation. They must share a common understanding of the venture's needs and be sensitive to their potentially destructive interference. Achieving such a relationship often requires substantial time, effort, and commitment to make it work.

Corning, unlike many other companies that have tried and failed, has had considerable success with joint ventures. Since 1924, Corning has initiated thirty-seven joint ventures and only six have failed. They attribute much of their success to the trust, compatibility, and commitment between them and their partners. Corning is careful to ensure that they and their partners share the same basic business philosophy and have no fundamental conflicts of interest with each other or with the venture itself. They also believe that it is important to give the venture management team as much independence as possible, an observation that underscores the research data cited above. It is this mixture of ingredients that enables a design like the collaborative structure to work.

Overall, it is the strength of the relationship between the partners and their interest in wanting to do what needs to get done (or not do what may get in the way) that make an effective partnership. It is clear that the success of the collaborative structure rests on a set of conditions that enable it to work. These conditions are summarized in Table 4.1. If all or most of the questions asked can be answered with a yes, then a collaborative structure is suitable. When all or the majority of questions are answered with a no, then an instrumental structure may be the best alternative.

In the instrumental structure (Figure 4.7), one partner becomes dominant in the management and operation of the venture. The other partner adopts a passive role. The board of directors again consists of managers from both partner organizations, but their primary role is general oversight. The venture general manager reports directly to the dominant partner and assumes a reporting relationship to the board (dotted line). In this design, the venture reports, in practice, to the dominant partner much like a wholly owned subsidiary. The venture manager and the venture staff in this design would typically come from the dominant partner.

This design is instrumental in that it avoids all of the conventional problems that can besiege a working partner relationship.

Table 4.1. Conditions That Enable the Collaborative Structure to Work.

Do the partners . . .	Collaborative Structure	Instrumental Structure
Trust one another?	Yes	No
Agree on venture autonomy?	Yes	No
Have compatible business philoso-phies and styles?	Yes	No
Agree on a process to resolve differences?	Yes	No
Each make a contribution that the other respects?	Yes	No
Agree on long-range goals?	Yes	No
Understand the business?	Yes	No
Agree on minimal direct involvement?	Yes	No
Commit time to their relationship?	Yes	No

Figure 4.7. Instrumental Structure.

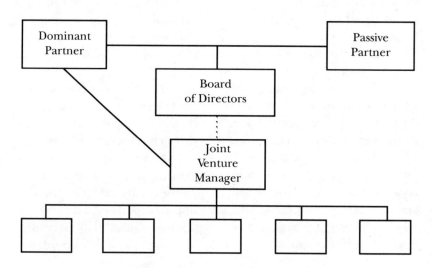

It provides a functional form of management while circumventing the difficulties that can arise between partners whose relationship is not now nor is ever likely to become collaborative. It is also instrumental for those partners who are not willing to commit the time required to turn their relationship into a partnership.

Assuming the role of passive partner is a difficult task for some firms even though they may have sanctioned their partner as the dominant partner in the venture. This is particularly a problem for those who have not worked with each other before. Many passive partners discover that they need to achieve a minimum level of comfort in knowing what is going on and how the venture is doing. Such firms should try to satisfy their need to know without doing things that disrupt the venture or lessen its chances for success. The board of directors typically satisfies this need. When more information is needed, however, some other nonobtrusive approach may have to be used. One option would be to consider the formation of an executive committee consisting of one board member from each partner organization and the joint venture general manager. They could meet on a regular basis to share information without convening the entire board and thus reinforce a perception of formal accountability and control. This committee could also be used to informally consider and discuss strategic inputs in an effort to provide the passive partner with yet another opportunity to feel involved in the venture.

Management Style

The best joint venture managers tend to be those who do well in matrix organizations, which are usually characterized by a high degree of ambiguity and uncertainty. The demands of a dual reporting relationship created by a matrix structure closely resemble the situation faced by a joint venture general manager having to satisfy the diverse information needs and demands of the partner firms. Although this is certainly more true of the collaborative structure, it applies to the instrumental structure as well. The manager must be able to resolve the controversies that arise and be prepared to handle the political circumstances that occur in either case.

When the responsibility for managing the operations is

shared, it is especially important that the venture general manager have a participative style. It is more likely that a venture proposal will be accepted and supported if the manager has solicited the input of subject matter experts from both partner organizations. Because these experts would likely be asked for their input by the partner firm anyway, their early involvement builds a coalition of support and commitment within the partner firms that facilitates the eventual decision regarding the proposal. It also avoids the divisiveness that can sometimes arise when experts have to defend their work to other experts whose input was not originally requested.

Another benefit of the participative style is that it lessens the likelihood that the venture manager will be seen as having favored one partner. By including others in an objective review of decision alternatives and focusing on the business requirements that must be satisfied, venture managers are more likely to have their decisions supported.

The venture manager needs to be positioned as the leader of the venture, the person who is in control. Partners who intervene directly in the venture (in the form of requests for information or directives) will serve only to undermine the authority of the manager and his or her efforts to achieve an organizational integration of the venture. It is imperative that the venture and its staff establish an independent identity and allegiance. The intrusion of partner organizations into the venture makes it more difficult for employees to sever the ties they once had to those organizations.

Support Systems

The joint venture should be staffed by employees from one or both of the partner organizations as suggested by the type of joint venture being adopted. In the collaborative structure, the employees typically come from both partner organizations, depending on the functional units or resources that are being combined in the venture. In the instrumental structure, the employees should come from the dominant partner organization. As a general rule, employees should not be employed from the passive partner organization; doing so will create allegiance problems and potentially lead to managerial interference from the passive partner.

It is imperative that the partners not use the joint venture as a personnel dumping ground. Staff should be seen as competent, respected, and qualified for the venture tasks they will be asked to perform. Some firms are hesitant to assign their most qualified people to the newly created venture. Their inclination is to retain those people for their own operations. In pursuing this strategy, they run the risk of lessening the probability of the venture's success and of sending an indirect message to their partner about their level of commitment to the enterprise. They may also lose an opportunity to tap the entrepreneurial tendencies of their most qualified managers and the contribution that the venture could make to their development.

The reward system that is used to compensate venture staff is an important personnel management issue. Like any good reward system, it should be consistent with the performance criteria and expectations of the new venture. It should strengthen employee identification with the venture and not reinforce that employee's former association with his or her parent organization. Allegiance will be hard enough to manage without an administrative system that serves as a constant reminder. Finally, the system should compensate employees for the higher risks they feel they may be taking in agreeing to join the venture.

Stage 3: Implementation

Many managers view the hard work as completed once the announcement of the new organization and its design has been made. Very little thought, if any, is devoted to what will happen next. The energy and enthusiasm characteristic of the initial design stage often do not extend to the implementation of that design. All three organizations are left with many unanswered questions. They soon learn that they must deal with all of the issues that typically arise when a major organizational change is introduced.

In the case of joint ventures, the change problem is even more complex. Besides its effects on the partner organizations, the joint venture itself and all of the uncertainties associated with it must be managed to ensure successful implementation. It, like any new organization, can quickly fail if ample managerial attention is not devoted to its startup.

The focus of stage 3, therefore, is on ensuring the successful startup and implementation of the joint venture. The underlying issue is the effective management of organizational change as it occurs in both partner organizations as well as the joint venture. How much change each partner experiences may well be determined by the decisions made in the design stage. Such issues as whether the joint venture alters the operations of the partners, establishes new cross-organizational relationships, or staffs itself with personnel from either or both partners will affect the degree of change experienced. At the very least, the anticipation of change and the uncertainty associated with it will create problems that must be handled effectively. The concepts of organizational change to be discussed below, therefore, apply to both the partner organizations as well as the newly formed joint venture.

The growing body of knowledge on effective change management has much to offer those involved in setting up a joint venture. Underlying this knowledge base is a concept originally proposed by Beckhard and Harris (1977), who saw the implementation of change as movement from a current state through a transition state to a desired future state. In its most general terms, the effective management of change involves achieving an understanding of the current state, developing an image of the desired future state, and moving the organization through a transition period from one state to the other. In the case of joint ventures, this typically means moving two separate organizations with no relationship to a state where the two share a common interest for a venture offspring, as shown in Figure 4.8. The formation of a successful offspring requires the active management of its startup.

When viewed in this fashion, the problems encountered in the introduction and startup of a joint venture are the same problems that arise with any major organizational change—problems with power, anxiety, and control (Delta Consulting Group, 1983).

Power

An organization is a political system made up of different individuals, groups, and coalitions competing for power. An understand-

Figure 4.8. Joint Venture Startup as an Organizational Change.

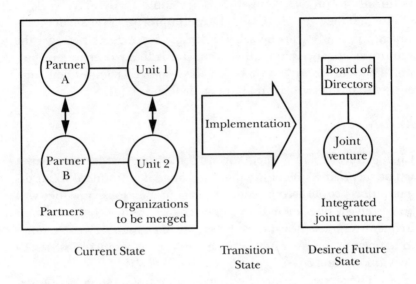

Current State   Transition State   Desired Future State

ing of political behavior is therefore fundamental to an understanding of how organizations function. During a period of transition, the established political dynamics are disrupted as the new set of circumstances is put into place. This change poses a threat to the balance of power among the various formal and informal interest groups. As the uncertainty about the future increases, so too does the political behavior of people who are concerned with protecting their positions.

Problems of this nature can easily emerge in the case of joint ventures. For instance, it is not unlikely that managers in both partner organizations would see the venture as an opportunity to gain power. The political behavior that results from the competition for control could very well interfere with what the joint venture really needs. Critical to these power dynamics is how the venture is perceived. If the venture is seen as a success, managers may vie for the select positions to be filled and promise appointments to others on their staffs. Staffing may thus proceed according to the desires of these networks rather than on the basis of job requirements. If, on the other hand, the venture is seen as too risky and not likely to succeed, the dynamics may be reversed. Fearful that they or their best people may be recruited for the venture, managers may act politically to protect themselves. They could easily make deals to ensure that they are left alone. The most unfortunate element of this strategy is that it can be self-fulfilling. If managers perceive the venture as not succeeding, their behavior is likely to ensure its failure. The venture will be robbed of the resources, commitment, and energy that otherwise could have made it successful.

Anxiety

Change implies a movement toward something that is unknown. It is not surprising, therefore, that as change is introduced to an organization people become concerned about their jobs, how they will be perceived, how their lives might change, and so on. The most frequent response heard during periods of change is, what's going to happen to me? As uncertainty about the future increases, so too does anxiety and stress.

The anxiety created by change often results in behavior and performance problems. People may be too anxious to hear the information they are being told. They are likely to resist the changes they perceive. People are more comfortable and secure with the status quo. Is it any wonder then that employees who are offered positions in a newly formed joint venture become reticent and concerned with the risky nature of the enterprise? How different will the job be from what I currently do? What will happen if the venture fails? Will I be out of a job? What does the venture have to offer me that I currently do not have? How will the new job contribute to my development and career? How difficult will it be for me to get back to my real organization and the career positions to which I aspire? Why should I leave my co-workers and the people with whom I work best?

The change becomes even more threatening as efforts are made to sever the employee's relationship with the old organization in favor of the new. Employees are asked to shift their allegiance from a secure, familiar environment to one that is uncertain and unfamiliar. They are likely both to be confused and to feel conflict in their approach to both organizations.

Managers who remain in either of the partner organizations

may resist the change out of concern for how their jobs and access to resources may be affected. Will they be robbed of people, functions, or financial resources? The possibility that any of those things could happen is enough to invoke many forms of resistance and opposition. Why should they cooperate and support the venture if it only means sacrifices and losses to themselves?

Control

Change tends to disrupt the normal course of events within an organization. Established systems of management control and structure may no longer be relevant to the new set of circumstances or may simply be seen as getting in the way. It is therefore easy to lose control during periods of change. As fundamental changes in strategy are made, it becomes increasingly difficult to monitor performance and move the organization toward the right goals.

Such is the case with joint ventures. Ventures often require the redistribution of work across all three of the organizations involved. As functional relationships are redefined and new ones established, many operations are likely to be disrupted. Specific functions, if not entire organizational units, are often redesigned in light of the resource or functional work flow requirements of the venture. This redistribution of people, tasks, materials, and systems is likely to result in a loss of managerial control and subsequent deterioration of performance in the units affected. If not anticipated and managed properly, it may be a considerable period of time before normal operations can be resumed in the partner organizations and before the venture can begin to engage in the business it was designed to conduct.

Discussion of the preceding three problems leads us to some very clear conclusions about what is needed to manage change effectively (see Delta Consulting Group, 1983, for a more thorough discussion of this topic). As shown in Figure 4.9, each of these organizational problems suggests how change should be managed. Problems of power require that the organization's political system be managed to shape the political dynamics in support of the change. A possible action that could be taken includes getting the

Figure 4.9. Management Implications of Problems Created by Change.

Problem		*Implication*
Power	⟶	Need to shape the political dynamics associated with change
Anxiety	⟶	Need to motivate constructive behavior in response to the change
Control	⟶	Need to systematically manage the transition state

support of key power groups within the organization. Another possibility is to shape the power distribution by having leaders behave in ways that support the changes required.

Other possible actions include using symbols (in language, pictures, acts, and so on) to reinforce identification with the newly formed venture and provide anchors to people so stability can be returned to the organization. Such anchors could be in the form of reassurances about what will not change, providing messages in advance to prepare people for the changes that do occur, and being consistent in the array of messages that are sent.

Problems with anxiety suggest the need to motivate constructive employee behavior in response to the change. Surfacing or creating dissatisfaction with the current state is one way to unfreeze people's perception of the present. It should be clear to employees in both partner organizations why a joint venture is necessary. Participation in planning and implementing the changes created by the venture as well as rewarding the behaviors that support its formation and development are additional actions that can be taken. Finally, providing the time and opportunity for people to disengage from the current state is necessary to help people achieve a sense of "psychological closure." Venture managers should acknowledge the feelings that employees are experiencing and allow them time to express and deal with those feelings. At the same time, managers should support and help those employees establish their identity and relationship with the new venture.

Managers can overcome control problems created by change if they devote the same degree of care, resources, and skill to managing the change as they would any other major project. By developing and communicating a clear image of the venture to be formed, managers can help shape employee perceptions of the venture and the behavior expected of them. Managers can also ensure effective management of the startup by ensuring that the internal components of the venture fit and complement the systems to which they may be linked in the partner organizations. Managers should think about what other changes might have to be made for the entire set of organizational systems to function effectively. Besides the changes directly affected by the venture, other changes may need to be made in organizational policies and programs, in the informal networks, or in the culture required of the business to be conducted by the venture.

To ensure the success of the startup, the partner organizations may want to provide specific resources or structures to support the venture manager in his or her efforts to establish the venture and its functional links to the partner companies. One final way to help maintain control during the startup is to monitor and evaluate progress through feedback. By collecting data on the progress of the startup, managers can target corrective actions where necessary and focus more attention on issues requiring their support.

Stage 4: Development

After the initial startup period, the venture general manager must continue to strengthen the identity and independence of the venture. The emphasis here is on enabling the venture to become as much like a separate operating unit or wholly owned subsidiary as possible. It must establish its own identity apart from the parent organizations. Establishing this independence implies the creation of a mind-set in which the venture is seen as different and distinct from the partner organizations. An allegiance must be built among employees to the venture, and formal ties to the partner organizations must be severed. It will be difficult to motivate employees to focus on the venture if they believe they can simply return to their parent organizations at any time or if things do not go well. They must be committed to the venture and its success. That commitment cannot be achieved when employees are tied both organizationally and psychologically to some other organization and job.

As the joint venture continues to develop and mature, it moves closer to the future state originally defined. Knowing what to do with the venture will depend on how well the partners have envisioned that future state and the purposes it was designed to serve.

A clearly defined strategic plan in which the role of the joint venture is also clearly defined and understood (as suggested in stage 1) can help guide the decisions required in the evolution of the venture. Managers can use such a plan to establish performance and financial criteria on which to base decisions to terminate, buy/sell, release, or continue to operate the venture. These criteria should, of course, reflect the purpose of the venture and what it was intended to provide the partner firm. This cycle of feeding back performance data through the internal assessment of the strategic planning process in each partner organization is summarized in Figure 4.10. It is also important, as suggested earlier, that the partners agree at the outset on some mechanism that enables either of them to take whatever action may be necessary as the venture matures. A buy/sell agreement like that described in stage 1 can be extremely useful in this regard. It allows either partner to invoke its option to terminate the partnership in as fair a manner as possible.

Figure 4.10. Joint Venture Process.

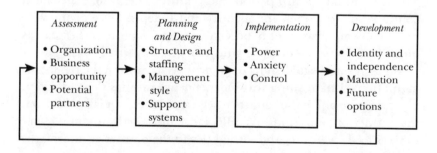

Summary

The preceding analysis can be summarized in the form of some specific actions that are likely to increase the effectiveness of joint ventures:

1. Develop a clearly defined strategic purpose and understanding for the necessity of the joint venture. Consider less complicated strategic alternatives. Use the products of this process to assess compatibility with potential partners.

2. Examine the willingness and readiness of the firm to accept the management and operating conditions required of a successful joint venture. Assess whether or not the organization can accept the conditions and circumstances (for example, structure, management philosophy and practices, independence, and partner relationship) implied in forming a venture.

3. Assess the readiness of the firm for organizational change. Identify both the range of changes that the venture is likely to create in the partner organization and the resources and plan that will be required to manage those changes.

4. Understand the business opportunity being sought. Do sufficient market research to ensure that the opportunity will, in practice, satisfy the strategic purpose originally envisioned.

5. Scrutinize potential partners. Select a partner based on as much real working experience as possible. Look at the profile of successful partner organizations when deciding what characteristics to examine.

6. Choose an organizational structure for the venture that reflects the nature of the relationship between the partners and what it can become. Use the checklist of enabling conditions to guide the selection.

7. Minimize the active involvement of both partner organizations in the direct management of the venture. Work to define a role for the partners that satisfies their need to be informed but minimizes their participation in operating decisions.

8. Select a venture general manager who is flexible, is able to deal with conflict, and can function effectively in matrixlike organizational arrangements. Encourage a participatory style of

management to achieve organizational integration and eliminate divisiveness.

9. Give the venture general manager as much autonomy and independence as possible. Allow the venture manager to control as much of the venture and its operations as possible.

10. Design reward and support systems to reinforce employee identification with the venture and be consistent with the performance criteria (including risk) expected of those employees. Encourage as much self-sufficiency as possible within the venture.

11. Manage the startup of the venture with a deliberate implementation plan that includes active management of the changes that also occur in the partner organizations. Support the implementation with resources and time as required.

12. Allow the joint venture to establish its own identity and allegiances independent of the partner organizations. Encourage the venture manager to focus the time and energy of employees on satisfying the business needs of the venture, not the information needs of the partners.

13. Use the strategic plan and preestablished evaluation criteria to guide the decision about what to do with the venture over time. Feed back data on venture performance and assess how well it continues to serve the strategic purposes of the partner organization.

As suggested at the outset, managers can maximize their chances of forming and managing effective joint ventures if they work to ensure the presence of critical success factors and the absence of potential areas of conflict and failure. The purpose of this chapter was to identify the array of these factors and their role in the evolution of successful ventures. We hope it has enabled managers to benefit from the experiences and lessons learned by others when they embark on their own efforts to manage future joint ventures.

References

Beckhard, R., and Harris, R. *Organizational Transitions*. Reading, Mass.: Addison-Wesley, 1977.

Delta Consulting Group. *Techniques for the Management of Organizational Change*. New York: Delta Consulting Group, 1983.

Harrigan, K. R. *Strategies for Joint Ventures*. Lexington, Mass.: Lexington Books, 1985.

Killing, J. P. *Strategies for Joint Venture Success*. London: Croom Helm, 1983.

Nadler, D. A. "Managing Organizational Change: An Integrative Approach." *Journal of Applied Behavioral Science*, 1981, *17*, 191-211.

FIVE

Designing High-Performance Work Systems: Organizing People, Work, Technology, and Information

DAVID A. NADLER, MARC S. GERSTEIN

Two black swans, aptly named Dream and Vision, serenely oversee the duck pond in front of American Transtech's Jacksonville, Florida, headquarters. Since 1983, when the company was established by AT&T to handle the dramatic increase in shareholder activity resulting from the creation of the Regional Bell Operating Companies, American Transtech has become a leader in work redesign in the United States.

Employing self-directed teams, a redesigned work process, and a virtually flat, three-level hierarchy in the operating business, the company has improved productivity from 100 to 300 percent and reduced its costs and staff in the core stock transfer area by more than 50 percent. American Transtech has taken in outside customers such as American Express to use the excess capacity necessitated by the cyclical nature of dividend payments and exploited its skills in phone customer contact to build a significant telemarketing business.

Employees monitor the performance and costs of their operations on a continuous basis and know their operations inside-out. In addition to their work redesign and operations responsibilities, they participate in hiring, career progression, and compensation decisions. Outsiders are universally surprised by the depth of employee knowledge, candor, and willingness to change. Although life is not perfect at American Transtech, as everyone is quick to admit, they are working on it.

110

A revolution is under way in the workplaces of America. It is a quiet revolution; there are few banners, no great battles, and relatively little publicity. It involves innovative thinking about how people, work, technology, and information can be brought together in new forms of organization capable of achieving significantly higher levels of sustained performance. The quiet beginnings of this revolution are setting the stage for profound changes in the way we think about the organization of work in the 1990s.

In fact, these efforts to develop new and better ways to organize human effort have been going on for some time. Since the late 1960s, innovation and learning about the organization of work has proceeded in a number of different companies under a variety of different names. Companies have experimented with autonomous work teams, sociotechnical systems, open systems planning, new plant designs, and other similar innovations. These efforts, however, have gone far beyond experimentation and pilots. In such corporations as Procter & Gamble, Digital Equipment Corporation (DEC), Corning, Inc., and AT&T, these new approaches to organizing have been implemented and have achieved sustained superior results.

In recent times, a term has emerged to describe these different innovations. The concept of *high-performance work systems* has been used as an integrating concept and a label to describe a variety of different specific innovations that all draw from a common set of principles and practices. The purpose of this chapter is to provide a perspective on high-performance work systems (HPWS), as a reference point for managers who are considering HPWS initiatives. This chapter is an attempt to integrate a number of different perspectives on this topic, with a focus toward practice and application. We begin with a short historical perspective to provide a sense of how this approach to organizing developed. We then describe what we believe HPWS means today. Next we focus on two core elements of HPWS. First, we identify principles of HPWS design and contrast them with traditional approaches to organization design. Second, we describe the basic HPWS design process, the steps involved in implementing the design principles. In a final section, we discuss the relationship of HPWS to some other organizational improvement strategies.

Historical Perspective

Traditional Models

Most of the conventional wisdom about how to organize dates back to two approaches developed close to a century ago. At the turn of the century, F. W. Taylor, an American, developed a "scientific" model of organization using the machines of the Industrial Revolution as his model (Taylor, 1911). Taylor believed in careful and comprehensive analysis of the work system and the removal of any possible cause of variation. At the core of his approach to organizing, called *scientific management,* were some design principles including specialization of work into the narrowest possible jobs, careful specification of work tasks in detail, repetition of activity with little (or no) variety, and removal of all discretion and "brain work" from operational personnel.

At approximately the same time, the German sociologist Max Weber, observing the organizational innovations of the German leader Bismark, articulated a management model called *bureaucracy* (Weber, 1947). Weber's bureaucracy was a coherent and well thought out theory of organizing containing the following important elements:

- Organizations should be built around a clear system of hierarchical relationships, with greater discretion in decision making as one moves up the hierarchy and with an established chain of command as the primary mechanism for coordination.
- Organizations should be governed by a clear and consistent set of written rules and procedures covering all positions, both operational and managerial.
- Job holders should be qualified to perform their assignments; therefore, technical competence should be the basis for filling jobs and for promotion.

Today it is difficult to understand the tremendous leap forward that these approaches to organizing represented compared with earlier feudal or tribal models. The "machine bureaucracy" that emerged from the fusion of Taylor's and Weber's ideas achieved

previously unattainable levels of performance through enhanced individual performance and vast improvements in coordination between organizational units. As this model of organization-as-
machine matured in the early part of the twentieth century, it established a template for industrial organization that persists to this day.
Though the basic principles of Taylor's and Weber's works may
seem obvious and perhaps dated as they are read today, they clearly
laid the foundation for an enormous increase in industrial productivity and established a pattern of beliefs about the right way to
structure a productive enterprise. In fact, this approach has become
so pervasive that we unconsciously equate the machine bureaucracy
model with the process of organizing; it is hard for us to think of
any other way of structuring work enterprises.

Human Relations Approaches

Despite the dramatic successes of the model of organization-as-
machine, productivity came at enormous costs. The enterprise was
frequently shortchanged of people's motivation and creativity,
which could not be harnessed as a result of narrow, repetitious jobs
that had little discretion. Coordination between units was difficult,
despite attempts to systematize interactions with rules and procedures. The bureaucratic system itself had a number of serious unintended consequences, such as communications bottlenecks, decision
making in the absence of the information necessary to make decisions, and an incapacity to act brought about by layer upon layer of
rules and managerial approvals.

In summary, the machine bureaucracy model, while tremend-
ously successful at first, ultimately suffered from three significant
problems, which became apparent by the middle of the twentieth
century (see, for example, Roethlisberger and Dickson, 1939; Argyris,
1957).

1. The model was built for the management of relatively stable and
    predictable situations. It broke down under conditions of uncer-
    tainty and instability because of the inability to reconfigure and
    the lack of emphasis on discretion by individuals. As rates of

change increased, organizations based on this model became less effective.

2. The model was built on the assumption that the work force was relatively uneducated, had little mobility, and was driven almost exclusively by economic needs. As more educated workers with greater mobility and a desire for noneconomic returns from their employment (pride, a feeling of worth and accomplishment, challenge, and growth) came into the work force, the organizations built on this model had a more difficult time motivating and satisfying workers.

3. Over time, organizations based on this model experienced their own entropy: they tended to become more complex, less responsive, more inwardly oriented, and more unwieldy.

Starting in the 1940s and continuing well into the 1970s, management theorists and practitioners responded with a variety of techniques to compensate for the inherent limitations of the machine bureaucracy (Argyris, 1957; Likert, 1961). These theorists worked from a very different set of assumptions based on the beliefs that people wanted to work and produce quality products; that through participation, people's energies could be enlisted in the service of organizational goals; and that there was potential power in groups or teams of people working together collaboratively. Such techniques included participative management, management style training, team building, job enirchment and enlargement, and other similar approaches. Despite the initial reports of the success of such innovations, in many cases their impact was short-lived. Frequently, these new approaches were "pasted on" the existing organization, which had been designed using the machine bureaucracy model. Two conflicting models of design were being employed, and these approaches had fundamentally different underlying values and design principles. Over time, these "paste ons" tended to have little positive impact.

Origins of High-Performance Work Systems

High-performance work systems can be traced back to a series of experiments conducted in the United Kingdom during the late 1940s.

Researchers from the Tavistock Institute, studying the introduction of new technology in British coal mines (and later in the weaving industry in India), discovered that technological innovation alone could not explain differences in performance (Trist and Bamforth, 1951; Rice, 1958). In fact, certain technological changes that were intended to increase performance resulted, instead, in performance declines. Research revealed that high performance resulted when the design of the technical system and the design of the social system of work were congruent. Building on group dynamics and general systems theory, the Tavistock researchers demonstrated that high performance required that the needs of the organization's social system and the needs of the technical system be considered equally and simultaneously in the design process. They argued that a set of design principles different from the classical "one man/one job" approach be used to construct work systems. Rather than fitting jobs (and thus people) to the optimum technical system, the joint optimization of both the social and technical systems would be required.

Research over subsequent years led to the development of an approach to work design called *sociotechnical systems* (Cherns, 1976). At the core of the sociotechnical model (Figure 5.1) is the concept of two work system elements—social and technical—designed deliberately to fit each other. Where a high degree of sociotechnical fit was achieved, performance increased. By the late 1960s, a large amount of experience (largely outside of the United States) had begun to accrue so that the principles of sociotechnical work design could be articulated. At the core of the approach are five principles (Hanna, 1988; Cherns, 1976):

1. Although rules and work processes critical to overall success should be identified, no more rules should be specified than are absolutely essential.
2. Variances, or deviations, from the ideal process should be controlled at the point of origin.
3. Each member of the system should be skilled in more than one function so that the work system is flexible and adaptive.

Figure 5.1. Sociotechnical Systems.

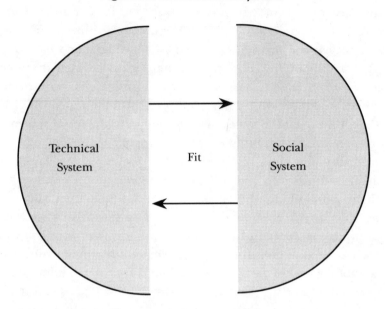

4. Roles that are interdependent should be within the same departmental boundaries.
5. Information systems should be designed primarily to provide information to the point of action and problem solving.

In practice, sociotechnical design also led to the heavy use of teams to manage interdependent work, with those teams empowered to manage their own work processes and flows. This approach, therefore became known as "autonomous work teams" and was prevalent in Europe during the 1970s. During the 1960s and 1970s, an additional element was added to the concept of sociotechnical design. A number of designers pointed out that most of the sociotechnical design work had been done with an internal focus. They argued that effective work system design needed to start with an external or "open systems" perspective, starting with the external stakeholders (customers, suppliers, competitors). Work system design would thus start with an understanding of environmental requirements, demands, and opportunities and then move to the design of specific elements of the social and technical systems (Lawrence and Lorsch, 1967).

At the same time, other experimenters were seeking to extend some of the concepts of sociotechnical design by applying them to larger work systems, in particular, complete manufacturing installations. The greatest success was gained in new plants that were designed from the ground up using sociotechnical principles. Notable examples were the General Foods Topeka dog food plant and the Volvo Kalmar assembly plant in Sweden. By the late 1970s, several hundred new plant designs had been implemented in the United States with a very high success rate (Lawler, 1978). These new plant designs used sociotechnical principles but went beyond them. The new plants also reflected significant changes in the design of the organizational architecture—the formal and informal structures and processes—that formed the context for the core work process (Lawler, 1986):

Employee selection. Peer selection and information sharing enable workers to select the new type of work environment.

Design of physical layout. Employees participate in the design of the physical setting and the work configurations that support team designs, team planning, and meeting areas.

Job design. Individual jobs within the context of the teams are designed to increase autonomy, variety of tasks, feedback, and the sense of completing a piece of work.

Pay system. Rewards are tied to skill acquisition for individuals, to encourage multiskill acquisition. Gain-sharing plans motivate improved performance.

Organizational structure. These plants typically are designed with fewer levels of hierarchy, with more self-contained or autonomous units, and in support of self-managing teams.

Training. The plants invest heavily in intensive training in skills, as well as training to provide the broad background knowledge that supports participation in decision making.

Management philosophy. These plants are run with an explicit philosophy of partnership between management and the work force, aimed at a common vision.

These new plant designs continue to be employed. Some notable examples are the Digital Equipment facility in Enfield, Connecticut, and the Procter & Gamble technician plant in Lima, Ohio.

During the 1980s, as more experience was gained with different design approaches, a growing number of companies began to integrate the sociotechnical, open systems, and new plant design concepts into an approach called high-performance work systems. It was a logical extension of the earlier frameworks.

Definition

The *high-performance work systems* (HPWS) approach to the design of human work organizations, in its simplest form, is an organizational architecture that brings together work, people, technology, and information in a manner that optimizes the congruence or "fit" among them (Figure 5.2) in order to produce high performance in terms of the effective response to customer requirements and other environmental demands and opportunities (Hanna, 1988; Sherwood, 1988; Nadler and Tushman, 1988; Tushman and Nadler, 1978; Brown, 1989; Nadler, 1989). High-performance work systems can be characterized as follows:

> *A way of thinking about organization.* Instead of fitting people to the requirements of the technical system with a focus on internal efficiency, the HPWS approach emphasizes the fit among work, people, technology, and information with an external focus on the effectiveness of the system in meeting the changing requirements of the environment.
>
> *A set of principles for designing organizations.* The HPWS approach comprises very specific design principles that guide the designer in making choices. These principles reflect a set of values about people and work.
>
> *A process for applying those design principles.* The HPWS approach also includes a design process—a series of ge-

Figure 5.2. High-Performance Work Systems.

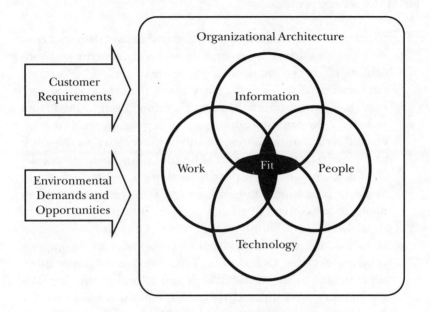

neric steps for the design (or redesign) of work systems and
organizations.

A variety of specific organizational design features. Very specific design devices or features, such as autonomous work
teams, enriched jobs, and flat hierarchies, are employed as
a consequence of using the design principles.

The historical view provided above described the evolution
of the HPWS approach. Now, we focus on what we see as the two
core elements of HPWS: the design principles and the design
process.

Design Principles

The HPWS approach is not a specific design or even a particular
design feature (such as autonomous work teams) any more than
machine bureaucracy could be equated to a seven-level hierarchy.
HPWS is a set of design principles that are applied to particular

organizational situations. Looking at a range of projects and initiatives, we see ten principles:

1. *Customer- and environmentally focused design.* Design must, over time, be driven by environmental requirements and conditions if an organization is to be successful. The primary environmental factor is the customer of the product or service that the organization produces. Therefore, design starts from outside of the organization (or unit), beginning with customers and their requirements, and then moves back to the work and organizational processes. The core purpose of HPWS design is to enable sets of people working together to produce and deliver products and services that meet customer requirements in the context of changing environments.

2. *Empowered and autonomous units.* Organizational units should be designed around whole pieces of work—complete products, services, or processes. The goal is to maximize interdependence within the work unit and minimize interdependence among work units. Obviously, there is still some need for coordination among different units, but the aim is to create loosely coupled units with the ability to manage their relationships with each other. Teams, as opposed to individuals, are the basic organizational building blocks. Rather than focus on how to break down work into the smallest units that can be performed by an individual, the HPWS approach emphasizes complete units of work that can be performed by sets of individuals, who are empowered to determine how they will do the work. Within the context of very stringent customer requirements, great freedom is provided to those doing the work to design and manage their own work processes. This implies minimum specification of the work and resources to enable empowerment, such as time, money, information, and decision-making authority.

3. *Clear direction and goals.* Although there is great latitude in determining how the work will be done, there is a great need for clarity about the requirements of the output. Therefore, the empowered autonomous work unit needs to have a very clear mission, defined output requirements, and agreed-on

measures of performance. Clear direction and goals provide the work unit with the information needed to design and manage its own work structure and process.

4. *Control of variance at the source.* Work processes and units should be designed so that variances (errors) can be detected and controlled at the source, as opposed to outside the work unit. It is much less costly to detect and correct variance at the point of creation than later on. This implies that the work unit is provided with the information and tools to detect and prevent error.

5. *Socio-technical integration.* The social and technical systems are seen as inexorably interlinked. The purpose of design is to achieve effective integration between the two. The technical system includes the work flow, the specific technologies employed, the movement of information, and the work processes. Rather than design the technical system for the people or select the people with respect to the technical system, the goal is to achieve joint optimization to create an integrated work system capable of responding to customer and environmental requirements.

6. *Accessible information flow.* As implied by many of the principles already articulated, information is critical to the effective functioning of a HPWS design. Members of the empowered autonomous unit need to have access to information about the environment, about the output, about the work process, about variances, and so on. The flow of information (as opposed to the flow of data) must be designed so that work unit members can create, receive, and transmit information as needed.

7. *Enriched and shared jobs.* The capacity of the empowered autonomous work unit is enhanced if people in the unit are cross-trained in a variety of skills. Broader jobs increase individual autonomy, learning, and internal motivation (Hackman and Oldham, 1980). The work unit's ability to reconfigure is enhanced. As individuals understand the nature of the work performed by others, their ability to participate in the design and management of the entire work process is also

enhanced. Learning, as well as performance, becomes an important driver for individuals.

8. *Empowering human resources practices.* Many of the human resources policies and practices in organizations reflect the machine bureaucracy model. The emphasis is on control, uniformity, and inspection of variance outside the unit. HPWS design implies the need to create human resources practices that are consistent with autonomous empowered units, such as local selection, skill-based pay, peer feedback, team bonuses, minimization of rank and hierarchy, and gain sharing.

9. *Empowering management structure, process, and culture.* HPWS units placed in the context of machine bureaucracies are like hostile, alien life forms. The larger system detects their presence and attempts to destroy or expel them. The literature on organizational change is abundant with examples of this phenomenon (Walton, 1977). The design principle is to ensure that the "host system" is consistent with and supportive of the empowered autonomous unit. In the early stages of HPWS design, this may mean the creation of a protective shield of sponsorship, but ultimately it will require redesign of the larger system according to principles consistent with HPWS: different modes of structure and coordination (for example, thinking about work units as linked together in sets of customer-supplier relationships), different approaches to planning and budgeting, different modes of decision making, different management styles, different types of information systems, and, ultimately, radically different management processes.

10. *Capacity to reconfigure.* The final design principle is in some ways an outcome of the application of the other principles. The work unit (or sets of work units) should have the capacity to reconfigure as required. An assumption is that organizations are designed to anticipate or respond to environmental requirements and conditions. If the environment is changing at an increasing rate, there is a competitive advantage for those who can anticipate and respond to those changes more quickly. This involves the creation of units that are able to learn—to collect information, to reflect on the consequences of their actions, and to gain insight. It requires units that have

the ability to act on their learning, either through continuous improvement or through large "leaps" of redesign.

These ten design principles constitute an interrelated set of concepts for design. When combined, they lead the designer to create organizations very different from the traditional machine bureaucracy model. To highlight this difference, we can contrast the principles of the two approaches (Table 5.1). It becomes apparent that HPWS is a fundamentally different paradigm for organizing.

Performance

Research and experience with HPWS have now yielded more than two decades of consistent evidence of the performance of units designed with HPWS principles as compared with those designed using traditional principles. In general, the data suggest that HPWS units produce the following results:

Reduced cost. HPWS units appear to be able to produce comparable products, with the same base technology, at significantly reduced cost, in general, 40 to 50 percent less than traditional analogs.

Increased quality. Many of the principles of HPWS are consistent with those of total quality. It is therefore not surprising that HPWS units have lower error rates and higher overall quality of service and product.

Enhanced internal motivation. The creation of high levels of ownership from this approach to design appears to lead to higher levels of commitment and higher internal (or "intrinsic") motivation. Employees feel that the work, the product, and the process are theirs, and they therefore feel internally driven to do well. They display increased feelings of pride and accomplishment.

Lower turnover and absenteeism. Feelings of involvement in and commitment to the team appear to lead to longer tenure, and lower levels of absenteeism and tardiness.

Table 5.1. Comparison of Traditional and High-Performance
Work Systems Design Principles.

Traditional	HPWS
Internally driven design	Customer- and environmentally focused design
Highly controlled fractionated units	Empowered and autonomous units
Ambiguous requirements	Clear direction and goals
Inspection of errors	Control of variance at the source
Technical system dominance	Sociotechnical integration
Limited information flow	Accessible information flow
Fractionated, narrow jobs	Enriched and shared jobs
Controlling and restrictive human resources practices	Empowering human resources practices
Controlling management structure, process, and culture	Empowering management structure, process, and culture
Static designs dependent on senior management redesign	Capacity to reconfigure

Increased learning. The emphasis on individual skill acquisition and the creation of responsibility for teams for the entire product and process lead to more openness to new ideas and, in fact, increased emphasis on the value of learning.

Increased capacity to adapt. As those close to the work and the customer have the ability to reconfigure or redesign the work process, these units appear to be able to respond to change more quickly and to adapt to shifts in environment, technology, or customer needs, which lead to a significant competitive advantage.

Although these benefits are impressive, there are some systems that seem to do significantly better than others. It appears that part of the explanation comes from the way in which the new design approach is introduced. The process of HPWS design can be as critical an element as the design principles themselves.

Design Process

Approach

The HPWS approach is more than simply a set of design principles. Inherent in the approach is a way of thinking about the process of design. Several assumptions underlie the design process.

The design process should be diagnostically driven. HPWS is not a universal solution; rather, it is a way of using organizational design to enhance organizational performance or to solve business problems. HPWS is not necessarily the solution of choice in all situations; therefore the design process needs to include a diagnostic phase in which the current system, its performance, and its problems are examined with an emphasis on understanding causes.

The design process must include data collection on both the social and technical systems. If sociotechnical integration is one of the core design principles, then the design process must include collection of data and analysis of those two systems and the nature of their interdependence before the design of new structures and processes begins.

The design process should be participative. The people who frequently have the best and most complete data on the true nature of the social and technical systems are those who work in them. It is therefore difficult, if not impossible, for outsiders to develop effective HPWS designs. The design process should mirror the values of the HPWS approach itself and, therefore, should empower and enable members of the work system to do the designing. Typically, this is done by creating a design team that includes members of the target work system as well as subject matter and technical resources. At the same time, because new tools and concepts are to be used in the design work, there is a role for a design consultant (either external or internal) to help teach design concepts and facilitate the design team.

Steps

High-performance work systems designers have developed a number of different design processes, but most of them follow a relatively consistent logic, as displayed in Figure 5.3. The process begins with an analysis of customer, environmental, and strategic requirements. If design is to be done "outside-in," then the nature of external requirements is critical. Typically, this step also includes some diagnostic work, focusing on the degree to which the organization is meeting environmental and customer requirements, with an emphasis on understanding the root causes of any problems.

The second step is analysis of the work process. This includes examination and description of the flow of work, the elements of the technical system, and the current formal organizational structures and processes used to manage the work. During this step, it is important to understand the inherent requirements of the work, as opposed to the steps in the work flow that reflect how the work is currently organized.

Concurrent with the work process analysis is the third step, analysis of the social system. This involves data collection on patterns of communication, emergent group structures, values, work practices, informal leadership patterns, norms, and other items.

The fourth step is to design the new organization. This involves application of the ten design principles (mentioned above) to the particular work unit(s). Perhaps the most critical activity in this step is determining what the new work flow will be and identifying the major pieces of work around which groups or teams will be constructed.

The fifth and sixth steps involve implementation. In step 5, a transition plan is developed that accounts for both the technical and social/organizational issues involved in managing the change to the new organizational design (see Nadler, 1981). The change strategy needs to understand, account for, and manage the predictable issues of power, anxiety, and control that arise any time a significant organizational change is implemented. In step 6, the transition plans are executed.

An important feature of the design process is a seventh step, which is continuous. Once the design is in place, there needs to be some form of assessment to determine how well the new work system is functioning. Even a new and innovative work system design can become rigid and unresponsive to change over time. There is a tendency to institutionalize practices and processes that have suc-

Figure 5.3. The High-Performance Work Systems Design Process.

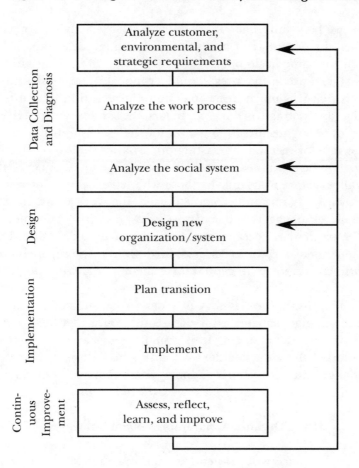

ceeded, and this institutionalization makes the work system less responsive to change. The key is to create some mechanism to ensure renewal and to build in the capacity to reconfigure the work design as the environment, customer requirements, or work technology changes. Periodic assessment can serve as a catalyst for renewal. Assessment, reflection, learning, and improvement activities provide the HPWS units with the ability to reshape themselves over time.

Design and Redesign

So far, we have talked about design as a generic activity, ignoring whether the design is of a new or an existing organization. Although the same basic process would be used in both situations, some significant differences should be noted. The most critical point is that it is much easier to design a new setting than it is to redesign an existing work system. In fact, the success rate for HPWS design of new "greenfield" organizations is much higher than the success rate for redesign of existing organizations. Most of this difference can be attributed to problems of change management—the natural resistance to change by those who have a vested interest in the existing organization. People outside the work units, such as middle-level managers and staff specialists, may feel threatened by HPWS, particularly because it reduces their day-to-day control. In addition, there are the costs associated with redesign, including downtime for transition, capital investment, and disruption of the work process.

The implication is that in redesign (versus design) initiatives, the change management issues require extra attention, particularly in the early stages. It is usually necessary to invest in education of those outside the work unit who will be impacted by the change and to develop a support system that can help manage the political dynamics associated with the redesign.

Other Organizational Improvement Strategies

High-performance work systems is one of a number of organizational improvement strategies and approaches that have come into broad use in recent years and will be increasingly employed in the years to come (Nadler, 1989). Of course, many other different improvement strategies are being discovered and employed by organizations, and to avoid confusion, it may be useful to briefly discuss the relationship between HPWS and some of these other approaches.

High-performance work systems is perhaps most directly linked with what might be called *strategic organizational design,* or the design of complex organizations starting from the top down. The focus of strategic design is on the architecture of major organizational units and the methods of linking those units together. Innovative strategic designs have begun to focus on new ways of structuring and linking groups through network organizations, joint ventures, alliances, flat hierarchies, and so on. HPWS is, in contrast, a "bottom-up" design process, starting with the work and the external requirements. HPWS and strategic organizational design are complementary. Although there are many examples of highly successful HPWS design efforts focusing only on a particular part or level of the organization (for example, manufacturing plants), HPWS units are likely to be more successful when the design of the larger organization is consistent with HPWS principles and is oriented toward responding to the same customer and environmental requirements. Similarly, strategic designs are more likely to be successful when they do more than just "move around the boxes" but rather lead to subsequent reconfiguration of the real work and how that work is managed.

Another organizational improvement strategy, *employee involvement,* is based on the research finding that when employees are involved they are more motivated to perform, their commitment to the organization increases, quality increases, and they contribute to better decision making. More and more organizations have moved toward adopting high-involvement management as a core principle (Lawler, 1986). In that context, HPWS is an intensive form of high-involvement management. It takes involvement to its extreme, by creating self-managed organizations.

In many organizations, HPWS work has occurred in the context of unionized environments. HPWS has thus been related to some form of labor-management collaboration. Indeed, the flexibility and ambiguity inherent in HPWS design run counter to the traditional orientation of the labor contract toward work rules, clear job specifications, and similar devices aimed at clarifying roles and responsibilities in the workplace. Where organized labor is involved, the more successful companies have therefore engaged the union as a valued partner in the work redesign effort.

Many other organizations have begun major drives toward *total quality management.* This strategy is based on the concepts of quality improvement, including fulfillment of customer requirements, statistical process control, management by prevention, and continuous improvement. Total quality management involves the systematic application of quality principles to the entire enterprise in a planned process of change over years. HPWS is highly consistent with total quality; in fact, many of the organizations that have pioneered HPWS have also been pioneers in total quality. Many of the principles of HPWS (for example, customer-driven design and control of variance at the source) are identical to principles of total quality. HPWS, however, does fill a potential void in many total quality approaches. Most total quality processes include a step where the work process is designed (or redesigned). Although methods to control the work process are specified, in practice there is little guidance as to how to design or configure these work processes. Therefore, people tend to fall back on their unconscious models of design (machine bureaucracy) and end up creating work processes in the one man/one job mode. HPWS provides the tools to aid in the application of total quality to major work processes.

Summary

The 1990s are a time of increasing change and increasing demands on organizations. The capacity to use technical and human resources effectively and to anticipate and respond to changing environments will be critical in sustaining a competitive advantage.

High-performance work systems is one approach to the problem of designing more effective organizations for the future. It has been forty years since the first sociotechnical studies were done, and there are now close to twenty years of consistent experience that indicate this approach has significant value. At the same time, the concepts are still being developed as organizations experiment and learn. In particular, as the HPWS model, which has largely been applied to manufacturing environments, moves out of the factory into the office and into "knowledge work" environments, we will learn more about the power of this approach. Clearly, however, it is a way of thinking about work, people, technology, information, and organization that holds tremendous promise.

References

Argyris, C. *Personality and Organization: The Conflict Between System and the Individual.* New York: HarperCollins, 1957.

Brown, J. S. "High Performance Work Systems for the 1990s." *Benchmark,* Fall 1989, 8–11.

Cherns, A. B. "The Principles of Socio-technical Design." *Human Relations,* 1976, *29,* 783–792.

Hackman, J. R., and Oldham, G. R. *Work Redesign.* Reading, Mass.: Addison-Wesley, 1980.

Hanna, D. P. *Designing Organizations for High Performance.* Reading, Mass.: Addison-Wesley, 1988.

Lawler, E. E. "The New Plant Revolution." *Organizational Dynamics,* 1978, *6*(3), 2–12.

Lawler, E. E. *High-Involvement Management: Participative Strategies for Improving Organizational Performance.* San Francisco: Jossey-Bass, 1986.

Lawrence, P. R., and Lorsch, J. W. *Organization and Environment: Managing Differentiation and Integration.* Homewood, Ill.: Business One Irwin, 1967.

Likert, R. *New Patterns of Management.* New York: McGraw-Hill, 1961.

Nadler, D. A. "Managing Organizational Change: An Integrative Approach." *Journal of Applied Behavioral Science,* 1981, *17,* 191–211.

Nadler, D. A. "Organizational Architectures for the Corporation of the Future." *Benchmark,* Fall 1989, 12–13.

Nadler, D. A., and Tushman, M. L. *Strategic Organization Design.* Glenview, Ill.: Scott, Foresman, 1988.

Rice, A. K. *Productivity and Social Organization: The Ahmedabad Experiment.* London: Tavistock, 1958.

Roethlisberger, F. J., and Dickson, W. J. *Management and the Worker.* Cambridge, Mass.: Harvard University Press, 1939.

Sherwood, J. J. "Creating Work Cultures with Competitive Advantage." *Organizational Dynamics,* 1988, 5–27.

Taylor, F. W. *The Principles of Scientific Management.* New York: HarperCollins, 1911.

Trist, E. L., and Bamforth, R. "Some Social and Psychological Consequences of the Long Wall Method of Coal-Getting." *Human Relations,* 1951, *4,* 3–38.

Tushman, M. L., and Nadler, D. A. "Information Processing as an Integrative Concept in Organization Design." *Academy of Management Review,* 1978, *3*(3), 613–624.

Walton, R. E. "The Diffusion of New Work Structures: Explaining Why Success Didn't Take." In P. H. Mirvis and D. N. Berg (eds.), *Failures in Organizational Development and Change: Cases and Essays for Learning.* New York: Wiley, 1977.

Weber, M. *The Theory of Social and Economic Organization.* New York: Free Press, 1947.

PART THREE

Transforming
the Informal Organization

Organizational Architecture

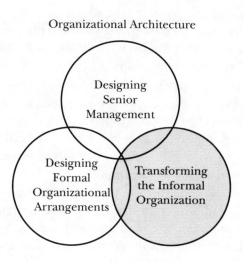

If formal organizational arrangements establish the framework for the organization, the informal organization adds depth, color, and texture to the design. As we all know from lifelong experience in organizations, a significant number of the rules that determine organizational behavior are not written. Rather, they are a combination of explicit values and beliefs and implicit assumptions.

Edgar Schein of the Massachusetts Institute of Technology has developed a model of organizational culture that articulates this point of view. According to Schein, organizational culture is the *learned behavior* of a group of people as they cope with problems presented by their external and internal environments. As solutions to ongoing problems emerge and are proven to work over time, they become so integrated into the accepted way of doing things they are almost invisible to people working in the organization.

At the highest level of Schein's model are the visible behaviors, or "artifacts," that we see every day. These include manner of speaking, standardized patterns of behavior, events, and rituals. The second level, values and beliefs, comprises the conscious reasons offered as explanations for all that occurs at the visible level. When one asks why things are the way they are, the response is typically at this level. The third level, basic assumptions, comprises the internalized, unconscious "views of the world" that have arisen over time as organizations successfully cope with their environment. Unconscious assumptions are heavily influenced by larger societal culture as well as local organizational history. As a result, organizations in the same country hold many assumptions in common.

The importance of Schein's model is that many critical organizational changes (such as shifting focus from internal to market driven, increasing employee self-management, and risking that improvements in quality will eventually pay off) often run counter to management's underlying assumptions.

In Chapter Six, Jeffrey D. Heilpern and David A. Nadler discuss the profound organizational changes necessitated by an organization's commitment to a total quality program. In particular, they examine the quality-hostile assumptions that underlie many current management practices. If an organization is to successfully sustain the new behaviors associated with total quality, it must eventually unlearn these old assumptions and replace them with new ones. As culture changes slowly, this process is likely to be painful. The acquisition of new assumptions related to quality provides a vivid example of the difference between changing the formal organization and changing the informal organization. We "engineer and build" the formal organization; we "plant and cultivate" the informal organization.

Chapter Seven deals with the difficult task of designing organizations in which people can address problems and implement solutions. Robert B. Shaw reports on a research project focusing on the causes, symptoms, and consequences of a complex phenomenon called *insufficient capacity to act*. Not surprisingly, many of the components of the capacity to act are found in the informal organization—for example, clarity of purpose, focus on critical priorities, and bias toward results. Shaw points out that when organizations are under stress, people often revert to behavior patterns based on their unstated cultural assumptions rather than their conscious values. In such circumstances, the behaviors consistent with a capacity to act may be lacking when we need them most.

In Chapter Eight, Robert B. Shaw and Dennis N. T. Perkins discuss an essential characteristic of organizational success in the decades ahead—organizational learning. That organizations face dramatically increased complexity and unprecedented change is quite clear. Less obvious, however, is that survival in such an environment requires a significant increase in the organization's capacity to learn and that a key to learning is "productive failure," the capacity to capitalize on mistakes.

In the immediate future, there will be an ample supply of mistakes to learn from. Implementing new organizational structures while transforming the informal organization will require many experiments, most of which will not work perfectly. Organizations need to learn from both successes and failures; the need to embrace failure in order to be successful is a paradox that many managers would rather avoid.

Reference

Schein, E. H. *Organizational Culture and Leadership: A Dynamic View*. San Francisco: Jossey-Bass, 1985.

Implementing
Total Quality Management:
A Process of Cultural Change

JEFFREY D. HEILPERN, DAVID A. NADLER

In the fiercely competitive 1990s, more organizations are pursuing total quality management (TQM). Senior executives considering companywide quality initiatives express their need to understand clearly what TQM is and how to implement it. Even in companies that have been pursuing TQM for several years, senior executives often report that they are not getting the return they anticipated from their efforts. On the basis of our experience with more than twenty companies in the 1980s, success is predicated on understanding, positioning, and managing TQM as large-scale organizational change that involves fundamental dimensions of corporate culture.

To help executives better understand TQM and how to approach its implementation, in this chapter, we focus on four topics:

- Why quality?
- What is quality?
- Total quality management and organizational change.
- Implementation of total quality management.

Why Quality?

In the 1950s and 1960s in the United States, monopolies or oligopolies existed in many markets, which severely limited choices for customers. For example, someone wanting to buy a car in the 1950s could choose only from a small number of models with a limited range of features and similar levels of (or lack of) quality. Increasingly, new competitors have appeared in almost all categories of products and services. Indeed, the increasing globalization of business enterprises has reduced barriers to entry and opened up borders dramatically. As a result, customer expectations have been raised and new requirements established. Customers first appreciate and soon take for granted the wide range of options. Through this process, customers discover they have real choices, and once that realization is made, there is no going back to the old days of the seller's market.

For suppliers this power shift is profound. To continue to be successful in terms of market share and retention, quality becomes a core competitive issue. Without the protection of limited competition and modest customer expectations, quality attributes become the key differentiator in the marketplace. In many highly competitive industries today, quality is not just a competitive issue; it is a matter of survival. Where competition is intense, companies without quality products and services that attract and satisfy customers cannot remain viable for long.

What Is Quality?

As organizations around the world have seriously begun to focus on quality, a common definition has emerged that reflects the leverage customers now have. *Quality* is defined as an offering (product or service) that meets or exceeds customer requirements. Although there are many technical definitions of quality, the focus on meeting or exceeding customer requirements provides an easily understood and powerful message.

Building on this definition, *quality management* can be defined as developing and operating work processes that are capable of consistently designing, producing, and delivering quality offerings. Central to this definition is the focus on process (versus functional) management as a primary means of continuous improvement. Further expanding the frame of reference, *total quality management* can be defined as creating and implementing organizational architectures that motivate, support, and enable quality management in all the activities of the enterprise. Put another way, *total* indicates that the entire organization and all of its functions are included; *quality* indicates that the product or service "offering" meets or exceeds customer requirements; *management* indicates that the core work processes are in control and capable, and quality is fully integrated into the management process.

Core Concepts

Several core concepts of quality and their relationships are illustrated in Figure 6.1. The main concept is the *customer/supplier model*. This model views all work as part of a process that is always focused on customers. All members of an organization have both suppliers and customers, and their work should be viewed as a value-adding process; customers receive the outputs (their work) and suppliers provide the inputs. Customers can be external, those who purchase the product or service, or internal, those who represent the next process in line.

Central to the process focus of the customer/supplier model are *process control and capability*. If a process is "in control" (that is, statistical not management control), its output is consistent and predictable over time. If a process is "capable," its output fully satisfies customer requirements.

In pursuing continuous quality improvement, a key concept is *management by fact*. To analyze and improve existing processes, products/services, and customer satisfaction, it is imperative that decision makers increase their reliance on data (measured and displayed through the use of specific quality improvement tools) rather than opinions, assumptions, and habits as the way to make decisions and operate the business. Management by fact is brought to life in most organizations through formal methods of *problem solving*. A variety of simple but powerful tools are used, including cause-and-effect diagrams (also known as "fish bone" or Ishikawa diagrams), histograms, pareto charts, control charts, brainstorming, and multivoting. The goal is to identify and define important gaps between what currently exists and what could or should be, analyze causes, develop and assess potential solutions, implement changes, monitor their impact, and continue the process of improvement.

There is significant financial benefit to be gained from total quality management because of the high leverage of *quality eco-*

Figure 6.1. Core Concepts of Quality.

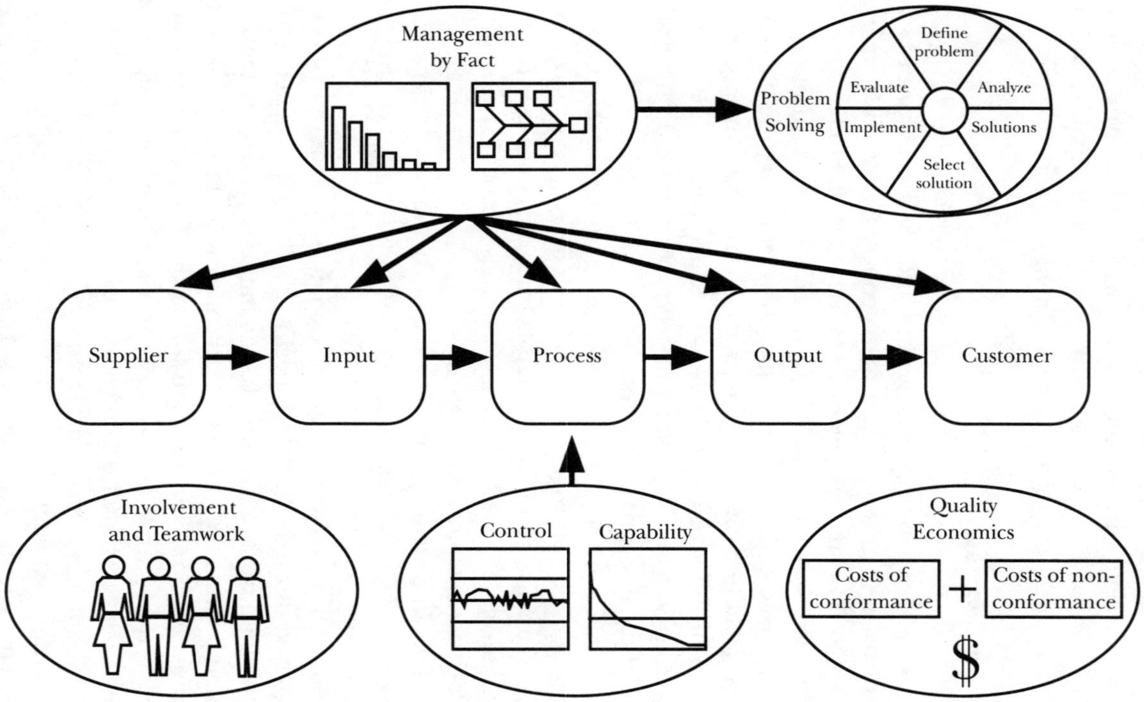

nomics. As shown in Figure 6.1, there are two costs of quality: costs of conformance and costs of nonconformance. Costs of conformance are basically positive investments and include prevention, incorporation of quality into the design, problem solving, and quality improvement efforts. Costs of nonconformance include scrap, waste, rework, and inefficiency and represent a huge target for reduction, estimated to be in the area of 20 to 25 percent of revenues.

The power of total quality management is greatly enhanced by *employee involvement and teamwork.* Quality improvement is the job of every single employee from the CEO to the hourly worker. Effective problem solving often requires that cross-functional or "family group" teams work together to pool knowledge, resources, ideas, and ownership of solutions for more effective implementation.

What Quality Is Not

Although total quality management is quite comprehensive in its perspective, activities, and benefits, it is important to recognize what quality is and what it is not. Many see TQM as a panacea for all organizational ills. It is not the single answer to all questions. In fact, this viewpoint is not only incorrect but dangerous. Quality improvement with increased management by fact is extremely important; however, it is not a substitute for knowledge, experience, and guts. Nor is it a substitute for good strategic decision making and effective corporate and business strategies.

Quality management is also not a substitute for effective organizational design. Quality improvement in itself will not eliminate outmoded or inappropriate structural arrangements that create internal focus and competition rather than coordinated and synergistic focus on customers.

Finally, quality is not a substitute for selecting the right people. Although we all would like to believe that everyone can change and adopt new attitudes and work practices, it turns out, to the disappointment of many executives, that some people, for a variety of reasons, either cannot or will not change. That reality needs to be recognized and dealt with, not wished away by well-intentioned but false optimism.

Total Quality Management and Organizational Change

Along with a better understanding of what quality is and why it is being pursued by more and more companies, it is important that executives also understand TQM as a large-scale organizational change. Without such an understanding, successful implementation is not likely.

Total quality management is a fundamental change in how an organization functions. It has an impact on almost everything that goes on in the organization. If we are to understand TQM as organizational change, we need some way to think about organizations and how they function and behave. In our work, we have used a model of organizational behavior and performance based on open systems theory (see the Nadler-Tushman model presented in Chapter Two). This framework views organizations as systems that transform input into output. Specifically, an organization is a mechanism designed and created to take strategy and turn it into a pattern of activity and performance.

Organizations are composed of four key components: the *work* that the organization has to perform; the *people* that the organization attracts to perform that work; the *formal organizational arrangements,* or structures, systems, and processes that are created to get those people to do the work; and the *informal organization,* which evolves over time and includes such things as values, beliefs, culture, and operating style. Organizations, in general, are most effective when there is high congruence among these components. Using this framework, we see that the shift toward total quality management has a significant impact on an organization. What changes does total quality imply?

- A change in strategy—in the definition of who we are, what we provide, and how we compete
- A change in output—in the increased focus on performance and improvement in quality and customer satisfaction, not simply financial results
- A change in the work—in what is important about the work and what are the core requirements for performing the work
- A change in people—in their roles, skills, and behavior

- A change in organizational arrangements—in objectives, measures, structures, systems, training, and rewards
- A change in the informal organization—in the beliefs, values, and assumptions that influence much of day-to-day behavior

Thus, moving toward total quality management requires the design and implementation of an entire set of changes that affect virtually all components of an organization.

Management of the Transition to Total Quality Management

To make progress toward the desired future state of total quality management, it is important to recognize the need for transition strategies. The most important transition strategies are highlighted in the cause-and-effect diagram presented in Figure 6.2. The eight elements on the ribs of the fish bone are critical success factors bringing about the desired effect, which is the transition to total quality management.

Tools. Central to TQM are the development and application of tools that managers and employees can use to examine their work processes, identify opportunities for improvement, analyze problems, and implement solutions. Four kinds of tools are most com-

Figure 6.2. Total Quality Management Transition Fish Bone.

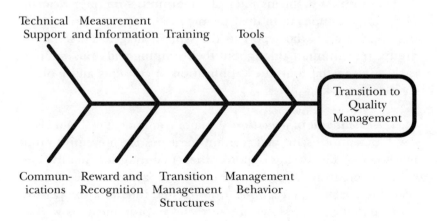

mon: (1) statistical tools to collect and analyze data for preventive problem solving; (2) formal problem-solving processes; (3) specific quality improvement processes, involving identification of customers and their requirements, translation of those requirements into standards for suppliers, measurement of outputs, and determination of why outputs do not meet the standards; (4) group or teamwork tools to enhance team effectiveness.

Training. Managers and employees at all levels require extensive training in the concepts and tools of TQM. Typically, training includes increased awareness of quality, its importance, and its costs; problem-solving tools and skills; specific customer-focused quality improvement processes; team skills; and, where appropriate, the role and required behavior of managers.

The training is delivered to large numbers of people, so the entire organization can speak the same language and work with compatible tools. For example, training employees in different parts of the company in different problem-solving processes may create cross-unit translation problems similar to the incompatibility between VHS and Beta video formats. Often the training is implemented from the top down, starting with senior management and working down through the hierarchy, so that the power structure of the organization fully "buys in" and no employee is trained before his or her manager. To maximize impact, the training must be relevant and immediately applicable, with early linkage to important business problems and real opportunities for improvement. Many organizations train their people in "family groups," or natural work teams who report to the same manager. These family groups remain intact throughout their training and, thus, support each other in the continued application of concepts and tools in their daily work.

Measurement and Information. A major component of TQM is the development of useful and relevant measures for preventive problem solving, identifying opportunities, planning for quality, and assessing progress. Often, new measures and data are needed that are linked to cusomer perceptions (external and internal), competitive benchmarking, process performance and improvement, as well as outputs. Some measurement of the cost of quality is important, although more as a catalyst for raising awareness, motivating change, and identifying opportunities for improvement than as a financial yardstick by which people are judged.

Technical Support. Frequently, training is not enough to help people effectively apply the quality tools to real problems, products and services, and work flows. To prevent frustration and difficulty, special support resources are often appointed, as either quality specialists or facilitators.

Management Behavior. Managers make or break the implementation of TQM. First, they need to provide the leadership to guide the organizational and cultural changes required for continuous quality improvement. Second, managers should actively participate in specific projects appropriate to their level. Third, managers need to create an environment that will encourage, support, and enable their subordinates to take responsibility for quality improvement.

Two important categories of management practices have a major impact on the success of TQM. First are those that specifically address quality management: Does the manager identify customer requirements and measure satisfaction? use quality tools when appropriate? inspect the work process? The second category comprises the establishment of clear objectives, definition of standards of performance, encouragement of open communication, and provision of specific feedback.

Transition Management Structures. To help the organization move from its current state toward the desired future state, a variety of transition management elements are useful and important, including the creation of special roles (quality officers, managers, facilitators, specialists), groups (quality implementation teams, councils, steering committees), and processes (quality reviews, quality goals). Although these structures are intended to be temporary, until quality becomes an inherent part of how the company is run, they appear to be necessary during the initial years of implementation.

Reward and Recognition. To most employees, producing a quality product or service is intrinsically rewarding; however, many companies have recognized the need to modify or replace existing reward and recognition systems. This helps to sustain quality improvement as a continuing process as opposed to a one-shot program. Both tangible (money, promotion, and job assignment) and intangible (recognition by management and peers, informal praise, and support) rewards are important in sustaining motivation over the long term.

Communications. A final component is intensive and systematic communications to employees at all levels via multiple methods and media. The content will vary at different stages of implementation, but typically progresses from awareness and need to commitment, activities, and rewards and recognition. The approach is critical. The focus should be on what is happening; hype should be avoided. Various methods should be used, including large group meetings, small group sessions, workshops, print media, and videotapes. Employees should be given opportunities to voice their concerns, perceptions, and suggestions. And in large organizations, it is important to let local units shape ownership of the communications, while ensuring that the crucial messages are conveyed to everyone in a consistent manner.

Total Quality Management as Large System Change

Our experience helping companies grapple with these issues has generated the following insights about TQM and the process of managing large system change:

> *Need for pain and crisis.* Making progress toward TQM requires persistence, discipline, and motivated action. Unfortunately, there appear to be no substitutes for pain and crisis as these are the most powerful forces motivating sustained commitment to change. Change may be easier for a company that has the resources and freedom that come from success; however, it is in the most competitive companies, which have all experienced some degree of pain and crisis, that the most progress has been made.
>
> *Quality as a way of thinking about the business.* Total quality management cannot be simply a program. Nor can it

be a separate stream of activity to be managed. It must be viewed as central to the strategic business proposition and the critical success factors around which the business is managed. Quality and customer measures must become as important in running the company as traditional financial outcomes and measures.

Quality as a total system intervention, social and technical. It is not sufficient to provide new technical tools, work on improvement of work flows, and focus on cost reduction. The human and social elements are due equal attention. Employee involvement and empowerment, team development and effectiveness, and enhanced communication and responsiveness are just as important as the technical dimensions.

Consistency across the organization and over time. If quality is considered important in only some parts of the organization or inconsistently over time, people at all levels will quickly get the message that it is not a fundamental management priority and progress will not occur.

Critical role of senior management. Active leadership, involvement, and commitment of senior executives are fundamental requirements for success. No lasting change can be achieved without them. Real and perceived power, decision-making authority, and ability to determine strategy and allocate resources all contribute to the critical nature of the senior executive role.

Critical role of unit management. Senior management alone cannot bring about organizationwide, lasting change. The managers of business units and functions must be actively involved, for they are the field commanders who implement TQM on a day-to-day basis throughout the organization. They control the resources and make the decisions that motivate or alienate the work force.

Importance of learning. Mechanisms for reflection, generation of insights, and dissemination of learning play a critical role in the transformation to total quality management. Managers so often focus on results and respond to short-term pressures that they fail to mine the successes and failures for the knowledge that might be gained. Effective learning organizations recognize the value of productive failure and the shortcomings of unproductive success and sufficiently examine both their successes and failures to ensure that useful learning occurs.

Quality as a cultural change. Total quality management cuts much deeper than the formal tools, work processes, and organizational arrangements involved in its pursuit. The basic mind-set, attitudes, and values of the organization are involved. Unless these less tangible aspects are tapped, the progress desired cannot be achieved. This area is of such importance that much of the remainder of this chapter focuses on aspects of cultural change.

For most organizations, the transition to total quality management will take at least five to seven years. Most executives who decide to pursue TQM believe the transition will take much less time. Why is it such a lengthy process? The main reason is the challenge of changing organizational culture. Here we see some of the more intractable problems and also find the keys to enhanced progress. Even in companies in which senior managers are aware of quality, where they understand the challenge of organizational change, and where they make the needed changes in strategy and organization, we still find leaders struggling with, and frustrated by, the problem of modifying corporate culture.

Quality and Organizational Culture

Edgar Schein of the Massachusetts Institute of Technology has proposed an approach to thinking about culture that we have found very useful in relation to quality improvement. Organizational culture, according to Schein, is the learned behavior of a stable group of people as they cope with their external environmental and internal problems (Schein, 1985). Schein sees culture existing at three levels (Figure 6.3). The first includes *artifacts,* or the daily observable activities, events, and rituals. The second level is *values,* statements about what is good or bad, which are offered as explanations of what is happening at the artifact level. The third level is *basic assumptions.* These are commonly held views of the world. They

Figure 6.3. Organizational Culture Model.

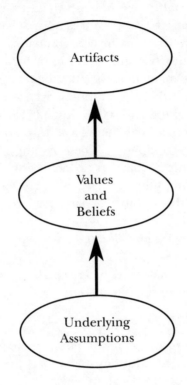

Source: Adapted from Schein, 1985, p. 14.

are frequently unconscious or implicit, having been formed over time, and (most importantly) they drive much of the organizational behavior that we see.

Using this model of organizational culture, our experiences in many different companies lead us to two observations: First, quality has been adopted by many companies at the artifact and value levels only. Therefore, what has been achieved is merely cosmetic quality; the basic assumptions remain unchanged. Second, the basic assumptions of many U.S. corporations are quality-hostile. They are at variance with the basic assumptions that underlie total quality management.

In our work with companies that are attempting to make the transition to total quality, we have spent time investigating the issue of basic assumptions. We produced a list of basic assumptions we observed in a number of major U.S. companies. We then sorted these assumptions into two groups: *quality friendly* and *quality hostile*. We identified many more hostiles than friendlies. For illustration, we have listed those assumptions we see most frequently, and we have organized them into five clusters (Table 6.1).

Our conclusion is that these basic assumptions reflect the cultures of many U.S. companies. These assumptions, where present, constitute significant barriers to achieving TQM. Without changes in basic assumptions, which is a difficult and lengthy process, there can be no true or lasting change.

Conclusions About TQM and Change

In light of the serious challenges described above, we have come to the following conclusions about the large-scale change that TQM represents:

1. *It is tough and requires a lot of work.* There are no shortcuts or easy, prepackaged solutions. Be prepared to work hard and do not expect results in the short term.
2. *It is a senior management job that cannot be delegated.* Although unit managers are pivotal to progress and employees at all levels need to be actively involved, the required senior executive role should not be given or assigned to those with less power, authority, influence, and stature.
3. *Do not do it unless*
   a. the current state is intolerable
   b. you are willing to make the needed investments over time
   c. you are prepared to stick with it permanently
   d. it is important to the success or survival of the business

This warning may be surprising and is not often stated by consultants; however, our experience strongly suggests that serious self-reflection about intention and motivation is essential before proceding.

Table 6.1. Quality-Hostile Assumptions.

Cluster	Illustrative Assumptions
Corporate purpose	Our primary and overriding purpose is to make money—to produce near-term shareholder return. Our key audience is the financial markets and, in particular, the analysts.
Customers	We are smarter than our customers; we know what they really need. Quality is not a major factor in customer decisions; they cannot tell the difference.
Performance	The way to influence corporate performance is portfolio management and creative accounting. It costs more to provide a quality product or service and we will not recover the added cost. Strategic success comes from large, one-time innovative leaps rather than from continuous improvement. We will never be able to manufacture competitively at the low end.
People	Managers are paid to make decisions; workers are paid to do, not to think. We do not trust our people. The job of senior management is strategy, not operations or implementation. The key disciplines from which to draw senior management are finance and marketing.
Problem solving and improvement	To err is human; perfection is an unattainable and unrealistic goal. Quality improvement can be delegated; it is something the top can tell the middle to do to the bottom. Celebrate success and shun failure; there is not much to learn by dwelling on our mistakes. If it ain't broke, don't fix it.

Implementation of Total Quality Management

Questions arise when an organization seriously considers the pursuit of TQM: How do we get started? What do we do first? What will all this involve? Figure 6.4 presents an implementation "template" for TQM that was developed from our experience working

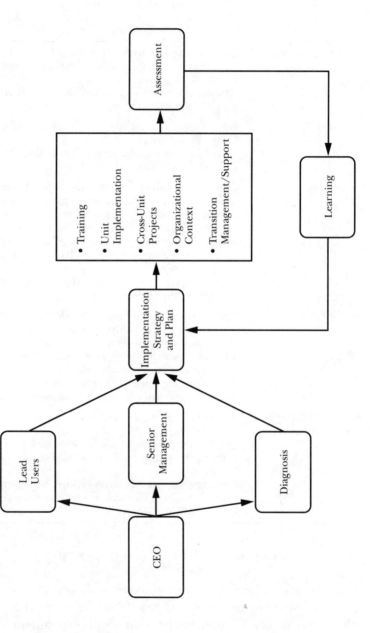

Figure 6.4. An Implementation Template for Total Quality Management.

with a large number of companies on TQM. Evidence strongly suggests that effective companywide implementation of TQM must begin with the commitment and active leadership of the CEO. A CEO can view TQM in one of four ways:

1. Intervention is not necessary because quality is viewed solely as a function in the organization.
2. Quality is a program, so it can be delegated and supported where people want to do it, but it does not seriously alter the focus, work tasks, and management process of the CEO and the senior team.
3. Quality is one of the few (three) core CEO themes and drivers over a period of years.
4. Quality is the overriding concept and core paradigm for all initiatives and activities in the organization.

    To make real progress, the CEO must embrace the third or fourth view. The first two views are not adequate to create the changes necessary in the organization. Views 3 and 4 both generate sufficient energy, commitment, and continuity to move the organization forward over time toward the desired future state.

    Once the CEO is sufficiently engaged and has decided to create a serious total quality process, the next steps, as portrayed in the template, are to conduct an organizational diagnosis and explore the progress being made by lead users in the organization. Usually, certain divisions with farsighted managers have already begun to implement quality management. Capturing the knowledge gained from both the successes and difficulties of the lead users is helpful in diagnosing the barriers to and enablers for moving forward with TQM.

    Senior management team members need to be interviewed as part of the diagnostic process, and the senior team is the appropriate body, after a one-on-one session with the CEO, to receive the resulting feedback and determine the priorities for going forward. The full team needs to be on board and share ownership in the decision to adopt TQM.

    The senior team typically enlists an internal transition team of key managers from units across the company to help create an implementation strategy and plan. Key elements of the plan include education and training, unit implementation, cross-unit projects, organizational context (management process, goals, measures, reviews, rewards and recognition, technical support, communications), and transition management and support. For each element, clear objectives, strategies, plans of action, and measures of results must be established. As implementation continues over time, periodic assessments are necessary to ensure things are on track, to identify where and why things go right or wrong, and to create an ongoing feedback process. Such assessments frequently have been catalysts for major improvements in the effectiveness of implementation. They also bring about continuous improvement on the organizational level.

Summary

As we move toward the next century in our rapidly changing global village, quality has become a very powerful competitive tool and, possibly, a matter of survival for an increasing number of companies in almost every industry. Total quality management, the multifaceted pursuit of quality in all functions, activities, and parts of an enterprise, is a large-scale and profound organizational change. It requires significant investments of time and effort, particularly by senior management. It should not be undertaken without a clear understanding of the complexity of the journey and the continuing commitment required. Because no two organizations are exactly alike in terms of history, culture, and strategic priorities, diagnosis is critical before jumping in or mimicking even highly successful efforts of others. Different situations pose different challenges and opportunities, and as Arthur Miller's famous salesman, Willy Loman, said, "Attention must be paid."

Reference

Schein, E. H. *Organizational Culture and Leadership: A Dynamic View*. San Francisco: Jossey-Bass, 1985.

SEVEN

The Capacity to Act:
Creating a Context for Empowerment

ROBERT B. SHAW

Each merger or leveraged buy-out involving corporations of significant size raises anew the question of whether any organization "that large" can be efficiently managed. The people who feel that small is beautiful point again to statistics that show it is primarily small companies that have created new jobs in the past two decades. Others make an equally compelling case that the competitors who are outstripping us are international giants, such as Matsushita of Japan and Siemens and Philips in Europe. Size, it seems, is not the best barometer of an organization's ability to be successful. The challenge to management is to create large organizations that remain competitive.

One impediment to organizational competitiveness is what we call an insufficient *capacity to act,* a disease that afflicts many large organizations. It is most clearly defined in the words of the president of a major corporation: "For an issue to get resolved, it always seems that it has to get raised up to my level. When we make a decision, we find out later that it hasn't been implemented! People out in the organization can't seem to identify a problem, develop a solution, and implement actions on their own."

Why is the capacity to act important? It is one measure of an organization's ability to use its human resources to achieve its goals. The success of any organization depends on the ability of its people to identify and address critical problems. A company loses its adaptability when known problems persist, when conflicts have to be brought to senior management for resolution, and when solutions are not efficiently implemented in a timely manner.

The material discussed in this chapter is drawn from a series of studies that we conducted over the past four years at four large corporations to learn more about insufficient capacity to act. It is also drawn from a "capacity-to-act" survey that was used in a broad-based study within a Fortune 100 company (the name of which we cannot release due to our promise of confidentiality). The survey consists of items that we developed from the research literature and initial interview data that we acquired from the host organization. The survey was completed by seventy-eight midlevel managers, all of whom were attending management-development courses in the host corporation.

Characteristics of the Disease

What are the symptoms of insufficient capacity to act? The first symptom is the failure to address key organizational problems. This occurs when important problems do not reach the stage of decision making and action. Organizational problems remain unsolved for three basic reasons:

- *Suppression:* People who should know about the problems are not aware of them.
- *Complacency:* People recognize a problem but treat it as a given that will not change. No one takes action even though it is obvious that harm is being done to the organization.
- *Confused priorities:* People select less significant problems to work on because there is no pressure to look at important problems. Over time, urgent or auditable problems drive out the vital business problems.

A second symptom of insufficient capacity to act is *implementation failure.* People identify organizational problems, develop solutions, and make decisions, but the solutions are not implemented or are implemented inefficiently. At least four types of implementation failure are possible:

- *Delivery failure:* People fail to recognize an opportunity to implement good ideas.

- *Derailment:* Good ideas are recognized but get lost in the process of implementation. Solutions are never fully developed.
- *Investment overload:* People implement good ideas but only after investing excessive time and effort. This process takes a tremendous toll on all those involved.
- *Replication failure:* Successful ideas are fully implemented in certain areas of an organization but are not spread to other areas of the organization.

Insufficient capacity to act results in the failure to address organizational problems and the poor implementation of solutions that are developed. In the long term, the consequences are significant, particularly in those organizations that must operate in turbulent environments. First, business decreases because the organization is unable to implement strategy, loses business opportunities, uses resources inefficiently, and fails to satisfy customers. Second, human resources are drained; employees are unwilling to take risks or address ongoing problems, become frustrated, and leave. Third, senior management becomes so involved in middle management problems and decisions that they lack the time needed for strategic thinking and customer contact. Figure 7.1 summarizes the consequences of insufficient capacity to act.

Causes of Insufficient Capacity to Act

What leads to an insufficient capacity to act? Three factors appear to be critical: (1) priority stress—managers fail to focus on core priorities; (2) a bias toward activity versus results—managers value the security of standard operating procedures over organizational performance; and (3) perceived powerlessness—managers believe they lack the authority and power necessary to make important decisions.

Priority Stress

The problem for managers in this company is that they have so many things to do. They're constantly asking themselves which one will get them killed versus being able to sneak by and get away with it. There is just too much on everyone's plate with no clear view of the top items versus the other forty.

Figure 7.1. Consequences of Insufficient Capacity to Act.

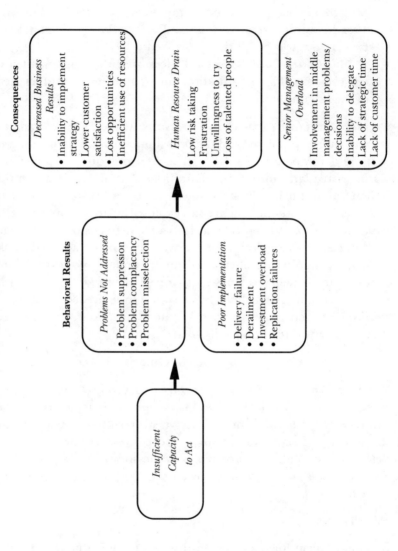

Behavioral Results

Consequences

Insufficient Capacity to Act

Problems Not Addressed
- Problem suppression
- Problem complacency
- Problem misselection

Poor Implementation
- Delivery failure
- Derailment
- Investment overload
- Replication failures

Decreased Business Results
- Inability to implement strategy
- Lower customer satisfaction
- Lost opportunities
- Inefficient use of resources

Human Resource Drain
- Low risk taking
- Frustration
- Unwillingness to try
- Loss of talented people

Senior Management Overload
- Involvement in middle management problems/decisions
- Inability to delegate
- Lack of strategic time
- Lack of customer time

Unclear Strategy. Many companies have unclear business strategies and operating guidelines. For example, less than half of the managers we surveyed in one firm believed that associate managers had a clear vision and purpose. In these situations, managers face unrelenting pressure to balance the conflicting priorities that come about because of unclear organizational strategies. In some cases, unclear strategies derive from conflicts at the top as to the direction in which a firm should move. We see many cases where this type of conflict is either denied or accommodated through halfway measures in which only moderate support is given to the conflicting strategic initiatives within an organization. The net result is that an organization attempts to do too much and fails to clarify which activities are critical to its long-term success.

No Vital Few. Priority setting involves the ability to select critical business issues from among many competing demands. Priority stress arises from role ambiguity ("I don't know what to do"), role conflict ("I have competing and conflicting priorities"), and role overload ("I have too much to do and cannot accomplish it all"). A manager can also end up with too many competing priorities because of unanticipated problems and a lack of organizational discipline. Increasingly, resources (time, money, and so forth) become stretched to the point that senior managers want to exert more control over resource allocation decisions. Some managers respond to competing priorities and resource limitations by reducing the areas in which they are willing to delegate authority. Under stress, they seek more control and see centralization of decision making as a way of obtaining that control. As a result, an increasing number of decisions are made by senior management. This often produces a type of decision making that blocks the timely and effective resolution of problems. "We're in a gridlock situation," complained one senior manager. "We've got to fight for the attention of the senior staff. But we can't schedule any access to them."

Bias Toward Activity Versus Results

Too many people in this company play by the rules. That is, they follow commonly accepted procedures without questioning if those procedures produce desirable business outcomes, such as profit and customer satisfaction.

A bias toward activity versus results occurs when people focus more on the processes they use than the results they obtain. In many companies, for example, managers rigidly follow standard operating procedures without considering what needs to be done if their organizations are to be successful. Similarly, organizational members can come to believe that staying busy is the same as being effective. There is no lack of activity within most corporations; if anything, the overall pace is frenetic. Still, most managers do not accomplish the vital work that needs to be done. Over half of our survey sample felt that managers worked hard but rarely accomplished the important work that needed to be done. The critical issue is whether people act in a manner that leads to the organizational results desired.

The characteristics of organizations and the characteristics of individuals can promote a bias toward activity versus results. Some organizations fail to reward risk taking, and some individuals are averse to taking risks. Both factors hinder successful organizational adaptation.

High Risk-to-Reward Ratio. Most managers in the companies we studied believe the risks of trying to solve problems are equal to or greater than the rewards (see Figure 7.2 for the survey results of a sample of seventy-eight midlevel managers from one U.S. corporation). Many managers do not believe they are rewarded for taking initiative, nor do they believe that mistakes made in an effort to improve business performance are acceptable in their organizations. This, of course, leads to a decreased willingness to act.

Organizational members can come to believe that the outcomes of taking risks to solve problems and implement solutions are unclear at best and career threatening at worst. The individual effort required may be too high and the likelihood of achieving the task too low. The result is low risk-taking behavior and a decreased willingness to take initiative. Organizations, particularly large bureaucratic organizations, often fail to sanction risk taking despite any pronouncements to the contrary. As a result, many strive to

Figure 7.2. Survey Results: High Risk-to-Reward Ratio.

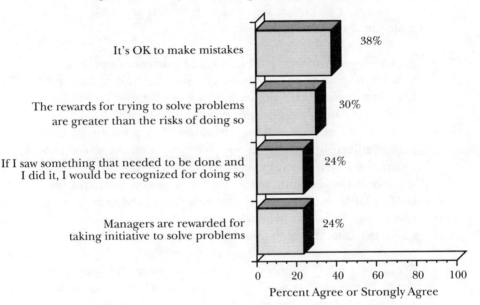

accomplish activities that will keep them out of trouble but not necessarily result in the best outcomes for their companies.

By design, most people focus their attention on those tasks that drive measurement systems or for which there is a strong senior management advocate. Thus, the organization reduces personal accountability for larger nonauditable problems and directs effort to formal measures of performance. The perceived inflexibility of most evaluation systems discourages people from implementing ideas that require a different form of measurement. An organization can discourage its members from taking actions that might jeopardize achievement of a formal operating plan but may be in the best interest of the company.

There is little room for failure if an organization's operating plan requires results beyond the limits of its capabilities. Everything a manager sets out to do must succeed. This leads to a low tolerance for creativity and risk taking. Overambitious goals encourage managers to conclude that they cannot win and the best they can do is try not to lose. The goals also lead to measurement and evaluation systems that tightly focus the attention of the work force. Auditable tasks can eventually drive out the vital tasks as suggested in the following examples:

- An employee who implemented an innovative preventive maintenance program for his company's primary product received his worst performance evaluation in years because he was measured on the number of service problems he handled.
- When senior managers in an international corporation diverted people and equipment from one country to another to meet the competition, the general managers in the two countries resisted the moves because they were afraid they would not make their profit plans. In the words of one manager, "The measurement system precludes people making good business decisions. We don't get into the economic optimization discussion. We get into the performance measurement discussion."
- A manager who had received a company award for innovation stated, "Several years ago I offered someone else this technology for their product. They were polite but basically said, 'It's not in my plan. Nobody's beating me up to do this and they are on other things.' The line guys don't get evaluated on the new opportunities they seize, but on whether they've done what they said. If it's not in their operating plan, they have to go through another planning cycle before they can address it."

Risk Averseness. An individual's reluctance to act is what we call risk averseness. Many managers are unwilling to take risks and appear to lack the courage needed to make tough business decisions. For instance, less than one-third of the managers we surveyed believed that managers in their corporation were willing to take risks to solve problems. Over half felt that managers in their corporation were tired and burned out. A significant number of managers may not have the energy necessary to initiate solutions to complex organizational problems and overcome the obstacles encountered in doing so.

Risk-averse people usually need an overwhelming body of evidence before they make decisions. Their need for evidence can outweigh their ability to use sound managerial judgment. This is not to say that individual managers are to blame for being risk-averse. Organizations often operate in a way that undermines managerial initiative and risk taking. Consider the midlevel manager who spent her entire career in a regulated industry where compliance with rules and regulations was of paramount importance. Although the company encouraged more risk taking after deregulation, this manager found it extremely difficult to buck twenty years of conditioning that had in a multitude of ways discouraged individual initiative.

Perceived Powerlessness

I have less authority to act now than ever before in my twenty-plus years with this company. It is due to the management style of my boss, which right now is dictatorial because of great pressure and poor results. I can only make decisions that he doesn't know about, and there's a high risk if he finds out. It's depressing for me and most people around here.

Powerlessness refers to the perception on the part of managers that they lack the authority and control needed to solve problems and implement solutions. Three primary factors tend to heighten the perception of powerlessness: unclear accountability, overcontrol, and inadequate resources.

Unclear Accountability. A majority of managers in our study believed that the lack of clear accountability was a significant problem within their companies. For instance, fewer than 20 percent of the managers surveyed believed that it was clear who had responsibility to solve key business problems in their organizations. This is particularly important when the development and delivery of products and services cut across different business units, increasing the likelihood of diffusion of responsibility. Unclear accountability regarding complex and often ingrained problems is the norm in many large corporations, as suggested by a midlevel manager in a Fortune 100 company: "One of the problems with this company is that it is hard to find people who are responsible. We have put so much energy into functional specialization that we have created wide seams between parts of the corporation. The biggest puzzle in the place is who is responsible. It's really diffused."

When people in the organization are not clear as to who has the responsibility for solving problems and implementing solutions, a chain of events occurs that consumes managerial time and effort. Cross-functional problems arise that increase the number of people involved as well as the number of levels required to reach a decision. A general lack of skill in dealing with cross-functional issues and conflicting interests forces ongoing input, debate, and negotiation. Evidence, sometimes taking the form of massive data analysis, is required to support a recommended course of action. The consequences are investment overload, delivery failures, and other costs resulting from lost time.

Overcontrol. Organizational control is exercised through the policies and procedures people are required to follow and the behavior of managers. Control mechanisms in many companies make it difficult to solve problems and implement decisions in an effective and timely manner. Specifically, tight controls and too many levels of authorization inhibit the capacity to act.

A significant component of the control issue is the way managers respond to performance pressures. When organizational results suffer, managers usually feel pressure to show improved performance. Some managers become more controlling, reducing the autonomy of those under them and, thus, reducing their capacity to act. Certain situations, of course, warrant tight controls; however, ongoing, excessive control can become a general pattern for some organizations and managers. Then, people are unwilling to believe empowerment is a reality or that management will support their independent actions.

It is particularly difficult to act when power has historically remained in the hands of senior managers. There appears to be an empowerment gestation period before managers believe the authority is real, are willing to act on it, and feel comfortable exercising it. Personal experience in the use of the new authority and subsequent support for the authority used are two critical factors that increase the willingness to act.

Inadequate Resources. A final component of powerlessness involves the absence of the resources needed to implement solutions to organizational problems. Three-fourths of the managers in our survey believed that a lack of resources (for example, money, people) prevented the implementation of solutions to business problems in their organizations. Although many managers admitted problems with resource management in the past, some felt the push to cut costs had hindered their ability to solve problems. As one manager in our study observed, "The pendulum may have swung too far. In the past, you could go to the functional managers to form a team to look at something. Now it's almost impossible because everyone is stretched."

An Explanatory Model

Insufficient capacity to act decreases business results, drains human resources, and overloads senior management. These outcomes are due to priority stress, a bias toward activity versus results, and perceived powerlessness. Figure 7.3 outlines the causes and consequences of insufficient capacity to act.

Potential Solutions

The way we've traditionally worked has resulted in managers becoming conditioned to certain situations and not being focused on the real needs of the organization. A lack of ability in addressing and correcting obstacles has labeled our managers as being very political and ineffective. We need to refocus the management direction from a stagnant traditional approach to an action management approach. Let's fix things now while we are all still working here.

How do senior managers, particularly those in human resources positions, prevent or treat this disease? Some large companies, such as PepsiCo and Corning, have either avoided or cured themselves of this ailment. They have developed approaches to creating and sustaining capacity to act at all organizational levels. First, these companies clarify their purpose and direction. Second,

Figure 7.3. Insufficient Capacity to Act: An Explanatory Model.

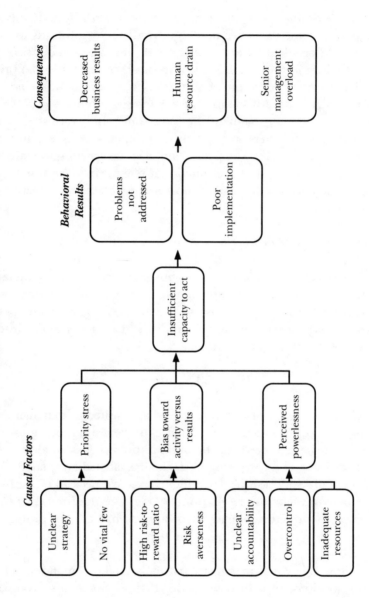

they focus on results by rewarding successful performance while learning from failure. Third, they empower individuals and teams.

Focus on Core Priorities

Managers must have the ability and flexibility needed to choose the methods that will best accomplish their organization's goals. All managers know that organizations try to manage more than they can do and that not all areas carry the same leverage. In many companies, there is a bias toward working on a very large number of priorities and focusing on the auditable tasks. Instead, managers need to identify the activities that will produce the desired results. This theme is not new but it is critical. An essential component of the capacity to act is the capacity to say no.

The ability to prioritize choices requires that managers exercise independent judgment in accordance with a common operating vision and strategy. A clearly focused endpoint is necessary if priorities at all levels of the organization are to be coordinated and synergistic. This vision is then disseminated throughout the organization in a manner that ensures collective understanding, a process that the Japanese call policy deployment (Newcomb, 1989) and that perhaps is best illustrated in the United States by Florida Power and Light (Tallon, 1989).

Effective companies establish a small number of very clear priorities—for example, total quality and return on equity (ROE) at Corning—and make sure that managers communicate those priorities throughout the organization. They also tend to set high standards and focus people on challenging yet feasible performance targets. As the CEO of Federal Express notes, "People who understand goals and how their jobs relate to them are much more inclined to exert their best efforts" (Smith, 1991, p. 18).

Managers can take certain actions to increase the focus on core priorities:

- Open the boundaries around the organization and insist on a customer-driven focus at all levels. An external perspective can help clarify business strategy and the appropriateness of internal operating principles.

- Ensure that all managers possess a clear vision and strategy for their company and their operating units.
- Identify the critical things that all managers must do (and must not do) and provide them with the freedom to choose the priorities that best accomplish their operating strategy. Hold managers accountable for the choices they make, with the emphasis on choosing the few areas of greatest leverage.

Bias Toward Results

A clear enabler of the capacity to act is the inherent motivation of many managers and employees. There are numerous examples of the widespread impact of individuals who became champions for the implementation of new ideas or products. The challenge is to channel this inherent motivation toward the needs of the company and to stimulate ongoing problem solving and innovation.

Individuals act when they sufficiently value the potential outcomes of their actions and when they believe they can accomplish the desired performance. An organization can motivate managers to act by increasing the perception that certain actions will bring rewards and by increasing the perception that they can solve key organizational problems.

Capacity to act requires an environment that encourages and supports individual initiative in the pursuit of clear organizational goals. It is important that people correctly identify those actions that lead to desired results and, if necessary, take risks to achieve them. Managers need to trust that when they take actions intended to improve their companies (but not specified in the operating plan or measurement systems), there will be a favorable impact on the evaluation of their performance. Of course, ongoing and systematic improvements in the business processes used to obtain results should not be ignored. In fact, results are often defined as improvements in the business processes that lead to achievement of long-term business objectives.

The rewards for taking initiative must be larger than the rewards for safe behavior. Companies that have effectively solved the insufficient capacity to act problem work to create meritocracies with rewards based on results rather than activity, and with very significant and tangible rewards for those individuals and teams that perform well (Lawler, 1990).

An intensive review and restructuring of formal and informal reward structures can increase the bias toward results. The measurement and evaluation systems must flexibly allow for new ways of operating and for new ideas that contribute to desired results. A key component of this action is a reassessment of how the organization defines and manages failure. Organizations must learn to differentiate between productive and unproductive failure. For example, if a good plan has a bad outcome, but learning takes place and the failure is not critical to the individual or the organization, it can be considered a productive failure.

Empowerment

The structure and practices of an organization can facilitate managers' attempts to take action and implement solutions (Block, 1987). Clear responsibility with the authority to act heightens the likelihood that people will resolve critical problems. The management style of the organization must carry the expectation that empowered managers are accountable for and supported in the exercise of their authority. Controls are minimized and resources freed for high-priority endeavors.

Some companies create organizational structures that facilitate autonomy. They ensure that units have the resources they need to manage their own work, make their own decisions, and solve problems. The following high-leverage actions support empowerment:

- Whenever possible, restructure organizational units to be smaller, less complex, and less dependent on other units for decision making and action.
- Reduce to a minimum the number of hard rules for the organization. These few rules or policies should clearly define how the organization will operate. Guidelines replace most rules and managers clarify and consistently reinforce operating norms.
- Drive a change throughout the organization that focuses on empowerment and personal accountability for delivering results.
- Provide the education and training necessary to enable people to

respond to opportunities for improvement. For example, quality tools and processes are essential in identifying and solving many organizational problems. Without understanding how to use and when to apply such tools, empowerment in and of itself will not result in significant organizational improvements.

In total, increased capacity to act is evident when there is a clear focus on core priorities, a bias toward results, and empowerment. The results are improved business, more highly motivated people, and enhanced senior management effectiveness. Figure 7.4 outlines the benefits that come with the capacity to act and the factors that give rise to it.

Summary

How prevalent is insufficient capacity to act? Our survey of a random sample of midlevel managers at one corporation showed that a majority felt that it took more effort than it should to solve key organizational problems. Only a minority felt that problems in their organizations were solved before they became major problems. Figure 7.5 illustrates the pervasiveness of the problem; our experience in other large corporations suggests that these findings are not unique.

A broader perspective can help us understand why organizations have historically restricted capacity to act. Max Weber argued nearly 100 years ago that bureaucracy emerged as the dominant mode of organizing because it improves on management based on the personal whims of a charismatic leader or the habitual following of traditional practices that can quickly become outdated (Weber, 1947). It provides a system that allows for impersonal coordination and control through the promulgation of rational rules and regulations. In this respect, bureaucracy was a sophisticated manner of ensuring an acceptable level of control and coordination. Bureaucracy also reflected a larger societal valuing of uniform justice in treating all people equally.

We believe that what Burns (1984) called organic forms of organization will come to displace more mechanistic structures in organizations that exist in a highly competitive environment. First,

Figure 7.4. Capacity to Act: An Explanatory Model.

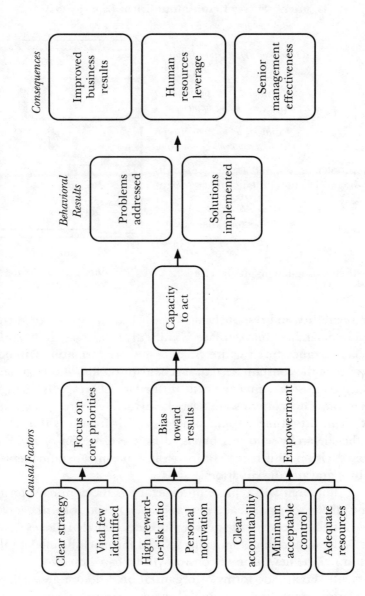

Figure 7.5. Survey Results: Insufficient Capacity to Act.

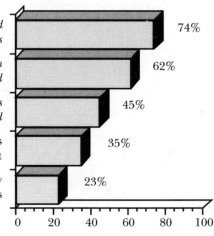

*It takes more effort than it should
to solve key problems*   74%

*I am frustrated because agreed on
actions are not being implemented*   62%

*Managers let known business
problems go unsolved*   45%

Important problems are solved at the lower levels
without the involvement of senior management   35%

Problems are solved before they
become major issues   23%

0   20   40   60   80   100

Note: Negatively worded items are italicized.   Percent Agree or Strongly Agree

the flexibility and responsiveness needed to survive in an increasingly demanding marketplace is difficult to extract from a traditional bureaucratic structure. Second, the transformation will occur because of the constant need in mechanistic organizations to elevate decisions to senior management in the face of a rapidly changing situation. This pattern soon overwhelms senior management, leaving them little time to plan strategy, and it frustrates those lower in the hierarchy who feel bypassed by the elevation of more and more decisions (Burns, 1984). Increasing the bureaucratic hierarchy only aggravates the situation.

But what will replace bureaucracy as the dominant form of control? We see signs that a new approach to control will evolve in the United States over the next few decades, one that moves beyond the Weberian notion of bureaucracy and the machine model inherent in it. The new form of control will be based on two key developments. First, new forms of organizational design are surfacing that stress group-level accountability in the context of entrepreneurial self-interest. These new systems create small, self-sustaining units within larger enterprises. These emerging organizational forms provide an alternative to the bureaucratic controls. Properly structured, the invisible hand of self-interest replaces the formalized control found in bureaucratic structures. Second, new forms of information technology are being developed that are capable of providing alternative coordination and control mechanisms. In the context of a self-managed unit, information is provided that allows the members of the unit to monitor and control their own behavior. Controls are built into the work process and the technology used by those doing the work, controls are no longer imposed through the use of rigid rules and regulations monitored from above. Increased spans of controls will also be possible when technology links together supervisors and perhaps hundreds of empowered individuals and groups.

Many leading companies, including Procter & Gamble, Corning, Hewlett-Packard, DEC, Xerox, and AT&T, are using this new approach. They are experimenting with new work architectures. The idea is to organize around self-managed "micro-enterprise units," work units that encompass an entire end-to-end work process related to a product or service. These structures, what some call focused factories or teams, are microcosms of a full enterprise, but they have the autonomy to structure and manage themselves. At the team level, they work without supervisors, design their own work processes, cross-train to create multifunctional people, and share in the financial benefits of their efforts.

We can move far beyond the machine bureaucracy that has been part of our heritage for close to a hundred years to new models based on autonomous teams linked together in organizational networks, with coordination achieved through relationships and information technology rather than a hierarchy. This concept, which started in the factory, is being expanded to office settings and knowledge-intensive environments. It has been applied in environments as diverse as Citibank's mortgage application unit, AT&T's stock transfer organization, Corning's administrative center, and Xerox's customer service teams. On a more general level, we increasingly find leaders like Percy Barnevik, chairman of Asea Brown Boveri Ltd., who has organized his 240,000-employee organization into 4500 profit centers overseen by a 100-person corporate staff (Peters, 1991).

Many U.S. workers value innovation, entrepreneurship, autonomy, teamwork, and diversity. Indeed, many American workers do not desire to rise through the ranks to the middle management of a large corporation; they dream of starting their own businesses, leveraging their own innovativeness and creative energies, and getting a piece of the action. Capacity to act builds on these values. When organizations tap the inherent creativity, diversity, and entrepreneurial spirit of their people, they create a competitive advantage that is not easily replicated by others, particularly foreign competitors whose societal values are at odds with notions of empowerment and entrepreneurship.

A major strategic challenge for U.S. corporations in the 1990s will be to avoid the maladies usually associated with large organizations. Hunting down and eliminating the organizational factors that inhibit the capacity to act will be important in meeting that challenge. Human resources professionals will play a pivotal role because the capacity to act is fundamentally the challenge of using the full potential of people within organizations. But the challenge requires more than programs to increase empowerment; it involves nothing less than a dramatic transformation of the way we view, structure, and manage our organizations.

References

Block, P. *The Empowered Manager: Positive Political Skills at Work*. San Francisco: Jossey-Bass, 1987.

Burns, T. "Industry in a New Age." In D. S. Pugh (ed.), *Organization Theory*. (2nd ed.) New York: Viking Penguin, 1984.

Lawler, E. E. *Strategic Pay: Aligning Organizational Strategies and Pay Systems*. San Francisco: Jossey-Bass, 1990.

Newcomb, J. "Management by Policy Deployment." *Quality*, 1989, *28*(1), 28–30.

Peters, T. "Letting Go of Controls." *Across the Board*, June 1991, 14–18.

Smith, F. "Empowering Employees." *Small Business Reports*, Jan. 1991, 15–20.

Tallon, R. *Executive Speeches*. 1989, *3*(7), 18–22.

Weber, M. *The Theory of Social and Economic Organization*. New York: Free Press, 1947.

EIGHT

Teaching Organizations to Learn: The Power of Productive Failures

ROBERT B. SHAW, DENNIS N. T. PERKINS

Each week, we are bombarded with reports of the national crisis in education. Another crisis is brewing in America of equal or even greater proportions. It is a crisis of learning that afflicts the organizations in this country. Simply put, many of our great companies have lost the capacity to learn. We frequently hear about the problems of competitiveness, cost, quality, customer focus, and so forth. But beneath these specific concerns is a more fundamental problem: the inability of organizations to learn and keep from making the same mistakes over and over. True competitiveness is achieved when organizations are learning-efficient systems.

What is organizational learning? It is the capacity of an organization to gain insight from its own experience and the experience of others and to modify the way it functions according to such insight. Why is organizational learning so critical? Part of the answer is that companies face intensified competition and increasing rates of change. The companies that prosper into the twenty-first century will be learning-efficient systems capable of anticipating shifts in their environment and growing smarter over time (De-Geus, 1988). The rate at which organizations learn may become the only sustainable competitive advantage, especially in rapidly shifting and knowledge-intensive industries (Strata, 1989).

We recently conducted several studies to examine organizational learning as a tool for increased organizational effectiveness (Delta Consulting Group, 1988, 1989, 1990). Our intent was to identify mechanisms for increasing an organization's ability to benefit from its own experience. This chapter summarizes the findings of our studies and includes a model of organizational learning, common barriers to learning, and recommendations.

A Model of Organizational Learning

The ability to gain insight from experience is the essence of organizational learning. When learning-efficient companies try something new, be it a new technology, product offering, or management approach, they can comprehend what works, what does not work, and why. These companies can examine their overall strategy in relation to what is learned and incorporate new learning into their day-to-day practices. And, they do all this in a short period of time.

Beliefs, Actions, and Outcomes

Our model of learning begins with the beliefs that influence behavior. In the broadest sense, beliefs are a combination of values, knowledge, and expertise. Belief systems encompass core values, many of which are implicit and taken for granted, and more everyday assumptions about the way the world functions. Individuals see the world through the "lenses" of these belief systems and take action based on their belief systems. These actions influence particular outcomes (such as success or failure in an endeavor).

Reflection, Insight, and Dissemination

Effective learning occurs when people reflect on the consequences of their actions and thereby gain insight (a richer and more accurate understanding of the key factors in their environment). This is particularly important in understanding cause-and-effect linkages. The relationship between actions and outcomes is complex and often subjective. Still, effective reflection can add to an individual's existing knowledge base and result in a better understanding of the relationship between action and outcomes.

Group learning cycles are similar to those for individuals: belief promotes actions that influence outcomes. Effective reflection helps a group modify, if warranted, its existing belief system. For example, a team chartered to develop a new product learns a great deal while completing its task. Successes and failures, if fully examined, result in a better understanding of what works and what does not work. The group's learning influences the strategies employed by the group in completing its work. These insights occur at a group level in that no one individual in the group embodies all the learning of the group as a whole.

Diffusion of what is learned through reflection is more than a simple transmission or exchange of cold facts. Sharing information among organizational groups is critical in facilitating reflection and action. Effective learning systems surface differing perspectives to better interpret experience and spark innovation. Without exchange, effective reflection is more difficult because those engaging in reflection lack the information they need to interpret the consequences of their actions. For example, a work team was set up to develop software for its firm's line of computer hardware. Members of the software development team were constantly struggling to determine the proper course of action in relation to a shifting corporate strategy. In addition, those in the development team felt that the level of exchange with their contacts in the corporate office was woefully inadequate, given the rapid pace of change in the software industry. Learning is most likely to occur when individuals and groups effectively reflect on and interpret the outcomes of their actions, individuals and groups disseminate new learning throughout an organization, and individuals and groups act on their beliefs and leverage new learning (their own and others) to produce the greatest benefit to their organization. Our organizational model is illustrated in Figure 8.1.

Barriers to Organizational Learning

The model outlined in Figure 8.1 is one way of understanding the factors that impede learning in organizations (see Huber, 1989, for

Figure 8.1. Organizational Learning Model.

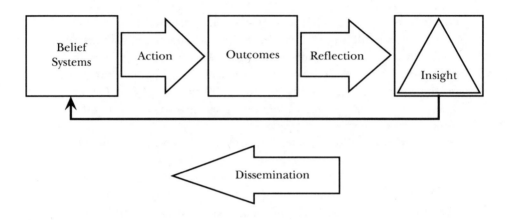

a general overview of organizational learning). Our studies suggest that barriers to learning fall into three broad categories that affect different capacities within an organization:

- A capacity to reflect and interpret is achieved when people reflect on the outcomes of their actions to gain insight into their experience and its consequences. Without reflection, cause-and-effect linkages are not fully understood. Faulty or incomplete reflection results in limited or incorrect learning.
- A capacity to transfer and disseminate learning is achieved when there is a collaborative exchange of ideas in which differing perspectives are aired and understanding is shared. Without exchange, insights gained from action and reflection at the individual and group levels are not fully realized at the organizational level. The organization consequently repeats mistakes and fails to adapt to changing internal and external conditions.
- A capacity to act is achieved when people throughout the organization are empowered to act on their beliefs. Without action, alternatives to the existing state are not attempted. Experimen-

tation is critical if an organization is to meet the challenges posed by an increasingly complex external environment. A capacity to act also permits new learning to be applied throughout an organization.

These organizational capacities and the obstacles to them are outlined in Figure 8.2.

Insufficient Capacity to Reflect and Interpret

The problem of insufficient capacity to reflect can be defined as the inability of organization members to correctly interpret the consequences of internal and external factors in relation to organiza-

Figure 8.2. Barriers to Organizational Learning.

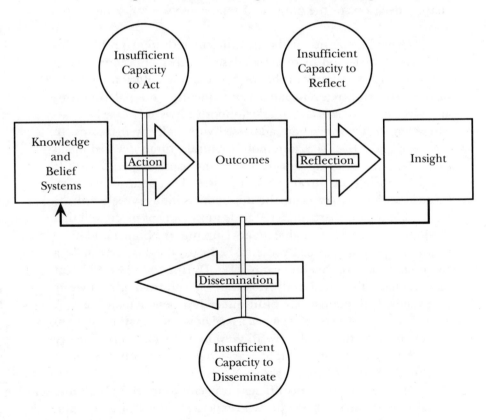

tional outcomes. People typically act on the basis of incomplete information and explore only a limited set of alternatives; they also have difficulty assessing the relationship between their behavior and observed outcomes (Simon, 1976). This tendency can become so extreme as to render an organization ineffective and unable to adapt to changing conditions.

Problem avoidance is one indication that an organization is having problems with reflection. Important problems never get to the stage of decision making and action. People may become complacent and ignore or deny the existence of problems, they may suppress problems, or they may select the wrong problems for action rather than the vital few that influence performance. United States automobile manufacturers, for instance, did not recognize the potential for quality to become a critical factor in consumer purchasing decisions or the progress the Japanese were making in this area.

Other symptoms of the insufficient reflection problem include incomplete and incorrect analyses. In this situation, organization members identify problems and develop solutions without fully considering relevant data. Consequently, internal problems are solved only to resurface; market opportunities are missed repeatedly; competitive threats are addressed with halfway measures. In the 1960s and 1970s, U.S. automobile manufacturers devoted much time preparing to compete with their American competitors while largely ignoring the threat of the Japanese. This occurred, in part, because senior managers in the automotive industry believed the low end of the car market offered little in the way of profit and that the Japanese would be unable to move up into the higher and more profitable product lines. By the early 1980s, the Japanese held a significant share of the total car market. During the 1980s, U.S. car makers closed thirteen North American car and truck plants while eleven new U.S. plants were built under Japanese management. A senior automotive executive, when asked how such a fall from dominance could occur, noted: "We all grew up with a lot of confidence that we were doing it the right way—that no one could teach us anything" (Keller, 1989).

What leads to an insufficient capacity to reflect? One cause is performance pressure. People who experience the strains of trying to meet short-term performance objectives often minimize the importance of reflection. In many companies, senior managers view formal reflection as a luxury that consumes time better spent on actions that meet clearly defined performance targets. Contrast this short-term financially driven business perspective with the approach taken by Toyota in introducing a new version of an existing commercial van. Toyota engineers spent more than six months riding through the streets of Tokyo with the users of the company's existing van, who were predominantly owners of dry cleaners and small grocery stores. The Toyota engineers did this to better understand their customers' needs and the changes needed in the van. The engineers who spent six months on the road with customers became the project managers for the new van. In this case, short-term costs were secondary to the design and manufacture of a quality product.

Organization members usually focus their efforts on doing what is measured, observed, or counted. As a result, they may ignore what is important if learning is to occur. High-level reflection is typically lacking when people are rewarded exclusively for meeting short-term financial targets. Consider the manager who was punished for taking time away from his regular duties to develop an innovative new approach to preventing service failures, which, if carried out, would have saved his company money. "I got beat up all year for not making plan," he complained. "I clearly got the message that I never should do this again."

Competency traps also can undermine effective reflection, particularly in settings where performance pressures are intense (Levitt and March, 1988). In such cases, individuals and groups become prisoners to the methods they understand the best, even when other approaches might be necessary, given changes in the marketplace. People often prefer to use standard operating procedures that they understand and associate with past successes. As a result, they may avoid investing the time necessary to develop new approaches that might be more effective in the long term. Successes of the past can become embedded in a host of organizational policies and practices that eventually become outdated and counterproductive.

A third cause of inadequate reflection is the absence of learning forums or structures. Part of the problem has to do with dominance of current practices and routines that guide behavior (Daft

and Weick, 1984). These standard practices or routines, which become part of an organization's culture, are independent of those
who execute them and can survive considerable turnover in individual actors (Levitt and March, 1988). Well-established routines often
block interpretations that are at odds with the status quo, and replacing old routines with new approaches is extremely difficult.
Few organizations help their members move beyond the dominant
set of core assumptions that guide behavior. Few help their
members test the validity of their beliefs about cause-and-effect relationships and examine what can be learned from their own performance. Instead, a host of defensive routines arises, usually
supported by the larger organizational culture, that prevent learning at either an individual or a collective level (Argyris, 1982, 1990,
1991). These routines, commonplace to the point of going unno-
ticed, serve to protect individuals and groups from the embarrassment, pain, and conflicts that arise when confronting the errors in
one's own reasoning.

Few organizations have structured learning processes that
encourage reflection and help with the complex task of interpreting
outcomes. The increasing emphasis on quality in many U.S. companies has provided some methods that promote reflection. But our
experience suggests that managers usually focus on how to improve
existing practices or processes and fail to engage in a broader analysis of an organization's strengths and weaknesses in relation to
external threats and opportunities. More generally, critical organizational actions often result in outcomes that take years to unfold
and interpret. Trial-and-error learning is much more difficult when
the cause-and-effect cycles stretch over years or even decades (Senge,
1990).

Figure 8.3 lists the symptoms and potential causes of insufficient capacity to reflect within an organization.

Insufficient Capacity to Disseminate Learning

The failure of people in different organizational groups to share
information and insights is commonplace. One symptom of this
phenomenon is problem ignorance. Individuals, particularly at
lower levels, recognize important organizational problems but do

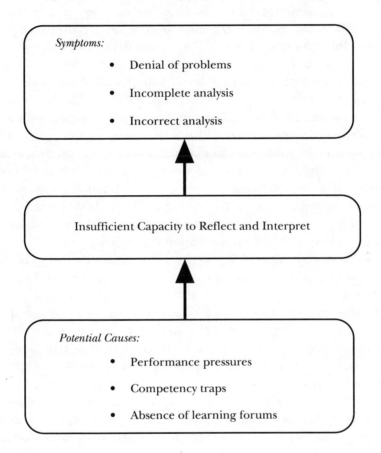

Figure 8.3. Insufficient Capacity to Reflect and Interpret.

not communicate with those in a "need to know" position. A related symptom is solution ignorance. Isolated groups identify problems and develop solutions but their approaches are not shared throughout the organization. An engineering group we studied solved a technical problem that was solved again in a different engineering group in the same organization, at considerable cost and expense, because of a lack of information sharing across these groups. Finally, companies often attempt the same approaches despite repeated failures in the past; the lessons from the past failures were never shared because of the stigma associated with failure. Redundancy of effort is all too common in many large corporations.

Many factors block dissemination of new learning. One is strong intergroup boundaries. "Functional foxholes," line/staff distinctions, and geographic dispersion generally inhibit the exchange of information among levels and groups. Individuals and groups can come to focus more on internal rivalries than the external threats faced by the organization as a whole. Information sharing is reduced when internal politics become more salient than the need to work in a coordinated manner. This is particularly true in companies that face little or no competition or compete in very stable environments. In more extreme cases, organization members actively camouflage their intentions or actions; believing that information is power, they seek to sustain or increase their level of funding and status within the organization through deception.

A second cause of ineffective information exchange is the myth of uniqueness. When individuals and groups believe they are different from their counterparts, they view the experiences of others as largely irrelevant to their own situation. Those in one geographic region of a company, for instance, may come to believe that those in another region have little to offer in the way of insight because their markets are seen as different. Thus, the experiences of others are not solicited.

Narrow bandwidths for acceptable information exchange can also inhibit the communication necessary for in-depth learning. Many companies view only short-term financial information as relevant. This approach can eliminate much of the richness in communication that is essential if learning is to occur. For example, long-term trends in consumer preferences and competitor offerings may be ignored if people exclusively focus on short-term financial indices. Companies can also view outcomes exclusively in terms of success or failure. The tendency to view experience in a black or white manner, what we call dichotomous thinking, blocks a fuller understanding of what does and does not work in a given situation. This is particularly true when assessing the outcomes of innovations, most of which fail over the long term but nevertheless offer valuable insights to those open to learning from experience. The ability to learn from attempted innovations, particularly when they fail, is essential given that the success rate for innovations is small.

Figure 8.4 lists the symptoms and potential causes of insufficient dissemination of learning throughout an organization.

Insufficient Capacity to Act

The insufficient capacity to act problem can be illustrated in the words of a senior manager in a major United States corporation:

Figure 8.4. Insufficient Capacity to Disseminate Learning.

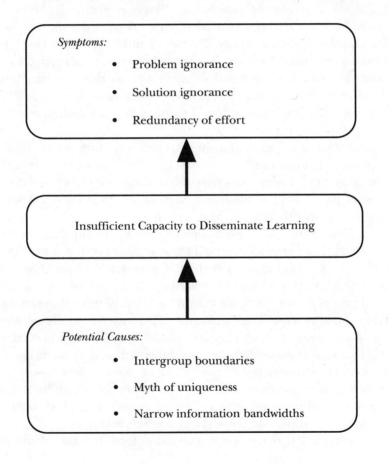

I have a good mind, good ideas, and a desire to see this company succeed. But I live in an environment where unless everything is checked out I run a great risk of being cut off at the knees for taking the smallest of risks, even when they are in the best interests of the corporation.

One symptom of an insufficient capacity to act is a lack of experimentation with new approaches. In such cases, organization members embrace standard operating principles and policies. The assumptions that underlie these principles are taken for granted and rarely challenged, even when evidence suggests that a new and better approach might be attempted. Practices continue because "things have always been done that way." A second symptom involves implementation failure. People identify problems, develop solutions, and make decisions, but the solutions are not carried out. Frequently, solutions are derailed; often, they are implemented, but only after inordinate time, effort, and money have been spent. In other cases, the implementation is so poor that the desired results do not accrue as predicted.

Our work suggests that three factors contribute to an insufficient capacity to act (see Chapter Seven). First, priority stress results when people experience the strain of too many priorities or confusing objectives. They are paralyzed or misdirect their efforts. A second obstacle to productive action is a bias toward activity versus results. This occurs when people focus their efforts on doing what is measurable or observable, even if these activities do not contribute to effective performance in a particular situation, because they are punished for mistakes and not rewarded adequately for success. As a result, people work hard, but not on the right things—those issues vital in the long term. The third cause of an insufficient capacity to act is powerlessness. Managers and employees often feel that they cannot make things happen, so why bother? In more extreme cases, there exists a pervasive fear of risk taking or of being seen as a rebel or troublemaker. Powerlessness develops where accountabilities are unclear and where individuals and teams are overcontrolled. Inadequate resources (time and money) can also inhibit action.

Figure 8.5 lists the symptoms and potential causes of insuf-

Figure 8.5. Insufficient Capacity to Act.

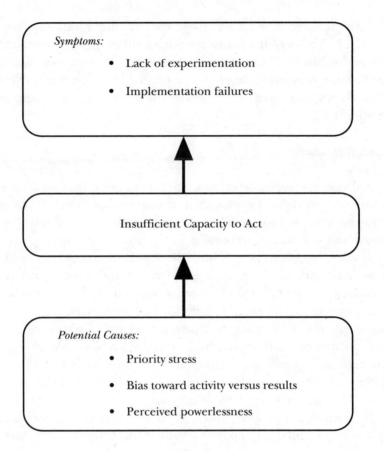

Symptoms:

- Lack of experimentation
- Implementation failures

Insufficient Capacity to Act

Potential Causes:

- Priority stress
- Bias toward activity versus results
- Perceived powerlessness

ficient capacity to act in an organization. The learning problems outlined above do not always undermine organizational effectiveness. Historically, some companies have existed in protected industries—they faced few threats because of monopoly, regulation, technological superiority, or weak competition. The ability to reflect, disseminate, and act is not as important in these environments. In other cases, problems develop only after restructuring and the resulting change in goals that renders existing organizational practices obsolete.

Teaching Organizations to Learn

Few American companies have been effective organizational learners. The bad news is that many companies fail to speak the language
of learning and lose opportunities. Still, some American companies
have begun to invest in developing a capacity to learn. Five general
elements are important in creating a learning-efficient company
(Nadler, 1989).

Open Boundaries

Closed systems are, by definition, not open to new ideas and information. A first step in promoting learning is to open the boundaries
of the organization to new ideas and information. This can be done
by sending out scouts, importing ideas through speakers or semi-
nars, and bringing in people from the outside (approaches the Japanese have practiced for decades). One of the most productive
boundaries to open is that between a company and its customers.
Effective learners constantly listen to their customers. They bring
customers in to talk about their perceptions of the market, of competition, and of the company itself. Jack Welch of General Electric
dreams of a "boundaryless" company free of the walls that separate
companies from their customers and suppliers. Boundaries are
opened by such events as DEC World, an annual gathering drawing
more than 50,000 people; Corning, Inc.'s management meetings,
which feature outside speakers; or Citibank's customer laboratory.

Motivation of Risk Taking

Learning cannot occur without experimentation. Effective organizations create an environment in which people feel both motivated
and able to experiment. This may be brought about by allocating
special funds for experiments (as done at Xerox or 3M) or by telling
people, as one company does, that 15 percent of their time is theirs
to explore or do whatever they want. Most experiments do not result
in successes. New approaches will occur if people feel they have
permission to fail productively and that experimentation alone will

be rewarded. They must also be able to look around and see organizational role models who are experimenters.

Experiments Structured for Learning

Learning-efficient companies recognize the value of productive failure and the shortcomings of unproductive success. A productive failure is one that leads to insight and thus adds to the knowledge of the organization. An unproductive success occurs when something goes well, but nobody quite knows how or why (other than to say, "We must be doing something right!"). No one can generalize from or reproduce such a success. Productive failures, in contrast, provide the capacity to create productive successes, where organization members know what they are doing right and where they can apply the lessons of success. Learning-effective organizations thoroughly examine their successes and failures to ensure that productive learning occurs in both cases.

Not all experiments or innovations necessarily lead to learning. There is a theory and method of experimental design that helps create experiments that yield productive successes or productive failures. Learning-efficient companies set up experiments with clear objectives, ensure that the experiments are executed well, and document the results. Not coincidentally, many of these companies also have instituted major total quality processes throughout their organizations and provide training in statistics, experimental design, and problem analysis that enables employees to design, implement, and analyze experiments.

Environments That Extract and Disseminate Learning

Good experiments alone are not enough. Learning requires an environment in which the results of experiments are sought after, examined, and disseminated throughout the organization. Effective learners spend much time and effort holding meetings, offsite sessions, conferences, and training programs to disseminate learning. Procter & Gamble gathers thousands of its managers each year to exchange information, and Xerox and Corning hold annual events where teams of employees present their projects, experiments, and innovations. Some companies have designed what might be called "inefficient offsites"—meetings that provide the time and opportunity for managers to meet informally and share their experiences. Other companies write case studies about successes and failures and use these cases in meetings and training programs.

More generally, norms are needed to encourage people to examine their own beliefs and, as needed, modify them. Letting go of existing beliefs and assumptions is difficult at best. Most of us would rather cling to that which we know than experience the discomfort of embracing a new paradigm. Those organizations and managers who have not experienced failure over their histories are particularly prone to defensive reasoning. Nystrom and Starbuck (1984, p. 59) note that "organizations succumb to crises largely because their top managers, bolstered by recollections of past successes, live in worlds circumscribed by their cognitive structures. Top managers misperceive events and rationalize their organizations' failures."

Encouragement of the Capacity to Act

Ultimately, the payoff for organizational learning is more effective action over time. Real leverage comes from applying learning throughout the organization. This requires overcoming the "not invented here" syndrome that leads to resistance to ideas thought of elsewhere. Organizations need to free up and motivate people to use what others have learned. Part of this comes from rewarding people who apply the insights of others, as opposed to rewarding only those who come up with ideas. Frequently, the only organizational heroes are those who do something new, rather than those who apply the insights of others. Chapter Seven offers examples of how companies have developed approaches to creating and sustaining a capacity to act.

Summary

Two themes run through the experiences of learning-efficient companies. One is the notion of the experimenting organization—the company that is constantly trying out new things through innovations and experiments. Combined with this is the concept of the reflective organization—the company that can look at its experiments and experiences, win, lose, or draw, and gain insight that can be applied in the future. Too often, we worship at the altar of unproductive, short-term successes and shun productive failures.

These themes indicate that organizations must recognize the importance of learning and continuously evaluate the basic assumptions that often inhibit learning. Organizations typically encode the learning of the past into a complex web of beliefs and practices that are extremely difficult to change. It is clear, however, that organizations open to inquiry and ongoing learning will be at a competitive advantage relative to those who cling to what worked in the past but will surely fail in the future.

References

Argyris, C. *Reasoning, Learning and Action: Individual and Organizational.* San Francisco: Jossey-Bass, 1982.

Argyris, C. *Overcoming Organizational Defenses—Facilitating Organizational Learning.* Boston: Allyn and Bacon, 1990.

Argyris, C. "Teaching Smart People How to Learn." *Harvard Business Review,* May/June 1991, 99–109.

Daft, R., and Weick, K. "Toward a Model of Organizations as Interpretation Systems." *Academy of Management Review,* 1984, *9*(2), 284–295.

DeGeus, A. "Planning as Learning." *Harvard Business Review,* Mar./Apr. 1988, 71–81.

Delta Consulting Group. "Organizational Learning Methods from Benchmark Companies." Unpublished study, Delta Consulting Group, 1988.

Delta Consulting Group. "Capacity to Act." Unpublished study, Delta Consulting Group, 1989.

Delta Consulting Group. "Organizational Learning Case Studies." Unpublished study, Delta Consulting Group, 1990.

Huber, G. "Organizational Learning: An Examination of the Contributing Processes and a Review of Literature." Unpublished paper prepared for the NSF-sponsored Conference on Organizational Learning held at Carnegie-Mellon University, May 18–20, 1989.

Keller, M. *Rude Awakening: The Rise, Fall and Struggle for Recovery of General Motors.* New York: Morrow, 1989.

Levitt, B., and March, J. "Organizational Learning." *Annual Review of Sociology,* 1988, *14,* 319–340.

Nadler, D. "Even Failures Can Be Productive." *New York Times,* Business Forum, Apr. 23, 1989.

Nystrom, P., and Starbuck, W., "To Avoid Organizational Crises, Unlearn." *Organizational Dynamics,* Spring 1984, 53–65.

Senge, P. *The Fifth Discipline: The Arts and Practice of the Learning Organization.* New York: Doubleday, 1990.

Simon, H. *Administrative Behavior: A Study of Decision-Making Processes in Administrative Organization.* New York: Free Press, 1976.

Strata, R. "Organizational Learning—The Key to Management of Innovation." *Sloan Management Review,* 1989, *30*(3), 63–74.

PART FOUR

Designing Senior Management

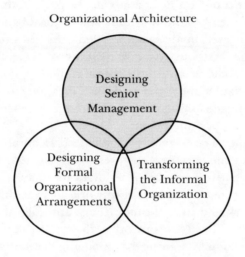

Organizational Architecture

Designing
Senior
Management

Designing
Formal
Organizational
Arrangements

Transforming
the Informal
Organization

The preceding chapters of this book established senior management's leadership agenda. As senior managers are the organization's "architects," by all rights we could stop the book here, leaving them the task of designing, experimenting, and eventually finding solutions to the issues we have raised. Such a treatment would be incomplete, however, because a major issue facing organizations is the design of senior management itself.

There is ample evidence that the very complexity and pace of change that are giving rise to the changes in organizational architecture are stretching the single chief executive or traditional CEO/COO pair to their limits. In response, a movement toward collaboration and teamwork has been observed in a number of organizations as many of the same ideas being applied organizationally through total quality programs and high-performance work systems are being implemented at senior levels.

The chapters in Part Four deal with emerging issues of senior management, specifically the selection of senior management, the nature of teamwork at the top, and collaborative approaches to the development of strategy, (perhaps senior management's most important function).

In Chapter Nine, David A. Nadler and Marc S. Gerstein analyze the complex process of assembling a senior executive team. To be successful, this process must analytically assess both the requirements of team membership and the capabilities of the individual candidates. However, analysis alone often does not produce a successful outcome. Without an understanding of the emotional and political issues that surround succession at the top, good decisions are not likely. Nadler and Gerstein discuss these sensitive issues and provide some suggestions to prevent them from overwhelming careful analysis and sound judgment.

In Chapter Ten, David A. Nadler and Deborah Ancona address executive teamwork in a comprehensive fashion. Specifically, they define executive teams and the forces that have created them, describe the nature of executive teamwork and the differences between such work and that of other teams, and identify the factors that contribute to effective teamwork at the top. In addition, Nadler and Ancona develop a "contingency model" of executive teamwork by specifying the types of teamwork required in a variety of environmental and structural contexts. Finally, the authors diagnose a number of problems that uniquely plague executive teams and offer a number of suggestions to avoid or remedy them.

Chapter Eleven deals with that most critical agenda item for executive groups, the formulation and implementation of strategy. David R. Bliss asserts that the spotty track record of executive groups in developing and implementing their strategic plans is due to three factors: the wrong people participate in the process, driving assumptions and beliefs are not addressed, and decisions are made in a "one-off" manner. Bliss then provides an alternative approach to strategy development that emphasizes that "the value is in the planning, not in the plan." In this approach, the emphasis is on collaboration, teamwork at the top, and willingness to confront tough issues openly.

NINE

Strategic Selection: Staffing the Executive Team

DAVID A. NADLER, MARC S. GERSTEIN

Many senior executives report that the most important decisions they make during their tenure involve staffing, specifically those selections that fill key senior team positions. While every CEO we have worked with confirms this view, from candid conversations it appears that the quality of the decision-making process is not consistent with the importance placed upon it. Senior executives use sketchy data, fail to discuss the requirements of the job separately from the characteristics of the individual, and focus on the individual as generally "good" or "bad," rather than on his or her specific strengths and weaknesses in the context of the job.

This state of affairs is not necessarily inherent to senior management. During the past decade, we have been working to develop, test, and use an approach for significantly enhancing the quality of decision making for staffing a wide variety of senior jobs. Earlier, Gerstein and Reisman (1983) presented a conceptual framework for matching people to business conditions. On the basis of this work and other research on executive selection (for example, Sorcher, 1985; Craut, Dunnette, McKenna, and Pedigo, 1989), we have developed a methodology for senior management selection. In addition, we have experimented with the use of information technology to create a cost-effective, efficient process, supported by computer. The results of this work appear to be positive: managers report significant improvement in the quality of the decisions made.

This chapter is intended to provide an overview of the approach we call *strategic selection*. First, we briefly review the conceptual basis for the approach. Second, we discuss in detail how we have implemented this approach and turned it into a series of action steps. Third, we step back and look at the question of CEO selection from a broader perspective. In the first two sections, the focus is on developing a rational-analytical approach to the selection process. In the third section, we consider other perspectives on executive selection, focusing specifically on the emotional and political dimensions of selecting people for executive positions.

The Concepts

The broad objective of strategic selection is to ensure that optimally effective decisions are made about the placement of people in senior-level jobs. The individual should have the highest probability of success in the job, and should learn and grow from doing it. These two goals frequently are in conflict: the jobs that people can do well may not be those from which they will learn, and vice versa. Thus, any decision (except perhaps for a final career placement) needs to balance these two criteria.

To achieve effective placement, the following elements are important:

- Job requirements must be described clearly with respect to the strategic context of the work, the organizational environment in which the work will be done, and the nature of the work itself.
- The strengths and weaknesses a person brings to a job as a consequence of his or her experience, training, and skills must be specified.
- A language system and process are necessary to compare individual capacities with job requirements in order to determine the areas where there is fit (and therefore the prospect of effective performance) and where there are gaps (and thus the potential for development).

Gerstein and Reisman (1983) provide a starting point for building the elements required for effective staffing decisions. In their review of the literature on executive effectiveness, they define the concept of strategic selection. They argue that any job exists within a strategic context or situation that shapes the requirements of the job and thus influences the characteristics of ideal candidates.

Their model (shown in Figure 9.1) represents a way of thinking about senior management jobs. They view different strategic situations as shaping different job thrusts, or the core requirements for success on the job. These different job thrusts, in turn, indicate the requirements of ideal candidates.

In their analysis, Gerstein and Reisman (1983) identify seven different strategic situations and then develop the specific job thrusts and candidate requirements for each situation. In addition, they identify twenty-three specific rating elements for use in assessing the requirements of candidates. These factors fall into seven major categories: (1) problem solving, (2) operations management, (3) human resources management, (4) strategic management, (5) organizational leadership, (6) self-management, and (7) general management knowledge. Finally, they propose a six-step approach to staffing decisions:

1. Specify the business condition and strategic direction.
2. Confirm or modify the organization structure.
3. Develop role descriptions for each key job in the structure.

Figure 9.1. The Strategic Selection Conceptual Model.

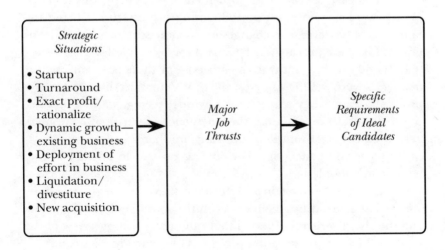

4.   Assess key personnel.
5.   Match individuals with positions.
6.   Implement.

Gerstein and Reisman thus provide some of the conceptual building blocks for a staffing process. They propose a strategy for thinking about jobs, provide a set of metrics for measuring jobs and
individuals, and outline a process for decision making.

The Process

Although the strategic selection framework is intuitively attractive,
it poses some significant practical problems. Early attempts to implement this framework met with significant resistance for a
number of reasons. In its initial applications in middle management positions, those involved in rating jobs and candidates did not
feel that those staffing decisions justified the time investment required. Second, many of those using the approach found it difficult
to organize the different pieces of data to make decisions. Third, the
process involved a large amount of manual calculation and paper-
work. This added time to the process and created issues about the
confidentiality of the information.

The early attempts to implement the strategic selection approach were therefore not overwhelmingly successful. During the
latter 1980s, however, two changes led to more successful implementation. First, the process was refocused on executive-level managers
(CEOs and other senior team members). For these positions, senior
managers were willing to invest the time demanded by a systematic
process, because they realized the obvious leverage gained in making better decisions. Second, the emergence of personal computers
permitted the creation of custom software that transformed a basically paper-and-pencil time-consuming process to an easy-to-use,
reliable methodology.

In practice, Gerstein and Reisman's seven strategic situations
are used as a backdrop; the focus is on the specific job requirements
and the characteristics of individual candidates. An overview of the
logic of the strategic selection process is presented in Figure 9.2.

Figure 9.2. Logic of the Strategic Selection Process.

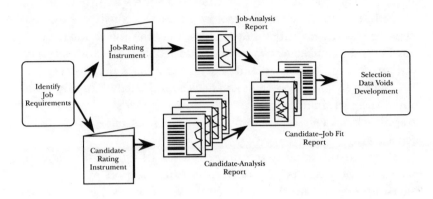

The first step of the process is identifying key job require-ments. The twenty-three rating elements of Gerstein and Reisman mentioned earlier are used as a starting point, but other items are frequently added. The elements have a number of uses. First, they are used to create a *job-rating instrument,* which describes the re-quirements of a particular job. The instrument is used by multiple raters and its results are displayed numerically and graphically in a *job-analysis report.*

While this is happening, the same elements are used to de-velop a *candidate-rating instrument,* which helps raters assess indi-vidual candidates. The data obtained from this tool are used to produce a *candidate-analysis report* for each candidate.

Finally, the *candidate–job fit report* offers an analysis that points out the areas where gaps exist between the candidate's capa-bilities and the position's requirements. This provides the basis for candidate selection.

In some cases, raters may not have adequate information to provide high-confidence assessments, which creates voids in data. Since the overall fit with requirements cannot be accurately evalu-ated without this information, raters will typically try to fill those voids before the selection process is completed. Finally, potential development actions might be identified based on the perceived gaps between a candidate's current abilities and a job's requirements.

In practice, the strategic selection process consists of thirteen steps, grouped into three major phases: (1) the job is rated or assessed; (2) the candidates are rated or assessed; and (3) candidate data and job data are compared and analyzed to make a decision (Figure 9.3). While each of these steps can be accomplished manually, computer support in the form of electronic spreadsheets and data-graphing packages or customized applications has proven to be beneficial.

We assume that two or more raters will rate both the candidates and the jobs. As part of the strategic selection process, these raters meet several times to work on the selection task. For purposes of illustration, we also assume that we are looking at one job with several candidates. The steps involved in rating the job follow:

1. *Identify jobs or job clusters.* Jobs to be rated may be individual positions or groups of positions with similar characteristics. Since a job may be a stepping-stone to another position, it is useful to identify this fact prior to moving to the next step.

Figure 9.3. Steps in the Strategic Selection Process.

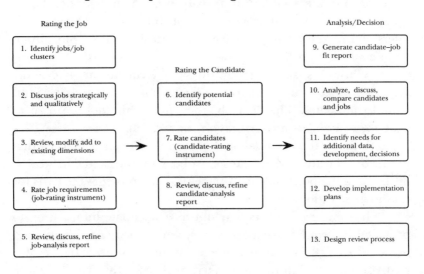

2. *Discuss job strategically and qualitatively.* With the Gerstein-Reisman concepts in the background, describe the strategic situation, identify major job thrusts, and list key job requirements. In a relatively unstructured discussion, talk through the raters' different perspectives.

3. *Review, modify, and add to existing dimensions.* Use the Gerstein and Reisman items as a starting point to create a framework that can be used to assess the job as well as the individual candidates.

4. *Rate job requirements using the job-rating instrument.* On a seven-point scale, indicate the degree to which strength in particular job requirements is required. An example of a strategic selection rating scale is shown in Figure 9.4. Indicate those requirements critical to a job by designating a "top five" group.

5. *Review, discuss, and refine the job-analysis report.* Combine the ratings to create numerical descriptors (and a graphic profile) that define the job—a job-analysis report. In practice, different raters have more or less information about the job. Therefore, the raters should discuss the ratings and, where appropriate, modify them to represent the consensus. In addition, review the "most im-

Figure 9.4. Example of a Strategic Selection Rating Scale.

Group management skills

Understanding when to work in a group as opposed to working individually; clearly establishing the group's agenda and objectives; conducting group discussion to maintain both participation and task focus; bringing closure to meetings by reviewing the results achieved and identifying any next steps to be undertaken.

   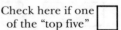

| 1 | 2 | 3 | 4 | 5 | 6 | 7 | Check here if one of the "top five" |

Low strength in this area is acceptable for this position. Moderate strength in this area is required for this position. Very great strength in this area is required for this position. *Notes:*

portant" nominations and decide on some "key dimensions," usually seven or less, that will be used later in the analysis.

    6. *Identify potential candidates.* Identify those who should be assessed as potential candidates for the job. Naturally, there are those who are logical successors and who have high potential. There might also be benchmark candidates, those who clearly could do the job, but are not currently candidates because they are not available or already have a comparable job. These people frequently are useful in calibrating the rating process. A third type of candidate would be the individual who is not yet ready for the job, according to conventional wisdom, but has high potential and might be selected if the decision makers are willing to take a risk.

    7. *Rate candidates using the candidate-rating instrument.* Assess the strength of candidates on each item, using a seven-point scale. The parallel candidate rating for the group management skills item presented earlier is shown in Figure 9.5. One key difference from the job-rating instrument is that the rater is asked to indicate the confidence he or she attaches to each rating (using a seven-point scale). This confidence rating has two purposes. First, when raters have lower confidence, they tend to move toward the

Figure 9.5. Sample Candidate-Analysis Rating Item.

Group management skills

Understanding when to work in a group as opposed to working individually; clearly establishing the group's agenda and objectives; conducting group discussion to maintain both participation and task focus; bringing closure to meetings by reviewing the results achieved and identifying any next steps to be undertaken.

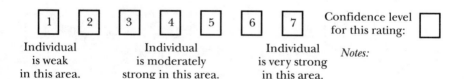

| | | | | | | | Confidence level for this rating: |
| 1 | 2 | 3 | 4 | 5 | 6 | 7 | |

Individual is weak in this area.　　Individual is moderately strong in this area.　　Individual is very strong in this area.　　*Notes:*

middle of the seven-point strength scale, confounding the data. Second, confidence ratings add important information by identifying when insufficient information is available to make reliable evaluations.

8. *Review, discuss, and refine the candidate-analysis report.* Combine the ratings of the candidate to create numerical descriptors (and a graphic profile) that describe the individual—the candidate-analysis report. As for the job-analysis report, discuss ratings and, where appropriate, modify them to represent the consensus.

9. *Generate candidate–job fit report.* Compare the ratings of individuals and job requirements by creating a report that highlights the degree to which each candidate fits the ideal profile. A sample report is shown in Figure 9.6.

10. *Analyze, discuss, and compare candidates and jobs.* Discuss the various options for placement or other actions.

11. *Identify needs for additional data, developmental actions, and decisions.* Assign candidates to the appropriate jobs. Fill data voids. Consider steps to develop candidates who have high potential but fall short on some requirements.

12. *Develop implementation plans.* Develop specific plans to implement the decisions made during step 11.

13. *Design review process.* Determine how the results of actions taken will be reviewed and how new data will be incorporated into the analysis.

Although the strategic selection process takes a good deal of effort and time, it has significant payoffs. The most obvious is improved decision making about job placement. In addition, the process leads to a better understanding of job requirements, which may be useful in future staffing decisions and helpful in managing the job. These requirements can be shared with the candidate who is placed in the job as a guide for action.

Since the process results in a more systematic assessment of candidates, those who manage the person in the job can be made aware of potential gaps and can compensate for them. In some cases, ratings have been shared with candidates as they start their new jobs.

The strategic selection process identifies data voids and thus indicates the information about the candidate that will be needed

Figure 9.6. Sample Candidate–Job Fit Report.

Dimension	1	4	7	Req.	MMJ
1. Problem identification and analysis				5.00	5.50
2. Solution implementation				5.50	7.00
3. Execution and control				5.50	5.50
4. Communications with others				3.79	5.50
5. Delegation				4.93	5.00
6. Crisis management				7.00	4.00
7. Negotiation skills				6.50	5.14
8. Integrated H.R. approach				6.00	7.00
9. Staffing				6.00	5.50
10. Development of subordinates				6.00	6.00
11. Conceptualizing the strategic environment				6.50	5.50
12. Strategic decision making				6.50	7.00
13. Strategic process management				4.00	6.00
14. Openness to innovation and change				3.50	3.00
15. Interpersonal empathy and influence				4.50	5.00
16. Group-management skills				5.50	6.00
17. Large-system "savoir faire"				6.50	6.50
18. Self-motivation				6.50	4.50
19. Emotional strength and maturity				5.50	6.00
20. Personal integrity				7.00	4.50
21. Technical knowledge				5.00	4.00
22. Functional knowledge				5.00	6.50
23. Environmental knowledge and perspective				6.00	4.50

Fit Statistic (1–100)	76
Average Confidence (1–7)	

> *Legend:*
> Requirements ●   Michael Jones ■

over time. In this way, it provides a guide for observing the candidate in subsequent assignments. The process also provides concrete documentation that can be used to describe the selection process to others. This may be important if the process is particularly emotional or political, as discussed in the next section.

Executive Succession

The strategic selection process is fundamentally a rational approach to making executive-level staffing decisions. It attempts to focus the decision maker on objective data through detached analysis, using a logical, disciplined sequence for making decisions.

Although movement toward rational decision making is admirable, it runs counter to much of what we know about how organizations function and how staffing decisions are really made (Cohen, March, and Olsen, 1972). It would therefore be naive to assume that one can or even should create a perfectly objective and rational process. In fact, several different perspectives exist on executive selection, particularly when that selection involves the CEO or jobs that lead toward the CEO position. Three different ways of looking at executive selection combine to provide a more integrated view of the process (Figure 9.7).

The first perspective, the one that has been emphasized so far in this chapter, is the analytical perspective. It views executive selection as a rational, analytical process aided by the collection and analysis of objective data through an explicit and defined work process. It emphasizes an understanding of the requirements of the job and of the strengths and weaknesses of individuals, an assessment of the trade-offs among alternative choices, and finally decision making on the basis of admittedly imperfect and incomplete data.

The second perspective is the emotional perspective. The choice of senior executives is a highly emotional event. Individuals are frequently involved in choosing those who will carry on their legacy. As there are often strong personal relationships between those making the decisions and those whose fates are being decided, feelings of obligation, guilt, and embarrassment may surface.

Figure 9.7. Executive Selection: An Integrated View.

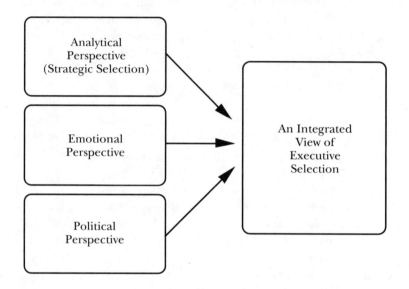

Emotions perhaps run highest when CEOs must decide on their successors (Sonnenfeld, 1988). There is a tendency to resist thinking about succession because they do not want to confront the issues of mortality inherent in retiring. Because the choice of successor is so critical and so leveraged, CEOs may become obsessed with making the right decision. This may lead to overintensive analysis, an inability to find a candidate who fills the bill, or in some cases, paralysis. Because many aspire to the position, the CEO, on making a choice, may have to deal with the negative consequences of decisions for other individuals who wanted the job. Finally, there is frequently an unconscious desire to replicate oneself. Although rational analysis may point to a need for a different type of individual, particularly when the company is in the midst of change, the natural tendency is for individuals to feel most comfortable with people whom they experience as similar to themselves.

In addition to the rational and emotional perspectives, there is a third point of view. Executive succession occurs within the context of an organization, which is a political system. The organization is made up of different individuals, groups, and coalitions that compete for power. The appointment of an individual to a senior position, particularly that of CEO, usually introduces profound changes in the political topography of the organization. The succession decision-making process therefore may be highly charged politically (Vancil, 1987).

The major political issues in succession concern the various stakeholders who feel they have something to gain or lose from the decision. In general, there are four types of stakeholders. First, there are the contenders, or candidates. They may become actively involved in attempting to influence the decision-making process, in particular in surfacing data about themselves or other candidates that they feel will help their prospects. In some instances, candidates engage in destructive conflict aimed at discrediting other candidates, frequently with major negative consequences for the organization. Second, there are the various internal constituencies who may support or undercut candidates. Over time, different groups and coalitions emerge who may view the choice of a particular candidate as positive or negative. They also may attempt to influence the decision-making process. Third, there frequently are external stakeholders, including unions, regulatory officials, large shareholders, suppliers, and major customers, who have an interest in the process and may attempt to intervene. Finally, for senior-level positions, and especially for the CEO position, the board of directors is a major stakeholder and potentially a key player in the executive staffing process.

Summary

The integrated view of executive selection presented in this chapter suggests that the selection process proceeds concurrently at three levels—rational, emotional, and political. Each level possesses its own dynamics, yet the three levels must be managed simultaneously. Therefore, a number of actions are important in designing, managing, and supporting an effective executive staffing process:

1. Start early.
2. Structure and manage succession decision making as a conscious, explicit process.

3.   Actively manage constituencies.
4.   Avoid horse races, which maximize the negative political dynamics associated with succession.
5.   Allow the emotional issues to surface.
6.   Build in needed staff support (human resources executives, consultants).

Staffing decisions at the senior levels of an organization are decisions with great leverage. The consequences of an ineffective choice can run into the hundreds of millions of dollars and may last years. Although these choices are recognized as important, little work has been done to develop the tools necessary to make effective decisions. The strategic selection process described in this paper is one such tool. It appears to be a viable approach with the potential of improving senior-level selection decisions. At the same time, we recognize that executive selection, and in particular the selection of a CEO, is a complex process and involves rational, emotional, and political perspectives that must be managed together.

References

Cohen, M. D., March, J. G., and Olsen, J. P. "A Garbage Can Model of Organizational Choice." *Administrative Science Quarterly,* 1972, *17*, 1–25.

Craut, A., Dunnette, M. D., McKenna, D., and Pedigo, R. "The Role of the Manager: What's Really Important in Different Management Jobs." *Academy of Management Executive,* 1989, *3*(2).

Gerstein, M. S., and Reisman, H. "Strategic Selection: Matching Executives to Business Conditions." *Sloan Management Review,* Winter 1983, 33–49.

Sonnenfeld, J. *The Hero's Farewell: What Happens When CEOs Retire.* New York: Oxford University Press, 1988.

Sorcher, M. *Predicting Executive Success.* New York: Wiley, 1985.

Vancil, R. F. *Passing the Baton: Managing the Process of CEO Succession.* Boston: Harvard Business School Press, 1987.

TEN

Teamwork at the Top:
Creating Executive Teams That Work

DAVID A. NADLER, DEBORAH ANCONA

Chief executives in firms based in the United States have discovered something new—teamwork. Team-based organization designs are replacing traditional executive structures. In fact, in many companies such titles as president and chief operating officer have disappeared from the organization chart and been replaced with management committee, policy committee, or corporate office. Although the two-person chief executive officer/chief operating officer (CEO/COO) structure still appears to be prominent, the team model seems to be emerging as a strong and viable alternative. A recent study of 277 firms drawn from the *Fortune* Service 500 and Industrial 500 revealed that during the 1960–1964 period, the team mode appeared in only 8 percent of the companies in the sample but, by the 1980–1984 period, increased to 25 percent (Vancil, 1987).

The emergence of teamwork at the top poses a number of questions for the executive who shapes and designs senior jobs: What do teams at the top look like? Why have these team-based designs emerged? How are senior teams different from other types of teams? How does one design and lead an effective senior team? What types of teamwork are needed in different situations? What types of special problems plague senior teams?

During the past eight years, we have explored these questions through a combination of research and in-depth consultation. The research has focused on discovering the determinants of team performance in different work settings (Ancona, 1987, 1989) and has included senior business teams, product development teams, and sales teams. The consultation has involved intensive work with

seven executive-level teams and approximately twenty other senior
business management teams of *Fortune* 500-type organizations for
periods of one to eight years. The work has included close interaction with team leaders and members as they tackle different tasks,
challenges, and problems.

Through this joint research and consultation effort, a picture
of the effective executive team has emerged. In particular, we have
found that three issues drive the need for and management of executive teams: responding to the complex and often changing external environment of the firm, managing the diverse yet interdependent units inside the corporation, and shaping the process of
executive succession. The recognition and management of these
issues need to be kept in mind as we discuss the nature, effectiveness,
and management of executive teams.

What Is an Executive Team?

During the 1960s, an approach to structuring executive roles and
work called the CEO/COO model emerged in the United States.
This structure (shown in Figure 10.1) typically includes a chairman
of the board serving as the chief executive officer, a president serving
as chief operating officer and reporting to the CEO, and a number
of executives each responsible for particular units and reporting to
the COO.

Work is allocated so that the CEO is responsible for strategic
issues, external relations, and overall corporate governance, whereas
the COO has primary responsibility for running internal company
operations. The COO might meet regularly with his or her executives. The role of the individual executives is to manage their own
pieces of the organization consistent with the strategies and direction established at the top. Although specific roles varied from company to company, by the 1960s this two-person structure became the
dominant form of organizing major U.S. corporations at the executive level (Vancil, 1987).

During the 1980s, a different type of organizational design
emerged: a *team* of executives reporting to the CEO. This group
collectively assumes the role of the COO in managing internal operations and may even take on some of the CEO's role in formulat-

**Figure 10.1. Chief Executive Officer/Chief Operating Officer Model:
Typical Two-Person Structure.**

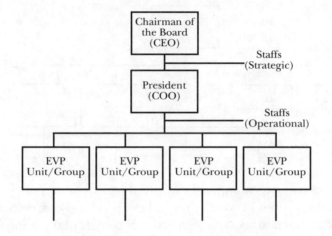

ing strategy and managing external relations. If set up effectively, such a group is more than a set of individuals who work together; it is a truly interdependent, interacting team (Schein, 1969). Team members have a sense of identity (they perceive themselves as a unit), they are interdependent (they depend on each other to produce their output), and they have joint outcomes (their rewards and punishments are affected by each other).

Figure 10.2 displays an example of this type of executive team, in this case a corporate management committee, which is the senior team of a diversified technology-intensive manufacturing and services company. The corporate management committee is composed of three group presidents, each responsible for a particular strategic sector of the company, and two vice-chairmen, one for technology and one for all corporate staff functions. This team was created when a new CEO was named on retirement of the existing CEO and COO who had been part of a traditional two-person structure. The new CEO announced that he was going to run the company differently. He created the corporate management committee and spent a good deal of time with the group developing a shared vision for the company, including a set of strategies, a statement of values, and operating principles. The group presidents, in partic-

Figure 10.2. Corporate Management Committee: Diversified Technology-Intensive Manufacturing and Services.

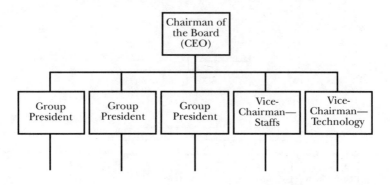

ular, found themselves suddenly involved in corporate policy and direction discussions in which they had not previously participated, as they were asked to take the perspective of owners of the company.

An increasing number of organizations are adopting organization charts similar to that shown in Figure 10.2, although the nomenclature may be different—for example, office of the chairman, policy committee, or corporate office. New organization charts alone do not make an executive team. The core defining characteristic is that there exists a group of people who collectively take on the role of providing strategic, operational, and institutional leadership for the organization. Each member is responsible for her or his own unit but also wears another "hat," that of corporate leadership.

Why Have Executive Teams Emerged?

The fundamental rationale for establishing any team, including executive teams, is the creation of synergy—effective coordination of functions and activities so that the performance of the whole is greater than the sum of its parts. Synergy, or what has been called a group "assembly bonus" (Collins and Guetzkow, 1964), is realized when the added value of the team is greater than the process loss or overhead incurred as a consequence of having to coordinate and manage the collective work (Nadler, 1985). This capacity to initiate and execute collaborative effort to create added value is at the core of designing and managing executive teams. Effective teamwork is reflected in the quality of strategic and operational decisions made, in the ability of the team to translate decisions into actions, and, ultimately, in the quality of organizational performance.

Why has the shift to executive teams seemed to have accelerated recently? Again, three factors seem to account for team formation: external demands, organizational complexity, and succession. There seem to be several environmental trends which, when coupled with some specific internal conditions, lead to the emergence of executive teams.

At the broadest cultural level, teams have come to be viewed as a more acceptable form of organizing, particularly because of the effective use of team structures by the Japanese and other foreign competitors. In contrast to the bias toward rugged individualism that prevailed for many years in U.S. organizations, the idea of managing through teams at the executive level is seen as a more legitimate concept today.

External business pressures have also played a role in intensifying the demands on corporate leadership and the demands on the CEO in particular. Increasing global competition, technology-based change, and turbulence in financial markets have added to the burden of the CEO. The need to spend more time on strategies to meet environmental instability has had to be balanced with a focus on short-term performance, driven by shareholder demands and concerns about takeover. As a consequence, CEOs have found themselves looking for help in both strategic and operational tasks.

Not only have environments been changing, but the pace of change itself has increased. As a result, large-scale strategic changes are occurring in organizations at a very fast pace (Tushman and Romanelli, 1985). CEOs seem to feel the need for a broader base of participation in providing leadership for the organization.

Although these environmental trends appear to necessitate the formation of an executive team, the more immediate catalyst for this design is usually events occurring inside the organization. In addition to external events, executive teams emerge because of the need to manage diverse yet interdependent organizational units or because of the need of the CEO to manage succession-related issues. One way of thinking about these various elements is to describe the three distinct scenarios that we have observed in relation to the formation of an executive team. The first is related to the internal management challenges, the second two are related to management succession.

The Business Diversity Scenario

This scenario is driven by the diversity and complexity of the parts of the organizations. In those companies where diversification has created multibusiness or multi-industry activities in the context of a more unstable and demanding environment, the CEOs may feel that it would be difficult for individual COOs to provide the needed direction and integration across the diverse units, so they form executive teams to perform the COO function. Furthermore, many companies have begun to experiment with new organizational forms such as networks, neoconglomerates, and alliances (Galbraith and Kazanjian, 1988). These new forms add to the amount and complexity of the demands on the senior operating executive, often creating jobs that no one individual can perform effectively and, thus, leading to the creation of multiple COO roles through a team structure.

Thus, the complexity of managing diverse businesses and new structures motivates the CEO to form a team to take on the work that would be difficult for a single COO to accomplish. The CEO believes that through the team, many minds will be working on a problem and the company will benefit from the collective wisdom and intellect of the team. Examples of this scenario are the office of the chairman structure used at AT&T for years and the management committee that CEO Jamie Houghton created and led at Corning, Inc.

The New Chief Executive Officer Scenario

When new CEOs take office, particularly when they were not COOs prior to succession, they often hesitate to designate COOs for several reasons. First, the new CEOs may want to maintain direct contact with those parts of the business with which they are less familiar. Second, they may not want to put a layer of management between themselves and the major business units during the initial stage of their terms when they are creating a leadership agenda and putting their stamp on the organization. Third, they may not want to designate a successor through the appointment of a COO, because such a move narrows the ultimate choices and perhaps leads other executives to believe they have less opportunity. Therefore, new CEOs create teams that work directly with them in leading the organization. Examples of this approach are seen in John Reed's structuring of the Citicorp senior management following succession from Walter Wriston and, similarly, Walter Shipley's creation of the three-president structure at Chemical Bank in the early 1980s.

The Executive Selection Scenario

As CEOs contemplate the choice of a successor, they modify the structure, frequently by retiring the current COO, to create an executive team which includes a number of the succession candidates. The team then becomes an arena for assessing, selecting, and preparing successors. This team provides the CEO and the board of directors with an opportunity to observe the candidates as they work together on business problems. The CEO is able to test the quality of the candidates' thinking, their leadership skills, and their relationships with others in senior management. Notable examples of this scenario are seen in the structures created by Reginald Jones at General Electric, Ted Brophy at GTE, and Walter Wriston at Citicorp during the early 1980s.

The three scenarios develop over time. For example, at Citicorp, Walter Wriston, the chairman and CEO, created a team of three vice-chairmen, which he referred to as the "vice squad," following the retirement of President William Spencer in 1981 and used this team explicitly as part of his selection process. One of those vice-chairmen, John Reed, who spent most of his career in consumer banking, was chosen as the new CEO. Reed chose not to designate a president and COO and, instead, created an "open management structure." He initially devoted much time and attention to the investment and institutional banking activities, rather than the consumer bank from which he had come. Despite the fact that

Reed became familiar with the nonconsumer activities in the organization and put his strategic and management agenda in place, he continued to use the team structure, consistent with the business diversity scenario. Thus, CEOs may manage and create teams through different scenarios, and they may move in and out of using team approaches.

How Are Executive Teams Different from Other Teams?

Are executive teams any different from other management teams that might be encountered in an organization? Our research, consultation, and observation indicates that very significant differences exist between executive teams and other teams we have observed. Members of nonexecutive teams are often unprepared by their previous experiences for the dynamics they encounter in the executive team. These differences also pose some unique challenges for the structuring and managing of these teams:

> *Salience of the external environment.* The executive team is uniquely influenced by external forces, particularly customers, competitors, financial markets, the board of directors, and shareholders. Understanding and managing that environment are more important for the executive team than for other teams.
>
> *Complexity of the task.* As noted above, the executive team today faces a set of tasks or work requirements that are potentially more complex than most other teams. The combination of internal operations management, external relationship management, institutional leadership, and strategic decision making creates a task that has many more interrelated elements and greater uncertainty than the tasks facing most other teams.
>
> *Intensified political behavior.* The essence of the executive team is power, or the exercise of influence over the behavior of others. In that environment, therefore, the presence of politics is much more pronounced, and explicit political behavior appears to be more frequent than in other teams.

Fixed pie reward contingencies. While there are many rewards for executive team members, the ultimate reward is succession—who ends up as the CEO or team leader. By definition, succession creates a zero sum game and thus a perception of a fixed pie of rewards. If one person wins, others have to lose.

Increased visibility. The executive team is the symbol of institutional leadership; therefore, the actions, interactions, and dynamics of the team are carefully watched by others in the organization. What might otherwise be small and inconsequential interactions become major events. Executive team watching is a popular spectator sport in many organizations, and this may magnify some of the win/lose dynamics among individual members.

Composition. Individuals become members of the executive team through a multiyear process of selection. Although it is dangerous to generalize, in the firms we have observed, individuals selected for the executive team tend to be power seekers and high achievers. They also have histories of distinguishing themselves through individual achievement, rather than through their work with or through teams. Thus, in many companies based in the United States, the executive team is composed of people who have been brought up and rewarded for their successes in the "rugged individualism" model of management; therefore, they may be less prepared than their colleagues at lower levels, to either lead or participate in effective teams.

Special meaning of team membership. While membership and inclusion are important issues in many teams, membership in the executive team has special meaning. Just being a member of the ultimate team in the organization has special status and symbolism. Frequently people talk about the importance of "sitting at the big table" as a shorthand for membership in the executive team. As a result, the questions of who becomes a member, how members are initiated, what it means to lose membership in the team, and so forth become of much more concern than in other teams.

Unique role of the chief executive officer as team leader. A key difference in the executive team is that the team leader is the CEO. As a consequence, there may be more social distance between the leader and the team members in an executive team than in other teams. The CEO is not only the team leader, but the ultimate determiner of rewards, particularly succession. Unlike other teams, there is usually no recourse beyond the CEO; if there are relationship or performance problems that arise between individual team members and the CEO, there is no place else to go. The CEO's tenure is also more defined than in other teams. It is at the same time more finite.

In light of these factors, the dynamics of the executive team significantly differ from those of other teams. There are some features that are specifically unique to the executive team: the role of succession, the salience of the external environment, and the intensity of the political processes and issues. Some of the features of executive teams occur in other teams (for example, complex tasks and special meaning of membership) but what is unique is that all of these tend to occur concurrently and intensely in the executive team.

What Contributes to Effective Teamwork at the Top?

The approach to executive teams shown in Figure 10.3 is based on some general models of group performance (Hackman, 1983; McGrath, 1984; Shea and Guzzo, 1987). Because traditional models often deal primarily with internal processes, we have expanded the model to emphasize two issues that are particularly salient for senior teams: external relations and succession. Executive team performance is determined by how three core team processes are managed over time. These processes are, in turn, shaped by certain critical aspects of executive team design.

What are some of the key features of the model? To begin, team performance is seen as having two dimensions. *Production of results* reflects the team's ability to effectively meet the demands of

Figure 10.3. A Model of Executive Team Effectiveness.

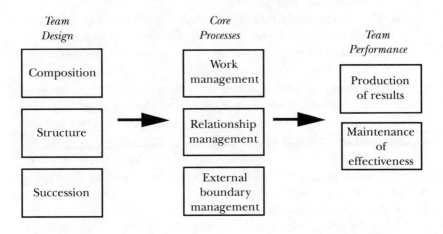

its role. At the executive level, this includes consistent positive re-sults (earnings, growth, returns), maintenance of organizational performance in the face of strategic and environmental challenges, quality of decision making, ability to implement decisions, and quality of institutional leadership.

Maintenance of effectiveness, the second dimension of team performance, requires that the team satisfy its members' needs, that team members work together over time, and that the team is flexible in response to challenges.

Executive team performance is seen as being directly influ-enced by the quality, effectiveness, and appropriate shaping of three core processes:

> *Work management process.* This includes how the team or-ganizes and manages itself to perform work: how it shares information, how the work agenda of the team is set, how the team goes about making decisions, how the team coor-dinates the activities of different individuals and groups, and so on. In executive teams, the work is primarily strat-egy, policy, and operating decisions. Work management,

therefore, concerns how the team gets those decisions made and implemented.

Relationship management process. This involves how the team manages the nature and quality of relationships among team members. Some key elements include the degree of openness between members, how conflicts are resolved, the nature of support expressed among members, the cohesiveness of the group, and the degree of trust. In executive teams, the issue is how to manage relationships in the context of the political, symbolic, and succession factors mentioned above, particularly when team members may be geographically distant or not in direct daily contact with each other.

External boundary management process. This concerns how the team deals with factors and elements outside of the team and outside of the organization. As mentioned above, this is a particularly important process for executive teams. It includes how boundaries are defined, how key external actors are identified, and how boundary management approaches or strategies are developed. In executive teams, boundary management may focus on actors outside of the organization such as financial markets, the media, key customers, competitors, and governments, but these teams also manage the boundary between the team itself and the organization that it leads.

The effectiveness of an executive team is determined by how well the team manages these three processes to meet demands and exploit opportunities. While the three core processes can be directly managed and fashioned by the team leader, they are also highly influenced by several factors that can be shaped ahead of time. We call these *elements of team design:*

Composition. The mixture of skills and experience in the team obviously has an impact on the team's ability to work on different problems and tasks. In addition, the extent to which the team shares values and perspectives also greatly impacts relationship management issues.

Structure. Different teams may have varying formal structures. In executive teams, team structure is determined by the organizational design decisions that establish the positions in the team. Structure also includes the size of the team, the boundaries, the specific formal roles, the goals, and the nature of team and individual rewards.

Succession. Succession reflects the scenario that has been created for the team, the resulting perceptions of team members about succession, and expectations about how their performance and behavior affect their succession prospects.

What Types of Teamwork Are Needed in Different Situations?

The executive team effectiveness model identifies some of the key elements that have an impact on team performance. Yet we have shied away from identifying the set of universal characteristics of a good team. Effective teams facing different strategic environments and created in disparate scenarios require different types of teamwork. Investing time and effort in the work management, relationship management, and boundary management processes where teamwork adds little value does not make sense. The decision to develop and work on the executive team has cost or overhead associated with it, including the time required, the potential delay in decision making, the creation of added interfaces and thus coordination costs, and the increased burden of managing more relationships.

Effective executive teams appear to be those that focus their efforts on the appropriate core processes given the strategic context of the team. Two contextual factors must be considered. The first is the *environmental context*, or the nature of the external demands that are placed on the organization by the environment. These demands are determined by the degree of threat posed by the environment, the pace of change in the environment, the complexity of the environment, and the degree to which important factors in the environment are outside the control of the executive team. Obviously, the greater the demands of the environment, the more attention the team needs to pay to external boundary management processes.

A second dimension is the *structural context* of the executive team, or the degree of interdependence (and, therefore, requirements for coordination) among the major organizational units. The degree of interdependence is determined by several factors. One determinant is the strategic choices the organization makes concerning its portfolio of businesses and the resultant strategic interdependence that exists among them. For example, a vertically integrated company has higher interdependence at the top level than a company following a strategy of unrelated diversification (Michel and Hambrick, 1988; Rumelt, 1974). Another determinant is the organizational design decisions that result in more or less interdependent organizational units. A company grouped into business units typically exhibits less interdependence than if it is grouped by functions. The greater the internal coordination requirements, the greater the demand for focus on internal work management processes and the greater the requirements for focus on the relationship management in support of effective work management.

This contextual approach is shown graphically in Figure 10.4. Those situations with low coordination requirements and low environmental demands (context 1, the upper left-hand cell in Figure 10.4) require relatively little team process management. What is required is the most minimal level of work management around the broadest institutional issues where there is some common fate or interdependence. In practice, this means that the executive team merely needs to focus on information exchange among members.

Organizations in this category might be holding companies in industries with relatively low levels of market and technical change. Here the top team is more like a set of portfolio managers, pushing managerial decisions down to the diversified businesses at a lower level in the organization. High levels of integration are not needed in these teams, and therefore studies have shown that establishment of a cohesive group is not related to performance (Michel and Hambrick, 1988; Song, 1982). Teams facing low coordination and environmental demands need only develop rudimentary group process skills such as the ability to call meetings, follow agendas, and surface information relevant to the few joint decisions team members must make. Meetings can be formal and infrequent.

Context 2—high internal coordination requirements but low

**Figure 10.4. Critical Processes for Senior Team Performance:
A Contextual Approach.**

		Structural Context (Internal Coordination Requirements)	
		Low	High
Environmental Context (Complexity/instability of external demands)	Low	1. Minimal work management (information exchange)	2. Internal work management and relationship management
	High	3. External boundary management	4. Multiprocess management

environmental demands—is best typified by the large integrated business in a relatively stable industry. In fact, a decreasing number of large organizations fall into this category. Currently, only those companies that hold monopolies, are in protected industries, or are part of an oligopoly face environments that are stable and do not make significant new demands. Consequently, many organizations previously categorized as context 2 now face different conditions and must change their processes accordingly.

For those teams that remain in context 2, the focus is on the internal work management and relationship management processes. In contrast to organizations in context 1, the companies are often functionally organized; thus, decisions are not easily delegated to lower levels and organizational units need to be more tightly coupled. Top management teams end up making major decisions about products, markets, technologies, structures, and stance toward the competition. These teams need to be cohesive, engage in frequent and open communication, and have well-managed meetings. Coordination across members is key to success. The smooth work and relationship management processes required in context 2 are facilitated by a relatively homogeneous, long-term executive team.

In those situations where there are low coordination requirements but high environmental demands (context 3), the team should focus its greatest effort on the external boundary management process. Academic institutions, professional service firms, and diversified companies in dynamic, heterogeneous environments exemplify this context. Much of the operational work is delegated to the executives responsible for particular segments of the organization. There is relatively little operational interdependence among those groups, and sometimes there is also little strategic interdependence. Examples include industrial companies that have developed significant financial services businesses separate from the core manufacturing business.

In context 3, the team is not involved in management of the interdependent work among the units. It focuses on the corporation as an entity, its strategy and policies, and its relationships with various external groups. Team members in this context must represent the corporation externally, negotiate agreements with outsiders, promote the organizational image to competitors and allies, work with the media, scan and monitor key external groups, and ward off unwelcome advances from other corporations.

Finally, in those situations where there are high internal coordination requirements and high environmental demands (context 4), the team needs to manage all three processes effectively at the same time, or engage in multiprocess management. Computer firms and other high-technology companies, for example, face turbulent markets and are often integrated businesses. Here, teams face the difficult challenge of adapting to changing demands while needing to show internal leadership in setting the priorities and direction that mobilize people. The external monitoring and communication with outsiders who have different values, priorities, and viewpoints that are needed to meet environmental demands in context 3 breed conflict within the team as the multiple perspectives are juxtaposed and evaluated (Dougherty, 1987); however, because teams in context 3 have relatively low coordination requirements, this conflict can be easily managed. In context 4, however, the conflict must be managed and the team must exhibit sophisticated processes.

Teams in context 4 must bring together members with high social skills who are able to negotiate and compromise, to pool information from multiple sources, and to blend analysis and action (Bourgeois and Eisenhardt, 1988; Quinn, 1982). Team members must meet more frequently with each other and with outsiders than is the case in the other conditions. Team members must always work multiple agendas, trying to pull disparate individuals together toward an ever-changing target.

It is important to keep in mind that effective teams do not completely ignore any of the core processes. Rather, teams focus the bulk of their time and energy on ensuring that processes critical to the team's current context are developed and managed. When the prospect of strategic change faces the organization, the team may also work on developing competencies that, while not critical at the moment, may be critical in the near future as the organization's context changes.

Common Problems in Executive Teams

The approach presented in this chapter suggests how to manage in different contexts, but implementing the appropriate team process is often difficult. In our work with executive teams, we have encountered seven common problems related either to setup of the executive team or management of core processes.

Synthetic Teamwork

Many so-called executive teams do not actually engage in teamwork. The group is not a real team—it is synthetic. The leader of the team does not want or require increased coupling and coordination, and therefore nothing more than information sharing happens in the team. There is no coordinated effort and no synergy.

Thus, the team is formed and presented as being in context 2 or 4, but is really in context 1.

There are several negative consequences to synthetic teamwork. The creation of a team leads to expectations that the team will take action, make decisions, or lead. When this does not occur, there is often a perceived leadership vacuum, a loss of executive credibility, and frustration throughout the organization. To the extent that there is no one performing the COO function and coordination is indeed required, the lack of true teamwork may cripple decision making and implementation.

Cosmetic Teamwork

In certain executive teams, while the trappings of teamwork and cooperation are created, the day-by-day behavior of the team members not only indicates lack of teamwork, but frequently reveals intensely negative relationships among the members. In cosmetic teamwork, there are surface level behaviors, particularly in formal team meetings, which affirm the team, the value of teamwork, and the importance of trust, openness, and collaborative effort. In truth, however, effective relationship management processes are absent. Team members interact in subgroups, between meetings and in other settings, and complain about other members or plan noncollaborative or destructive actions (Eisenhardt and Bourgeois, 1988).

Cosmetic teamwork often occurs when an executive team structure is created to enhance collaboration and coordinated effort but the underlying scenario (including issues of rewards and succession) is one that motivates people to work in competitive as opposed to collaborative modes. Similarly, cosmetic teamwork occurs when the CEO claims to want teamwork but is unwilling to give up any control. Because teamwork is often articulated by the CEO as socially desirable behavior, the trappings of collaboration occur in the presence of the leader but are not carried into the day-to-day interactions among the members.

Underdesigned Teams

Frequently, executive teams run into trouble because they are "underdesigned"; the team has been established but composition has not been thought through, the structure (size, boundaries, goals, roles, rewards) has not been adequately developed, and the succession scenario has not been clearly defined. These teams gather together, but are incapacitated. In the worse cases, the wrong people are "at the table," attempting to do the wrong work, with unclear goals and roles, few rewards for true teamwork, and ill-defined succession scenarios that create relationship problems. In these cases, the CEO has not taken the time and effort to develop the needed design of the executive team and has not worked with the team to implement the design.

Consensus Management

Many CEOs have limited experience in team leadership and management. They create an executive team but have no idea of how to harness the energies of the team. They do not know how to create effective work management and relationship management processes. This is particularly problematic for teams that are moving into a multiprocess mode. Not wanting to dominate the team, the CEO mistakenly shifts to the other side of the spectrum and ends up providing no direction for the team; the result is consensus management. While there are a few situations where consensus is an appropriate method for decision making, the more effective teams we have observed tend to make different decisions in different ways; they choose the decision-making process that is most appropriate for the issue. Some decisions are made in a consultative mode, with the CEO receiving input and discussing options with the team but retaining the role of ultimate decision maker. Other decisions may be made through a negotiation between the individuals most directly involved in the decision and the CEO, while in some cases consensus is appropriate. When all decisions become consensual, however, the team usually gets bogged down and loses effectiveness.

In consensus management, the CEO mistakes participation and collaboration for a lack of direction and structure. The resulting laissez-faire work process results in ineffective decision making and risk aversion. The problem is usually not the team, but rather the inability of its leader to lead.

Good Plow/Wrong Field

Another common problem is that the team places its effort in the wrong processes. For example, an executive team that faces major environmental challenges but works on the internal work management processes to the point of neglecting the boundary management issues may be doing things right but is not doing the right things. This contextual misalignment results in an executive team that does not have the capacity to understand and manage the processes that are responsive to the critical strategic challenges.

Inertia

Frequently, executive teams run into trouble because they become so comfortable with the team processes that fit their context that they take those processes to an extreme. For example, teams in context 2 may excel in work and relationship management processes, but when cohesion is too high, negative consequences can ensue. Members of highly cohesive groups want to maintain cohesiveness so much that they do not critique each other and may follow decisions they believe are wrong to avoid conflict. Similarly, high cohesion leads to isolation of the group and the inability to detect warning signals and change in the environment (Dutton and Duncan, 1987; Janis, 1982). In contrast, team members in context 3 may excel at boundary management but become so engaged in external activity that they lose their allegiance to the team. These teams find it difficult to get members to commit to team decisions.

Succession Overhang

Succession is a fundamental issue that can hang over the team, shaping the nature of team relationships and, thus, the relationship management processes. Poisoned relationship management processes can, in turn, incapacitate work management and boundary management processes. The two succession-related executive team scenarios have different impacts, both negative. In the executive selection scenario, the "horse race" creates an inherently competitive situation that motivates individuals not to collaborate. This is the exact opposite of what is required for effective teamwork. Team members perceive that their individual stakes overwhelm the stakes deriving from the success or failure of the team as a whole, at least in the short term. Competitive and, in some cases, destructive behavior results. At the least, cosmetic teamwork starts to occur. Similarly, in the new CEO scenario, the aftermath of the succession decision can create interpersonal dynamics that make teamwork difficult or impossible. Losing candidates may be team members, and they may feel wounded or attempt to prove (consciously or not) that the choice was incorrect. In the new administration, team members may be anxious about their position and their evolving relationship with the new CEO who so recently was a peer and perhaps a competitor. Despite the statements of the new CEO, individuals may perceive that a COO will be named, so a secondary succession scenario begins. All of these factors potentially contribute to significant problems in the relationships in the team.

The aforementioned problems, though not all-inclusive, are fairly common and can severely undermine team effectiveness. Most of these problems can be prevented through thoughtful design of the team and deliberate management of the team's core processes.

Summary

The executive team has emerged as a viable alternative for organizing work at the top level of complex organizations because of three sets of demands: external demands posed by the environment, internal demands posed by the requirements of running diverse but interdependent organizations, and unique demands created by executive succession. Not surprisingly, effective executive teams need to be able to manage the three sets of issues raised by these demands. They must organize to manage external complexity and internal work requirements and relationships, while coping with both the reality and the perceptions associated with succession.

Teams in different situations face varying degrees of intensity and combinations of these demands. As we have illustrated through the contextual approach presented above, the more effective teams appear to be those that focus their time, energy, and resources on the issues critical in their context. Using composition, structure, and the succession scenario to create the core processes that meet internal and external requirements clearly is the most critical single challenge in creating effective executive teams. The executive team is a higher-risk/higher-reward structure than the traditional CEO/ COO model. The rewards are earned by a team that provides quality leadership that no single individual COO could ever hope to replicate. Yet, significant risks exist when insufficient thought and care is given to the design and management of the team over time. One implication is that executive team structures make sense in many, though not all, situations. A second implication is that the CEO who seeks to employ this approach must be ready to invest the time, effort, and energy required to understand the requirements of the particular situation, to develop an appropriate team design, and to work on nurturing the evolution of the right core processes. When this effort is made, the rewards of teamwork at the top can be very significant.

References

Ancona, D. G. "Groups in Organizations: Extending Laboratory Models." In C. Hendrick (ed.), *Group Processes and Intergroup Relations.* Newbury Park, Calif.: Sage, 1987.

Ancona, D. G. "Top Management Teams: Preparing for the Revolution." In J. Carroll (ed.), *Social Psychology in Business Organizations.* Hillsdale, N.J.: Erlbaum, 1989.

Bourgeois, L. J., and Eisenhardt, K. M. "Strategic Decision Processes in High Velocity Environments: Four Cases in the Microcomputer Industry." *Management Science,* 1988, *34,* 816–835.

Collins, B. E., and Guetzkow, H. *The Social Psychology of Group Processes for Decision Making.* New York: Wiley, 1964.

Dougherty, D. *New Products in Old Organizations: The Myth of the Better Mousetrap in Search of the Beaten Path.* Unpublished Ph.D. dissertation, Sloan School of Management, Massachusetts Institute of Technology, 1987.

Dutton, J. E., and Duncan, R. B. "The Creation of Momentum for Change Through Strategic Issue Diagnosis." *Strategic Management Journal,* 1987, *8*(3), 279–296.

Eisenhardt, K. M., and Bourgeois, L. J. "The Politics of Strategic

Decision Making in Top Teams: A Study in the Microcomputer Industry." *Academy of Management Journal,* 1988, *31*(4), 737–770.

Galbraith, J. R., and Kazanjian, R. K. "Strategy, Technology, and Emerging Organizational Forms." In J. Hage (ed.), *Futures of Organizations: Innovating to Adapt Strategy and Human Resources to Rapid Technological Change.* Lexington, Mass.: Lexington Books, 1988.

Hackman, J. R. "The Design of Work Teams." In J. W. Lorsch (ed.), *Handbook of Organizational Behavior.* Englewood Cliffs, N.J.: Prentice Hall, 1983.

Janis, I. *Groupthink.* Boston: Houghton-Mifflin, 1982.

McGrath, J. E. *Groups: Interaction and Performance.* Englewood Cliffs, N.J.: Prentice Hall, 1984.

Michel, J. G., and Hambrick, D. C. "Diversification Posture and the Characteristics of the Top Management Team." Working paper, Columbia Business School, 1988.

Nadler, D. A. *Designing Effective Work Teams.* New York: Delta Consulting Group, 1985.

Quinn, J. B. "Managing Strategies Incrementally." *Omega,* 1982, *10*, 613–627.

Rumelt, R. P. *Strategy, Structure, and Economic Performance.* Boston: Harvard University Press, 1974.

Schein, E. H. *Organizational Psychology.* Englewood Cliffs, N.J.: Prentice Hall, 1969.

Shea, G. P., and Guzzo, R. A. "Group Effectiveness: What Really Matters." *Sloan Management Review,* 1987, *3*, 25–31.

Song, J. H. "Diversification Strategies and the Experience of Top Executives of Large Firms." *Strategic Management Journal,* 1982, *3*(4), 377–380.

Tushman, M. L., and Romanelli, E. "Organizational Evolution: A Metamorphosis Model of Convergence and Reorientation." In L. L. Cummings and B. M. Staw (eds.), *Research in Organizational Behavior,* Vol. 7. Greenwich, Conn.: JAI Press, 1985.

Vancil, R. F. *Passing the Baton: Managing the Process of CEO Succession.* Boston: Harvard Business School Press, 1987.

ELEVEN

Strategic Choice: Engaging the Executive Team in Collaborative Strategy Planning

---

DAVID R. BLISS

Organizations around the world continue to seek ways to make strategic planning a significant value-adding effort. The tools have become very sophisticated, an army of experts stands ready to provide the answers, and executives at all levels devote significant time to the annual planning process. Despite more than forty years of evolution, however, strategic planning continues to fall short of the mark for many organizations. The laments are heard in the halls and conference rooms of organizations large and small:

> My judgment says we are going in the wrong, or different directions, but there is no place in our process for us to have that debate.

> I brought in the experts and they developed a strategy for us, but nothing is happening.

> They call this strategic planning, but it feels like budgeting.

> We spend all of our time in meetings, but we never have the time to deal with the real issues.

At the same time these complaints are being voiced, the rapid pace of change and increasing pressures of global competition require organizations to make strategic planning an integral part of the way they manage the business. Rapid reaction and the capacity to act effectively require a clear, coherent strategic envelope for distributed decision making and execution. The increasing demands of employees, shareholders, and the financial markets raise the stakes significantly.

Why are so many organizations frustrated by the results of their strategy development efforts? Part of the answer lies in the fact that the planning process has taken on a life of its own and does not provide the environment and mechanisms for senior management to debate the significant choices that may be required to achieve or sustain real competitive advantage. The analytics have taken over from judgment, experience, and honest debate. In some cases, debate does not occur. In the rapidly changing and uncertain environments faced by many organizations, this can lead to the dissipation of limited resources and organizational wandering.

If strategic thinking is to be reflected in the day-to-day operation of an organization, then the thinkers and the doers cannot be separated by the process. Mechanisms must be found to harness the judgment, experience, and perspectives of the senior team that controls the resources of the organization.

From 1986 to 1991, we developed and refined an approach to strategy development that engages senior management teams directly in debating strategic direction. We call this approach *strategic choice*. It is both a way of thinking about the critical assumptions that influence strategy development and a process for effectively engaging the senior team in the task.

We begin this chapter by providing a perspective on strategy and strategic planning. We then discuss three major issues encountered in strategy development. Next, we present an approach to collaborative strategy development that addresses these issues. In the final section, we describe some of the signs that indicate this approach may be appropriate for an organization and guidelines for implementation.

Perspectives on Strategy and Strategic Planning

The knowledge, tools, and techniques available to management engaged in strategic planning today are overwhelming. However, the proliferation of techniques has not necessarily resulted in better strategic thinking and action. In fact, the processes have become so complex that the true purpose of strategy development has become obscured. It is useful to separate the three defining concepts: strategy, business strategy, and corporate strategy.

Strategy

Strategy can be thought of as a set of intentions, often expressed as a strategic plan. The plan states the firm's mission, the scope of its operations and goals, and the actions required to fulfill its goals in the broad context of its competitive environment.

At the same time, strategy is also behavioral, suggesting that strategy is a pattern of resource allocation decisions. Looking at intentions is not enough. How intentions are translated into resource allocation decisions must also be addressed. When viewed this way, two things become clear. First, every firm has an implicit intentional strategy that can be constructed from its behavioral strategy: the way it allocates capital, facilities, and people, as well as the problems management addresses and ignores (Gerstein, 1987). Second, a successful translation from new explicit intentions to behavior is required before management can state that the firm indeed has a new strategy. Intentions are only half of the strategy creation process.

Business Strategy

The purpose of formulating a *business strategy* is to ask, What business are we in and how will we gain and sustain competitive advantage? Answering these questions involves bringing together the right data set and judgments to make decisions about *markets* (the customers and customer needs the organization will serve); *offerings* (the products and services the organization will provide and how it will provide them); and *competitive basis* (the reasons customers choose to do business with this organization versus its competitors). Our view is that the core of strategy development lies in addressing these three areas.

Corporate Strategy

Corporate strategy applies to multibusiness organizations and addresses the combination and balance of businesses needed to create a robust portfolio and lay the foundations for profitable growth. Corporate strategy usually is more than portfolio management: it looks at ways of combining different businesses, operations, and activities within one corporation to achieve maximum potential value.

The challenge for management is to identify, acquire, and nurture the core competencies required to build the foundations for profitable growth. Core competence is the collective learning in the organization—how to coordinate diverse production skills and integrate technology, the organization of work, and the delivery of value. These core competencies provide the vital elements for differentiation in the core products of the corporation and must be leveraged across the business units of the corporation to create and sustain competitive advantage (Prahalad and Hamel, 1990). The portfolio may include an array of arrangements with other organizations, for example, joint ventures, acquisitions, and spinouts. This increases the challenge of setting direction and allocating resources across units of the corporation to leverage core competencies.

Strategy can serve to guide and unify actions. It states a direction and establishes a foundation on which an implementation plan can be built. In a world of constant change, the more effective organizations have a strategy that is well understood by those who have to make it happen, that defines the relationship between the organization and its environment, and that serves as a compelling guide to day-to-day actions.

The Value Is in the Planning, Not the Plan

Industries and markets are changing overnight and organizations are being challenged from many directions simultaneously—new competitors, new technologies, shifting roles of governments, new forms of ownership and governance, and increasingly sophisticated customers. In this environment, the formal, written plans that are the prized output of many planning processes can no longer be the major conveyors of organizational direction. It is the strategic thinking behind the plans, carried in the minds of management and reflected in their daily decisions, that unifies and focuses the application of resources to the organization's mission.

With the pace of change ever increasing, the written plan will always be wrong. It is an artifact that has symbolic value. It is the shared understanding of the organizational context that evolves from strategic thinking that continues to be relevant and guiding. With a sense of the *why* behind the *what* that drives the *how,* managers are able to react rapidly and consistently to change and the inevitable, unforeseen obstacles that often arise along the way.

Three Core Problems in Strategy Development

Organizations are not led by written documents. Organizations are led by teams of individuals with different perspectives of the world. Many planning processes fail because they do not create mechanisms that address the powerful behavioral dimensions of strategy development. In our work, we have identified three problems that can significantly reduce the impact of strategic planning.

Failure to Involve the Right People

Our experience suggests that the process of struggling with the complexity, messiness, and conflicts inherent in strategy development produces a level of understanding more valuable than the final plan itself. All too often, the plan simply documents the resolution of these debates, not what was learned from them. Senior management allows itself to become isolated from these struggles. Staffs often see their role as protecting senior management from the dirty laundry of strategic planning. This can lead to a strategic planning process that builds complex forecasts about the future rather than focusing on the "big bets" and judgments that must be made to remain competitive. Strategic planning is critical precisely because the future cannot be predicted and the organization needs to be able to make decisions in the face of uncertainty without centralized approval of every move.

Increasingly, the real value added by strategic planning

comes from the shared understanding of the organization's mission and the factors critical to achieving success. The CEO is by definition the chief strategy officer of the organization, but he or she needs to engage the senior team in shaping the direction to ensure that it is both attractive and achievable.

Failure to Address Driving Assumptions

It is not uncommon for organizations to encounter difficulties in reaching closure on strategic direction. Countless hours are invested in debating issues that never seem to be resolved; staff get trapped into doing endless cases or studies to break the deadlock. The question is, How can managers who live in the same environment and share a common history with an organization come to different conclusions on strategic direction when presented with the same facts? Part of the answer is that members of a senior team may not, in fact, see the world or their organization in the same way. Each senior team member carries an implicit model of how the business operates and what kind of actions will lead to success for the organization. These models are based on individual backgrounds, education, positions held, and past successes and failures. Therefore, although they see the same facts, they perceive the situation very differently, weigh the data differently, and envision different consequences. In many cases, the use of a common language is misinterpreted as common understanding of circumstances and their implications. People who have worked side by side for many years and who think they know each other may suddenly realize that fundamentally they disagree (Drucker, 1973).

Positions on strategic options reflect these deeper, personally held assumptions about the company, the world in which they operate, and their own roles and values. These driving assumptions will not be addressed if the planning process focuses solely on complex data sets and analysis. If these strongly held but unstated and untested assumptions are not identified and debated, the day-to-day actions of the senior team will reflect their own interpretations within the "strategic umbrella," leading to a wide dispersion of effort down through the organization. Lack of true understanding, agreement, and support at the top significantly weakens the ability to focus resources and effort for competitive advantage.

Failure to Integrate Strategy

The third major problem is that organizations attempt to decide on the scope and direction of major supporting strategies in a "one-off" process. Concerns about the right direction for manufacturing, product development, R&D, marketing, distribution, and other matters may lead to detailed efforts to decide on a key functional or supporting strategy without reaching agreement on the larger strategic context. Without a larger, integrated strategic direction, these "one-off" decisions may conflict with each other, create disconnects among organizational units, and waste resources and time. Several strategic alternatives may be available to the organization, but success requires that all parts of the organization support the choice that integrates all of the actions.

Collaborative Strategy Development

Effective strategy development requires an approach that ensures that the right people debate the right issues and ask the right questions. Our experience has led us to develop an approach to strategy development that provides a logic for thinking about strategic alternatives and processes that get groups of executives to work together productively on strategy development. Strategic choice evolved as a way to address the three core problems we identified.

Strategic choice is a collaborative process that gives structure and support to interactions among the senior team members and creates an environment that encourages constructive debate. The process focuses on the driving assumptions that underlie the organization's potential direction. It also helps make the implicit models explicit so the team can create a shared model for forming strategic alternatives and making strategic choices. Strategic choice engages senior management in a collaborative effort to develop and debate integrated strategic alternatives as sets of linked decisions constituting a whole strategy. The process helps the management team articulate and debate these alternatives, leading to a choice that will determine the role of the key supporting strategies and decisions. In the end, there is an opportunity for the members of the senior team to make their own recommendations to the CEO.

In the following sections, we discuss the key elements of strategic choice as responses to the commonly observed problems of strategy development (Table 11.1). These elements include focused collaboration (getting the right people to participate); identification of driving assumptions (debating the right issues); and development of integrated strategic alternatives (asking the right questions). We then show why strategic choice is an integrated process.

Focused Collaboration

Involving the senior team in a collaborative process of strategy development generates reactions ranging from high expectations to deep concern. Some may feel threatened by the senior team working without staff support or may be concerned that they may do something dumb if they do not have all the data available. Others may feel that it would be a lot easier if the boss simply went off by himself or herself and figured out where the company should be headed. Many, including some of the participants, are concerned that a collaborative process will be messy and time consuming. To some degree, all of these reactions are valid. For many management teams, this significant change may disrupt long-standing roles. It will require that the senior team set aside uninterrupted time (one or more days at a time, for one or more times) to get away from daily pressures and struggle with hard questions and a lot of uncertainty.

The question, then, is, Why change? Much of the answer lies

Table 11.1. Problems in Strategy Development.

Strategy Development Problems	Response to the Problems in Strategic Choice
The wrong people participate.	Focused collaboration.
Driving assumptions and beliefs are not addressed.	Identification of driving assumptions.
Decisions are made in a "one-off" manner.	Articulation of integrated strategic alternatives (ISAs).

in the discussion of strategy and strategic planning presented earlier. At the heart of the answer, however, is the fact that competitive
leadership will increasingly require companies to make big resource
bets long before the data confirm what is happening and a consensus builds. By the time the competition's moves become obvious, the
opportunity to secure a position of leadership in the marketplace
will have passed.

Traditional planning processes have not been successful in
presenting the tough questions and challenging the driving assumptions. Form can take precedence over substance. Hard analysis
can drive out judgment. A company's strategic orthodoxies are more
dangerous than its well-financed rivals (Hamel and Prahalad, 1989).

A well-structured process that engages the CEO and senior
team in collaborative strategy development can break through these
barriers and introduce fresh perspectives. In this process, the tough,
and even unthinkable, questions can and should be posed. Here,
personal judgments, opinions, biases, hunches, and experience are
valuable commodities. The objective of the collaborative process is
to draw these out, debate the assumptions and implications, and
build a collective understanding. In our experience, this process has
a number of benefits:

- *Different points of view.* The challenge of different points of
  view sharpens thought processes and prevents the participants
  from reaching a consensus too quickly. There is no one right
  answer, and the answer never emerges as a logical conclusion
  from the facts. Significant strategic choices should never be
  made on their plausibility alone, should never be made fast, and
  should never be made painlessly (Drucker, 1973).
- *New ideas and perspectives.* Released from the constraints of
  more traditional planning processes, the senior team can think
  out loud and test new ideas with each other. Members of the
  senior team frequently carry ideas around with them until they
  have an opportunity to discuss them. Others are stimulated by
  the debate, which can lead to a number of big ideas that would
  not have emerged otherwise.
- *Broader understanding.* One of the most valuable outcomes of
  the collaborative process is that the senior team members test

their common understanding. This understanding helps make their individual actions more congruent.

- *Ownership and commitment.* Direct participation in the development and debate of integrated strategic alternatives builds greater ownership in the direction of choice, laying a strong foundation for more effective implementation. When the inevitable problem is encountered, each member of the senior team will have a personal appreciation for the trade-offs and choices that were made and can respond more rapidly and consistently.
- *Energy.* Senior teams that become directly involved in a collaborative strategy effort are energized by the exchange of ideas. They feel involved in a high-value activity that is the essence of their jobs. Working the real issues gives them a sense of achievement.

These benefits do not come without costs. Engaging the senior team directly in strategy development may expand the number of people involved and bring together individuals with very different backgrounds and orientations, which may slow the decision process. In many cases, including a wide range of people in the debate carries the risk that the real issues will not surface, that people will play it safe. Another risk is that the process becomes so consensual that no bold moves are initiated. The challenge then is to manage the methodology of collaborative work so the benefits are realized and unproductive overhead is minimized. This requires a focused and well-designed process, preparation, and some discipline on the part of the participants. In the end, the return on effort can be substantial and significantly higher than anticipated at the beginning.

In our experience, collaboration also has a special meaning in the strategic arena. Rarely do we see committees develop visions or bold strategies. Ultimately, the CEO is responsible for the development of vision and strategy. He or she is charged by the board and the shareholders to make fundamental strategic decisions. The purpose of collaborative strategy is not to undermine that role or allow the CEO to avoid responsibility. Rather, it is a way of helping the CEO to receive the advice of the senior managers who will ultimately have to participate in the execution and implementation of strategy.

Identification of Driving Assumptions

Each member of the senior team has his or her own model of the
business, the company, and the external environment. For many,
this model may be unconscious, but it directly impacts their reactions to events and strategic alternatives. Two views need to be
addressed. The first, which we call the *view of the world,* addresses
the external factors, positive and negative, that could significantly
influence a company's success but are beyond its direct control. The
second, the *view of the company,* addresses the organization itself
and the strengths and weaknesses that may help or hinder success
in the future. We have found that it is important to separate these
two classes of assumptions to better understand points of view and
differences of opinion. Often teams are unable to reach closure on
a strategic direction not because of the specific action suggested, but
because those involved in the debate have different views of the
world.

The objective is to make these implicit models more explicit
by identifying what each participant sees as the driving external and
internal assumptions that influence the success of the organization.
From this, the team members build a common model that they can
use to develop and evaluate strategic alternatives. Differences of
opinion should be noted; if the differences can be resolved by additional data, then the staffs can be asked to provide that data. If the
difference is a matter of judgment, then a decision can be made as
to how and when the judgments can be tested. If it is just a guess,
then the team can agree on a guess until additional information
provides a different perspective. Thus, the process moves forward
and time and resources are used efficiently.

Where possible, we find it useful to begin with the view of
the world. This ensures that the discussions begin with an external
perspective and creates a sense of realism. The objective is to identify the positive and negative forces that could impact achievement
of the mission of the organization. The topics to consider depend
on the organization and its industry and may include the industry,
market segments, competition, the role of government, economics,
politics, technology, demographics, and capital markets.

With the view of the company, the objective is to understand how the senior team's evaluation of the company's strengths and weaknesses may influence the range and possibility of future strategic options. Strengths need to be developed and areas of weakness need to be addressed. Areas to consider include human resources, management skills and succession, technology, products, reputation, financial condition, research and development, manufacturing, and marketing.

Articulation of Integrated Strategic Alternatives

Too often, strategic decisions are dealt with on a "one-off" basis. Strategic decisions are addressed as if they are independent of each other, with independent analysis, discussion, and decision. Our observation is that even in diversified companies, meaningful strategic decisions are not independent. They frequently are interdependent. A decision to move in one direction—to make an investment—may obviate another direction. Some are mutually exclusive. Part of the problem lies in processes that bring decisions to senior management on a schedule determined largely by the time line of the work and the schedule of regular senior management meetings. These pressures and constraints are real, but senior management cannot allow its own processes to undermine its ability to lead the organization effectively.

A separate issue is that many organizations fail to recognize the conflicts and waste that "one-off" strategic decisions can create. Unstated or untested differences at the top can create significant debates and missed hand-offs throughout the organization, as employees try to implement strategic decisions that are not integrated. Differences on individual strategic decisions are frequently manifestations of other more basic differences in the views of the world and views of the company held by management.

Therefore, the thrust of this approach is to have the senior team work together to identify, develop, and debate related decisions that make up *integrated strategic alternatives* (ISAs). An ISA is a set of related decisions that, taken together, define a coherent strategic direction. It is a linked set of decisions—investments and disinvestments—with a consistent pattern of resource allocation decisions including cash, capital, facilities, people, technology, and organization. An ISA is both a description of a destination and a path to reach the destination.

The objective is to define three to four ISAs that characterize different strategic directions. Together, they should define the boundaries of the strategic envelope within which the company can operate. They should be specific and different enough that the senior team can address certain questions: What would we do differently? What would we start? What would we stop? In our experience, ISAs usually exist in some form within the company, but have not been recognized, articulated, or debated. Individual interviews with members of the senior team frequently provide the information needed to formulate ISAs. ISAs can also be derived from "what if" questions stimulated by opportunities or concerns about mergers or acquisitions, moves by competitors, or changes to the industry.

Figure 11.1 provides an overview of the key steps in the development of ISAs by the senior team. The first step is to identify three to four ISAs. To facilitate comparison of the alternatives, a common framework should be used. To help sharpen the debate, it is helpful to construct the ISAs as pure strategies to make the differences clearer.

The next step is to address each ISA with a common set of questions, so that everyone understands their key dimensions. At this stage, the senior team should make the case for each ISA. If necessary or appropriate, a small staff support group could develop the ISAs more fully, including industry and market data, financial parameters, and any additional information that would help the senior team understand the consequences of each ISA.

The senior team should then assess the ISAs on two basic dimensions: attractiveness and achievability. The discussion should enable each member of the senior team to understand the pros and cons of each ISA for the organization. Each ISA carries risks, but the risks differ.

In the final step, each member reflects on the discussion and how it has influenced his or her own thinking. At this point, the CEO should ask the members for their personal recommendations—what they would do if it were their decision. We find it useful to build the recommendations around questions of interest

**Figure 11.1. Use of Integrated Strategic Alternatives (ISAs)
in Strategy Development.**

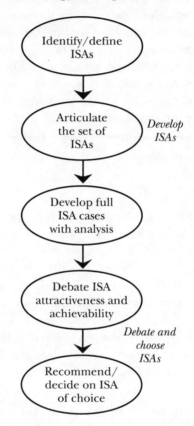

to the CEO: Which ISA would they choose? Why would they make that choice? Where do they see the risks? Why is this a good choice for the organization? What should be started? Stopped? This provides the CEO with specific and integrated input from the senior team. The CEO should ask questions to clarify input and to ensure that everyone understands each point of view and its rationale. If there is substantial agreement among the recommendations, the CEO may want to work on those areas with the greatest difference to see if additional discussion will close the gaps or sharpen understanding. If there are significant areas of difference, the CEO may ask individual members of the senior team to provide additional information or to elaborate on a point in question.

At this stage, the choice may be obvious, or a real significant difference of opinion may exist among the senior team. In either case, the CEO must make or confirm the choice. Having participated in the discussions, the members can be satisfied that their views were considered, and they must support the final decision. This shared understanding provides a strong platform for effective communication and implementation.

The Integration Process

Strategic choice is an integrated process that links the identification of the driving assumptions to the development, choice, and implementation of ISAs. We have discussed the role of collaboration and the key elements of the driving assumptions and the development of ISAs; Figure 11.2 diagrams the flow of the process. To help readers understand the approach, we briefly walk through the major steps. There are several types of input to the process. In some cases, this work may already have been done; other situations may require that work sessions focus on the definition of input. Specifically, two types of input are important: vision/mission of the enterprise and the current assessment of business units.

Vision/Mission of the Enterprise. At the beginning of the process, it is helpful to provide the members of the senior team an opportunity to discuss their understanding of the vision/mission of the enterprise. A vision may range from a set of principles or values to specific objectives, operating modes, and organizational structures. In most cases, the vision/mission encompasses values as well as performance (Delta Consulting Group, 1987).

If the vision/mission is written down, what are the sources? If it is less formalized, what is the team's understanding and how has that understanding been gained and reinforced? It is useful to have the CEO present his or her personal view of the vision/mission at the beginning or as part of the discussion. The important point is to identify areas of agreement and disagreement among the team

Figure 11.2. The Strategic Choice Process.

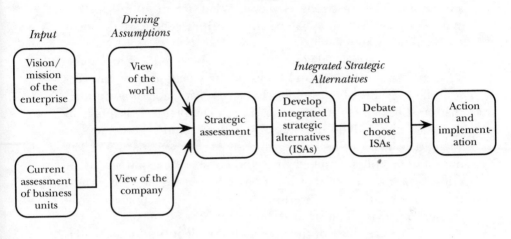

members. This input is important because it draws out the individual views of the team members and sets the context for the discussion of driving assumptions. During the remainder of the process the team may return to the vision for clarification or modification.

Current Assessment of Business Units. The work of developing a strategic direction should be grounded in an accurate assessment of the current status of the business units. Where possible, it is important that the members of the senior team reach a common understanding of the state of the businesses by participating in a structured business unit review. The objective here is perspective and relationships. The challenge is to find the most effective way to communicate the relevant information and insights with efficient use of time. This is a strategic planning effort, not an operating plan process.

Following the analysis of input, the next phase is identification of driving assumptions. As mentioned earlier in the chapter, the two major elements of this are view of the world and view of the company.

The integration of the input and the driving assumptions is what is called the *strategic assessment*. The team members have now reached an understanding of how they interpret the vision/mission of the enterprise and have identified and debated the driving assumptions. The questions now are, What are the implications? What does it all mean? What are the priorities? These are the focus of the strategic assessment.

In this phase of the process, the members of the senior management team step back and looks at the situation they have described. They identify the major challenges, gaps, and opportunities that must be addressed to gain or sustain competitive advantage in the years ahead. It is important that they identify both areas of strength, which can be leveraged, and areas of weakness. The key output of this phase is the identification of specific requirements, or critical success factors, that must be addressed by the ISAs. These criteria are then used to determine which ISA most successfully responds to the vision/mission and the strategic assessment.

The next phase of the process is the identification, articulation, development, debate, and choice of ISAs. This activity includes the various steps outlined earlier in our discussion of ISAs.

The final phase involves action and implementation. We return to our original defining concept of strategy as a pattern of resource allocation decisions to turn intent into reality. Strategic choice establishes a strong platform for implementation throughout the organization. Implementation will not occur, however, unless the senior team's work is connected to the formal resource allocation process. Additional effort is required to ensure that the strategic direction is well understood and reinforced through visible, day-to-day actions.

Summary

In this chapter, we proposed a collaborative approach to strategy development that provides a logic for thinking about strategic alternatives and a set of work processes to engage executive teams in working together productively on strategy development. Strategy can be thought of as a set of intentions; at the same time, it is also behavior, expressed as a pattern of resource allocation decisions. As such, the powerful behavioral dimensions of strategy formulation must be addressed.

We have identified three core problems that can significantly reduce the impact of strategic planning: participation by the wrong people, failure to address driving assumptions, and failure to integrate strategic decisions. The strategic choice process combats these problems by directly engaging the senior team in identifying driving assumptions and developing integrated strategic alternatives.

Although we have described this approach with respect to a CEO and his or her senior team, it applies to many types of organizations and different teams of executives across a wide range of industries or environments. The method of implementation can be modified to fit the particular organization. The CEO and senior team have been our focus because of the high leverage and the unique aspects of this group and their role (Ancona and Nadler, 1989).

With this in mind, what are the implications for those executives and organizations engaged in strategy development?

1. *Consider the advantages of collaborative strategy development.* The benefits and returns can be significant:
   - The process of identifying and discussing driving assumptions allows participants to explain their own models and gives them an opportunity to hear each other more fully. Real understanding will emerge from behind the words and phrases that are exchanged daily.
   - The development and debate of ISAs forces participants to recognize apparent conflicts and inconsistencies.
   - The people who control the resources will develop a common understanding that will guide their operational actions.
   - Direct participation in the strategy development process will set the groundwork for effective communication and implementation.
2. *Be alert to signs of need in the organization.* Observe patterns of behavior that signal the need for a change in approach or process to break the deadlock in strategy development. The patterns include:
   - A sense that members of the senior team are not in agreement about the strategy and may have competing or incompatible views of the firm
   - Continual resurfacing of the same strategies or approaches

- Low commitment to the strategies
- Lack of connection between strategies, creating wasted effort, turf battles, and missed hand-offs
- Discrepancies between the stated strategy and the day-to-day decision making—the words and the music don't match
- Feedback to the CEO and the senior team members that they need to do a better job of communicating the strategy

3. *Ensure that the conditions necessary for success are in place.* Collaborative strategy development can produce significant benefits and the returns can be substantial. However, the change in approach may challenge traditional processes, relationships, and roles. As such, a number of factors are critical:
   - The CEO must be willing to take personal ownership of the process and to run the meetings, with support from others as appropriate. This will require the CEO to prepare for the meetings in advance.
   - The CEO must be willing to let the senior team participate in the debate and must ensure that his or her behavior encourages others to express their ideas and assumptions. At the end, he or she must be willing and able to make a decision if differences of opinion remain. The CEO may need some coaching to develop these skills, depending on his or her personal style.
   - Facilitation support and resources must be available to give structure and support to both the process and the CEO in his or her role. This should include a small analytical support group to provide additional data and analysis as needed by the senior team.
   - The CEO should have confidence that the senior team understands the business well enough to construct and debate valid strategic alternatives.
   - The senior team needs to have command of a basic data set that allows it to work from a sound base and that provides facts to offset assumptions.
   - Prior to the senior team meeting as a group, it is very valuable for those responsible for supporting the team (such as external consultants or trusted staff within the organization) to conduct candid, confidential premeeting interviews

with the participants (and perhaps selected others). This
helps the team develop an understanding of how the issues
are viewed, to begin the identification of driving assumptions, and to identify emergent ISAs.
4. *Manage expectations.* This process will require that the senior
team set aside significant periods of uninterrupted time. The
time required can vary widely based on the size and complexity
of the business and the condition of strategic development in
the organization. The time between meetings can vary from one
or two days to several months. Success requires that the process
be designed to fit the organization's needs and style; it also
requires some discipline.

Strategy development is not simply objective analysis, tools,
and techniques. Ultimately, the development and articulation of
strategic vision and strategic decisions reflect the leadership of the
CEO. Experience indicates that significant benefits are to be gained
from a well thought out, focused, and disciplined approach that
enables senior management to collaborate in shaping the vision of
the CEO and putting it into action.

Collaboration, however, is a double-edged sword. For all the
benefits it provides, the costs are immense and the risks significant.
Our experience has led us to realize that the benefits of collaboration can be achieved, and the costs and risks minimized, by using
a process that enables the senior team to surface driving assumptions and debate alternative strategies through the device of integrated strategic alternatives. Under the right conditions, such an
approach can lead to the development of more effective strategies
that are understood and owned by senior management. This, in
turn, is the basis for more effective implementation, so that strategies become realities.

References

Ancona, D. G., and Nadler, D. A. "Top Hats and Executive Tales:
Designing the Senior Team." *Sloan Management Review,* Fall
1989, 19–28.
Delta Consulting Group. *Organizational Frame Bending: Princi-*

ples for Managing Re-orientation. New York: Delta Consulting Group, 1987.

Drucker, P. F. *Management: Tasks, Responsibilities, Practices.* New York: HarperCollins, 1973.

Gerstein, M. S. *The Technology Connection: Strategy and Change in the Information Age.* Reading, Mass.: Addison-Wesley, 1987.

Hamel, G., and Prahalad, C. K. "Strategic Intent." *Harvard Business Review,* May/June 1989, 63–76.

Prahalad, C. K., and Hamel, G. "The Core Competence of the Corporation." *Harvard Business Review,* May/June 1990, 79–81.

PART FIVE

The Road
from Decline
to Competitiveness

As presented in Chapter One, the history of physical architecture shows that good design is the product of matching architectural form to the functions the architecture must serve and the needs and aspirations of the people who must use it. A good design can endure for generations. Only with hindsight can we usually see the origins of mismatches between such designs and altered conditions or people's changing needs.

The multidivisional firm with its steep hierarchy, complex rules, and vertical division of labor into "thinkers" and "doers" was a social innovation of incalculable proportions. Without it, it is unlikely that society could ever have harvested the fruits of the machine age and the initial growth after the electronics revolution. Yet, for some time, evidence has been mounting that the organizational architecture that emerged nearly a century ago has run its course.

As David A. Nadler points out in Chapter Twelve, we are no longer what we once were. The assumptions that underlie our organizations—we own our customers, we can ignore quality, we can underestimate the competition, and we should not question financial success—are increasingly dangerous inhibitors to our future competitiveness. Although such ideas may not be consciously expressed, they are nonetheless real and, as Nadler explains, imprinted into the "genetic code" of our managers and built into the structures and processes of our organizations. In short, the basic architecture of many of our institutions is suited more to the past than to the future, and if we are to prosper, we must develop new architectures.

In the final chapter, Marc S. Gerstein and Robert B. Shaw identify some ways in which the "look and feel" of future organizations need to be reshaped to focus more on customers and quality, ensure continuous improvement, and institutionalize organizational learning. Although this architecture of the future is not yet fully clear, Gerstein and Shaw outline designs that point the way.

In reading this final part, keep in mind that this book was born in practice; its principal lessons were drawn from observing clients confront organizational problems and solve them through experimentation, innovation, and struggle. Together, we have learned that building a new organizational architecture is a monumental undertaking, one that is unlikely to be completed in our lifetime. Despite this, our clients have taught us that the chance to help frame the organizations of the next century is both an exciting possibility and an irresistible challenge. Besides, it's the only game in town.

TWELVE

Key Leverage Points for Improving Competitive Performance

DAVID A. NADLER

Not long ago, the German journalist Joseph Joffe, writing in *The New York Times,* commented that "the rivalry of nations in the democratic-industrial world has moved from the battlefield into the economic arena. Nobody expects the Germans to invade Alsace again: now they pay for the pleasure of owning the choice plots there, just as the Japanese are buying, not bombing, Pearl Harbor." This comment articulates an obvious but important observation. We have entered a period of intensified international economic competition. Although this global rivalry is not violently expressed on battlefields, it is still a real conflict with profound stakes. There are battles to be won and lost. There are tangible casualties from these conflagrations in terms of disappearing jobs, damaged or destroyed companies, and abandoned industries.

In this context, we believe we are witnessing the awakening of a sense of economic nationalism, both here and abroad. This means that we should be very concerned about, even obsessed with, the competitive viability and effectiveness of U.S. companies. Ironically, it also means that we need to think more globally.

A Perspective on Competitiveness

We come to the issue of competitiveness from the perspective of people who study the dynamics and effectiveness of organizations. Our primary focus is therefore on those internal factors that make individual companies more or less successful competitors. At the same time, we cannot discuss competitiveness without mentioning the very real external factors that influence competitive effectiveness. Four external factors seem particularly significant.

First, certain structural factors of the business environment in the United States make global competition difficult. These factors include changing patterns of ownership; the dynamics, expectations, and time frames of the capital markets; and the objectives of institutional investors.

Second, certain political factors in the United States undercut efforts to compete globally. In particular, we are referring to the crisis in education, the lack of an explicit and thoughtful national industrial policy, and antiquated ideas of antitrust law.

Third, certain economic factors in the United States, including the balance of trade, in particular the federal deficit and its impact on cost of capital, impair the ability of firms to access the funds they need to support competitive initiatives.

Fourth, certain international political-economic factors, in particular the behavior of Japan toward the United States, make competition on a level playing field nearly impossible.

We could discuss these four factors at length. Our objective here is simply to note that part of the answer lies outside the actions of individual firms. Although these external factors are consequential, there do exist companies that are significantly more effective competitors than others, even within the same industry. It appears that the actions of individual companies still explain much of the variance in competitive effectiveness.

The external factors are complex, problematic, and not amenable to quick fixes. In the near to medium term, corporate leaders can exert the greatest leverage on the internal factors that influence competitiveness—the characteristics of organizations that determine how well they can anticipate, respond to, and master the evolving environment of global economic competition. We intend to focus on the internal determinants of competitive success. We articulate some key leverage points for improving competitive performance. The core question we want to address is, How might we build organizations that are radically more effective and thus significantly better global competitors?

Sources of Decline

To answer that question, we turn it around and ask the opposite: What are the sources of competitive decline? Why is it important to understand decline? Almost all U.S. industries that face significant problems with competitiveness—consumer electronics, automobiles, office equipment, and machine tools—were dominant not so many years ago. How did we lose this dominance? Which actions and perspectives caused us to lose our lead to others?

We have put together an initial list of lessons, which you might think about as teachings in what we'll call a curriculum for competitive decline:

Lesson One: Assume the customer. Assume that you own the customer, you know what the customer wants (better than he or she does), and the customer will remain loyal to you no matter what you do. You are not to measure customer satisfaction and definitely not to respond to customer complaints.

Lesson Two: Disinvest in quality. Assume that the customer does not care about quality. Do not meet customer requirements, do not make quality a core strategy, and do not invest in improving work processes and reducing error.

Lesson Three: Ignore design. You do not need to worry about industrial design, the human interface, and the aesthetics of your products and services. Design costs money and customers do not care.

Lesson Four: Deemphasize manufacturing. Do not pay attention to how the product is made, how the manufacturing process can be improved, or what the relationship is between design, development, engineering, and production. Keep people with manufacturing experience away from the executive suite. The secret to success is to remain completely out of the business of producing things yourself.

Lesson Five: Avoid the low end. There is not much money to be made at the low end. The margins are small. It requires a focus on process improvements, sometimes to save pennies, and the competition is tough. Foreign competitors who enter the low end really do not have the capacity to move up in the market.

Lesson Six: Do it alone. If you really are any good, you will not become involved in entangling alliances.

Lesson Seven: Underestimate competition. You should not worry too much about competitors. They probably are not that good. Assume that the competition is standing still and that you can compete tomorrow against what they have in the market today. Competitors have been more lucky than good, and their luck cannot last.

Lesson Eight: Organize traditionally. The traditional organizational structures and processes (in particular, narrowly defined and fragmented work, steep hierarchies, centralized control, functional organizations, and large, powerful staffs) all work perfectly fine. Reduce cost by simply cutting heads or eliminating levels, but use the same basic approaches to organizing.

Lesson Nine: Develop talent narrowly. Keep your people, particularly managers, focused closely on their special function, discipline, product, or geography. Do not worry about the broad development of people over time.

Lesson Ten: Do not question success. Assume that the sources of success in the past will continue to be the seeds of triumph in the future. Do not dwell on failures or reflect on mistakes. If it worked before, it will work again.

Now, at first blush, this list seems ridiculous. Who would possibly teach such lessons? The sad fact is that many companies appear to be working straight from this volume. They may not have mastered all the chapters, but they have come pretty close.

From Decline to Competitiveness

Let us now return to our original question: How might we build organizations that are radically more effective and thus significantly better global competitors? Look again at our curriculum, as each lesson has an obvious corollary. We can push our thinking further and look at what would be called the root causes in quality terms. What are the critical success factors for competitiveness, the necessary and sufficient conditions for success? We believe there are four.

Strategy

A basic requirement for competitive success is viable competitive strategies. Many of the best international competitors, in particular the Japanese, have been markedly superior in the ability to gain focus and generate strategic momentum over a period of years. They have identified clear targets (often us) and specific objectives. They have exerted sustained effort to achieve those objectives, particularly their intent to gain global market share. Therefore, qualitatively different and better strategic thinking and execution are required. Fortunately, we are learning something about the content of strategy. C. K. Prahalad at the University of Michigan has begun to develop some very useful concepts such as strategic intent and core competence. Ultimately, the process of developing strategy may be as important as any particular concept. Specifically, we need to stop separating the thinkers from the doers. Recently, some companies have made significant progress in strategy formulation and implementation by engaging the executive team in collaborative strategy development.

Quality

There is now evidence about quality from companies like the Baldrige winners (Westinghouse, Motorola, Xerox, Milliken, General Motors, IBM, and Federal Express) and from other firms who have had comparable quality efforts and achievements, such as Corning and Alcoa. Sustained strategic work on quality can make a significant difference in the capacity to compete in tough global markets and can lead companies to recapture lost market share. These companies have done so through the implementation of total quality management and strategic, organizational, and cultural change.

We have learned a lot about total quality strategies over the 1980s. Providing a quality offering (one that meets or exceeds the customer's requirements) has become the means of survival. This means that although quality is critical, it does not by itself ensure success. Rather, innovation, design, and speed are also necessary.

Most difficult problems in implementing total quality strategies are not technical but behavioral. Quality technology is not that new, sophisticated, or complex. Changing the behavior of tens of thousands of people each day toward the customer, toward the product, toward the work process, and toward each other is the major challenge in implementation of total quality. Not surprisingly, we have also learned that changing behavior is tough; it takes time (often years) and requires the intimate, intensive involvement of senior management.

Organizational Design

Organizational design is just starting to gain recognition as a critical factor for success. Competitive success requires successful innovation and speed. The capacity to innovate quickly is emerging as a critical determinant of success in the marketplace. Innovation and speed lead us to think about radically different ways of organizing enterprises. Most companies are organized on the paradigm of the machine bureaucracy and the theory of scientific management, both of which evolved during the early part of the twentieth century. That approach to organizing has become so pervasive that it has become reflexive or, to use John Sculley's phrase, implanted in the genetic code. Intensive competition is forcing us to reexamine this approach, and advances in information technology are beginning to create the potential for new ways to manage work. Companies are experimenting with self-managed teams, networks, fuzzy boundaries, micro-enterprise units, flat hierarchies, and the computer-integrated enterprise.

We believe that a significant opportunity for improvement in competitiveness in the 1990s will be the design and application of new architectures of organization. In particular, we need to devise forms that play to the inherent competitive advantage of the American culture and the diverse American work force, rather than mimic the successes of others, such as the Japanese. Boldness and an ability to think outside the boundaries that define organizations today are required.

Organizational Learning

Even those companies with great strategies, total quality management, and innovative organizational architectures do not always get it right the first time. They make mistakes. The best competitors have that unique capacity to reflect on and understand those mistakes quickly and turn insight into action; they are learning-efficient organizations. They learn from customers, competitors, and suppliers. They learn from success and they learn from failure. They view "productive failure" as a key ingredient of the learning process. They recognize that the sources of success in the past are often the seeds of failure in the future.

Competitive effectiveness therefore requires that companies invest in the development of their capacity to learn. It requires significant improvements in the capabilities of individuals, groups, and organizations to reflect and gain insight. The key ingredients are the structures, processes, and environments that enable and encourage learning but also empower people to translate learning into action.

In reflecting on these four critical success factors—strategy, quality, design, and learning—another implication emerges. It is difficult for executive teams to work on these issues if they are consumed by the day-to-day operations of the enterprise. Building competitive effectiveness requires significant reallocation of senior management time, which in turn requires the empowerment of lower-level managers in the organization.

Summary

We find ourselves, in this last decade of the century, in the midst of profound change. The basis of the rivalry of nations is shifting to economic terms, at least in the industrial world. Competitiveness has become a critical national concern. Both the external and internal determinants of competitiveness require our attention and demand action.

The 1980s witnessed the financial restructuring of much of corporate America. If we are to succeed, the 1990s will need to witness the strategic, managerial, and organizational restructuring of our firms, and the design of new organizational architectures. That is our challenge.

THIRTEEN

Organizational Architectures for the Twenty-First Century

MARC S. GERSTEIN, ROBERT B. SHAW

The 1990s may witness the beginning of the end of the traditional organization. A century dominated by a single type of organization—the machine bureaucracy—is slowly giving way to a new era. Driven by the eight forces described in the Introduction (technology, competition, oversupply, globalism, customer expectations, government participation, ownership, and work force dynamics), organizations are being forced to reshape themselves to survive and to prosper.

Signs of this change emerged in the 1960s as firms used task forces and teams to achieve greater flexibility than could be provided by their formal structures. Some organizations, such as those in the aerospace industry, adopted dual reporting structures such as the matrix to seek a balance between functional expertise and program focus. In addition, throughout the late 1960s and 1970s, a number of companies aggressively experimented with alternative work organizations (such as those based on sociotechnical models) in an attempt to increase productivity and organizational responsiveness.

By the middle 1980s, many organizations were operating very differently from their own blueprints. In fact, formal structure explained only a relatively small percentage of the observable behavior. Repeated studies of communication patterns indicated that complex work processes, such as new product development, required a great deal of cross-functional interaction, relatively little of which was formalized. Furthermore, in a number of leading firms the total quality movement was in the process of redefining the roles of employees and supervisors in the problem-solving process, yet another work design innovation. By the end of the 1980s, although the hierarchical framework of the classical organization structure remained largely intact, a number of the other elements were undergoing a metamorphosis.

As organizations became increasingly complex internally, their relationships with the outside world also grew more complex. After decades of successfully going it alone, organizations often found themselves frustrated by failures in new technologies, new businesses, and new markets. To address identified shortcomings of expertise, capital, or market access and to mitigate the financial risk inherent in many new ventures, some organizations turned to alliances, including joint ventures, licenses, and comarketing deals. Even the once "treasonous" action of leaving the company to start up a related business could now be encouraged through spinouts launched with seed capital from the parent organization.

Although this catalog of experiments with new organizational forms is several decades old, our sense is that the change to a new organizational architecture is only beginning. Organizational design is one of the most useful tools in enhancing the competitiveness of organizations; we will thus see more frequent and more radical attempts to enhance effectiveness through innovative structures. How a firm organizes its resources can be a source of tremendous advantage when a premium is placed on flexibility, adaptation, and the management of change. Still, architectural evolution is inextricably tied to people's capacity to change and thus progress is measured in generations, not in years.

Although it is difficult today to tell exactly where we are in the transition to a new organizational paradigm, the purpose of this final chapter is to look forward and speculate as to the nature of organizations over the coming decades. Specifically, we try to describe the "look and feel" of future organizations, identify the more difficult problems that must be managed along the way, and develop a sense of the timing for the changes that lie ahead. Our intent is to concentrate on the general nature of the forces that are at work rather than to make accurate "point-estimate" predictions. In fact, one characteristic of most long-range social forecasts is that they inevitably both overestimate and underestimate. Large-scale change almost always takes longer than people predict, but it goes much further than people think possible.

The Future "Look and Feel" of Organizations

Organizations will exist in networks of suppliers, competitors, and customers who cooperate with each other to survive in an increasingly competitive marketplace. In the preceding chapters, we drew a picture of organizations of the future as global networks. Instead of the traditional firm containing all of the needed capabilities, future organizations will make various alliances to develop, produce, and market goods and services. More companies will evolve into a combination of wholly owned operations, alliances, joint ventures, spinouts, and acquired subsidiaries. They will be linked together in organizational networks that share values, people, information, and operating styles. Organizations will make arrangements with all links in the value chain, including customers for intermediate products and finished goods and suppliers of raw materials, production technology, capital, and financial services. The need for arrangements will encourage lifelong competitors to collaborate, and, driven by arrangements, historical allies may occasionally find themselves positioned as competitive adversaries. Experimentation will be the rule, with successful innovation the objective. As in any period of active experimentation, however, we can expect many failures.

Organizational boundaries will become fuzzy as various allegiances emerge. These fuzzy organizational boundaries, however, will be the result of strategic intent and constructed with much thought and skill. In this respect, boundaries will become more complicated and diverse, in proportion to the complexity and diversity found in the external environment. Mechanisms will evolve to create and manage these more complex organizational boundaries, and senior management will have the critical role of shaping boundaries to be consistent with strategy in any given market or product line. The days of rigid boundaries, where one structure and style was used in most situations, will end as new forms of interorganizational collaboration emerge.

At the unit level, process-oriented high-performance work systems that embody elements of total quality will tend to be the norm in offices, in factories, and in the field. The term *high-performance work systems* describes an organizational improvement approach that emphasizes the deliberate design and intergration of the social and technical systems used to do work. These new designs are characterized by simplified business processes and work flows, advanced technological tools (expert systems, knowledge-based tools, smart documents), and innovative human system design (autonomous work teams, enriched job designs, flat hierarchies). Implementation of high-performance work systems will result in dramatically more productive and innovative organizations—Paul Allaire of Xerox calls them "productive work communities." Movement toward these structures will be tightly linked to efforts in the area of world-class quality. To date, we have seen only limited linkage between high-performance approaches and total quality management. In the future, however, these two methodologies will be completely integrated.

Within organizations, teams will be the norm at all levels. Rather than a rigid formal structure, the organization will be more organic, adapting to changing conditions and the current work load. Most productive work will be accomplished by small teams assisted by technology support. Many teams will have full-time and part-time members who live and work remotely from the team's home base, but extensive communication systems will make this completely practical. Ubiquitous electronic communications will allow the organization to be reshaped as the work requires. Which distribution lists one is on and to which data files one has access will be more important than to whom one reports. In fact, a much more accurate picture of the "real" organization will be obtained by analyzing its electronic mail traffic than its organization chart.

Subunits and teams will be relatively autonomous in comparison to previous organizational eras. Rather than providing traditional supervision, managers will coach, assist with problem solving, and provide linkage to top management, to other organizational units, or to other organizations as required. Teams will have much more latitude to solve problems and much greater access to resources than in the past. Specialized resources, if necessary, will be assigned to teams (rather than to their managers). Because of the reduction of traditional supervisory responsibilities, organizations will tend to be flat, with few middle managers overall.

With large numbers of autonomous teams doing the work, norms and values rather than rules and direct supervision will furnish the cohesion necessary to provide direction and achieve coordination. Leaders will thus spend an increasing amount of time and energy shaping the vision and values of the organization. In addition, organizational leaders will spend a significant amount of time focusing on the development of people, particularly in selecting team leaders and managers. In the more diffused organization, the principal means of control will be a strongly held culture and a network of individuals who use their own leadership skills to build the organization consistent with an overall vision.

Organizational forms will be fluid and transitory. Organizations will be able to charter special groups of employees and outside contractors for each new project or task. Internal structures will evolve into a myriad of constantly shifting teams, partnerships, and units, more as a result of changing conditions than as a result of innate preferences. The freedom provided groups to optimize their work processes will encourage experimentation. Because a variety of solutions will inevitably be found to similar problems, and not all problems will be worthy of imposing standardized solutions, a wide range of design variations will evolve over time. With constant pressure for innovation and relative autonomy to initiate change, organizations will be better understood in "ecological" rather than "mechanical" terms.

A cornerstone of the new organizations will be an emphasis on system-level learning. The characteristic that will most effectively distinguish an effective organization from a less effective one will be its capacity to innovate and learn. Effective learning will require members to seek out new ideas and adapt them to internal use. The "right" organizational answer will not endure for long, because changing environmental conditions will force ongoing change. Organizational architects will seek designs that facilitate continuous improvement rather than static structures.

In a broader sense, learning will become the domain of senior managers as well as those producing products and services. Increased innovation and experimentation will result in successes and failures that will be analyzed to extract knowledge that can be applied to new situations. New learning forums and approaches will be applied as suggested in Chapter Eight. For example, an important feature of the more successful joint ventures will be their capacity to create organizational learning from those arrangements rather than just profiting in the short term. These learnings, once extracted, can strengthen both the joint venture and the larger corporate entities sponsoring the collaborative work. The availability of resources for experimentation and the natural variation that occurs within any large system provide opportunities for learning in large corporations. The key is to develop formal and informal structures to take advantage of these learning opportunities.

There will be a general emphasis on developing people who understand both the broader strategic issues and the specific tasks in all areas of the organization. We see a growing trend toward developing individuals and teams to be broader in their focus, providing the organization with the ability to reconfigure as needed. Cross-training and pay-for-skill reward systems, for example, are creating in some organizations a cadré of employees who can work at any point in the work process. These people can be viewed as craftsmen working within high-performance systems. Those working in the new structures of the twenty-first century will understand and help solve the larger competitive issues facing their companies.

Finally, a necessary characteristic of the successful organization will be a more balanced emphasis on short-term financial performance. Although positive financial results are obviously critical to any economic entity's long-term survival, overreliance on short-term financial measures can lead to costly mistakes. This will be particularly important in the creation of goal-setting and performance-management systems for autonomous teams. To ensure that teams make the right decisions, a full range of performance indicators will be used. In addition, to avoid a negative impact on motivation, teams will need to be largely isolated from shocks and windfalls arising in parts of the organization they cannot influence.

Achievement of the "State Change"

The future organization just described is much greater than the sum of its parts. In fact, many of the components identified are present in organizations today, though perhaps not to the degree described. The transformation we expect in future organizations might be analogous to a state change in a physical substance. For example, at a specific temperature and pressure, water may be a solid (ice), a liquid (water), or a gas (steam). If we concentrate on understanding these changes as changes in the nature of the substance itself, we miss the true phenomenon.

Organizations of the future will be in a different "state" relative to organizations of the past. They will be dramatically more flexible and efficient, they will learn more rapidly, and, overall, they will adapt more quickly to changing environmental conditions and to competitive initiatives. The benefits of this state change will arise from the subtle interplay of many architectural elements, not the presence of a single factor.

Designing and building the organizational architecture of the future will require that we solve a range of complex problems. Some of these problems are straightforward—figuring out how to make the new organizational forms work. Developing a compensation plan for team-based work designs is one such task. Other higher-order problems are only indirectly associated with making the organization work but must be solved nonetheless. Protecting our civil liberties in an all-electronic workplace is one such example. The list of problems outlined below is not exhaustive. We will discover most of the problems as we develop the new architecture.

Partners do not work for you. Arrangements are the result of mutual agreements between separate companies, which are bound by contracts that cannot be unilaterally altered. Unlike employees, partners are not obligated to follow the company's chain of command. Ending a joint venture that is not working is not like making a decision; it is like getting a divorce. Companies that have engaged in various alliances uniformly report that senior management must devote extensive time to maintain the alliances. Management of internal businesses of almost any size can typically be delegated, but even a modest-sized partnership requires ongoing attention by senior management. Therefore, the greatest challenge in successfully creating networks may not be setting them up, but managing them once they are going and modifying them when conditions change.

"Centrifugal force" must balance "gravity." The success of

the network organizational design depends on balancing the forces that tend to drive individual units toward increasing independence with the forces that would create leverage through overall coordination and the imposition of consistent, companywide practices. Historically, however, organizations have tended to oscillate between centralization and decentralization, often going too far in each direction at various points in time. Avoiding the extremes requires that senior management recognize the importance of balancing these opposite tendencies and of developing both the management processes and the culture to ensure that this balance is maintained. In particular, the selection of managers who seek balance rather than either extreme is crucial. Such managers will work to identify the areas in which coordination produces dividends that clearly outweigh the enormous organizational costs of reducing people's autonomy.

Groups are not individuals. Today companies are built on a contract between individuals and the organization in which money is exchanged for work. The shift to a group-centered organization design, although appearing to be an extension of the teamwork that has been building for decades, may represent a more profound change. At a minimum, an increase in group-based designs will require the working out of such complex issues as compensation systems and evalution, feedback, and discipline procedures. To do so, we must develop the means to separate the behavior that is causally attributable to individuals from that which is not. For instance, if a group develops antiorganizational norms and applies coercive peer pressure to ensure compliance with them, we must develop the means to fairly assess the responsibility of those individuals who disagree but feel compelled to go along. In addition, we have traditionally hired and fired people as individuals, moving them into and out of work groups principally at the discretion of management; however, as team-based designs flourish, entire teams may act as a unit, or prospective employers may hire groups intact from one organization to another. Whether group employment contracts will be used remains to be seen.

A high-tech world threatens civil liberties. The transition from conventional media to electronics will necessitate reexamination of many of the freedoms we currently take for granted. For instance, at present we generally consider our communications and personal files to be private, even if kept at work. We expect that fellow employees and management will not wantonly read our mail, listen in on telephone conversations, and snoop through our records. Legitimate criticism, such as complaining about a company policy to peers, critiquing the behavior of the boss, or expressing an opinion on an employee survey, is expected to be made in private or anonymously, unless one chooses otherwise.

The social conventions and laws that govern conduct today do not transfer intact to the world of electronic communications. Computer-based networks share characteristics with first-class mail, the telephone, publishing, broadcasting, and a town meeting without falling cleanly into any of these categories. As each of these modes of communication is subject to different expectations and legal precedents, it is difficult to know which norms and rules to apply. In addition, physical security is so much a part of our current protections that we may not fully understand the ramifications of files that can be read covertly from a distance or by monitoring traffic over the network. And although writing a letter using a company pen and paper would not affect its status as a private communication, the status of a memo composed on a company's personal computer and sent via a network consisting of company-owned and public carriers is much less clear.

The legal issues surrounding these matters are complex; however, we must remember that values, social conventions, and people's expectations are in many ways far more important than the statutory law. Senior executives must exert leadership to ensure that policies are developed consistent with enduring values concerning privacy and freedom and that the law is used to help shape the society in which we wish to live. Otherwise, we may find ourselves living in organizations and a society in which the extensive application of technology has caused us to lose far more in liberty than we have gained in productivity.

Change may occur slowly. The ability of managers to adjust to the organizational architecture we have outlined in this book will be one of the principal pacesetters for change. The new organizations will inevitably have critical success factors different from those of the past, and the managerial skills suited to the old world may no longer be appropriate. More important, radically different conditions require different instincts, and managers who can no longer trust their instincts will not be effective for long.

Movement away from the bureaucratic model will place significant demands on management. Those who work in highly functionalized control-oriented organizations will be required to develop radically new structures that bear little resemblance to their existing organizations or the organizations in which they matured as managers. Some will be limited by the narrowness of their experience. Managers who have only worked within functional organizations will find it extremely difficult to envision organizations that break with that model. Bureaucracy is in the "genetic code" of those who will ultimately be responsible for designing and managing new organizations. Imprinting of this sort exists even in those who can list all the problems and shortcomings of a bureaucratic organization.

The manager chosen and trained to prosper in the bureaucratic world may be a skilled incompetent in the highly participative, team-based network organization of the future. Some will learn; some will not. If the skilled incompetents are in important leadership positions, the organization must wait for the next generation of leadership before it can move on. This is one reason experimentation will be necessary—to provide examples of alternative organization models that managers can "touch and feel." Experimentation provides managers with an opportunity to transform their beliefs through the day-to-day management of new organizational models.

Recently, we conducted a seminar for 150 Japanese managers and consultants in Japan. One participant said he had visited American plants using high-performance work systems and was astounded at the knowledge and commitment of the workers. The workers he met on the plant floor knew the customers who would receive the product and the competitors the organization faced in the marketplace. He saw these plants as superior to most plants in Japan because Japanese workers, in general, understood only small pieces of the entire work process. He stated that these highly trained and broad-thinking workers and the self-managed teams in which they worked were what his country needed to fear most.

Intensified competition and ever-increasing customer expectations are forcing organizations to function at a level of effectiveness (high quality at low cost), speed (reduced cycle and product development time), and innovation that is far superior to that of the past. We believe classical expressions of the machine bureaucracy model will eventually "run out of gas," unable to respond to the myriad pressures facing organizations in the twenty-first century. Those who cling stubbornly to the machine bureaucracy model may find they can survive, but just barely and only at great cost. In writing this book, our goal was to provide organizational architects with the concepts and tools necessary to create and test new organizational forms. Our greatest hope is that they can take the perspectives contained in this book—ideas based on practice—and build better organizations. It's time.

INDEX